CRITICAL ACCLAIM
FOR *TRAVELERS' TALES*

"The *Travelers' Tales* series is altogether remarkable."
—Jan Morris, author of *Journeys, Locations,* and *Hong Kong*

"For the thoughtful traveler, these books are an invaluable resource. There's nothing like them on the market."
—Pico Iyer, author of *Video Night in Kathmandu*

"This is the stuff memories can be duplicated from."
—Karen Krebsbach, *Foreign Service Journal*

"I can't think of a better way to get comfortable with a destination than by delving into *Travelers' Tales*...before reading a guidebook, before seeing a travel agent. The series helps visitors refine their interests and readies them to communicate with the peoples they come in contact with...."
—Paul Glassman, Society of American Travel Writers

"*Travelers' Tales* is a valuable addition to any predeparture reading list."
—Tony Wheeler, publisher, Lonely Planet Publications

"*Travelers' Tales* delivers something most guidebooks only promise: a real sense of what a country is all about...."
—Steve Silk, *Hartford Courant*

"*Travelers' Tales* is a useful and enlightening addition to the travel bookshelves...providing a real service for those who enjoy reading first-person accounts of a destination before seeing it for themselves."
—Bill Newlin, publisher, Moon Publications

"The *Travelers' Tales* series should become required reading for anyone visiting a foreign country who wants to truly step off the tourist track and experience another culture, another place, firsthand."
—Nancy Paradis, *St. Petersburg Times*

D0956159

GRAND CANYON

TRUE STORIES OF LIFE BELOW THE RIM

TRAVELERS' TALES GUIDES

GRAND CANYON

TRUE STORIES OF LIFE
BELOW THE RIM

Collected and Edited by

SEAN O'REILLY   JAMES O'REILLY

LARRY HABEGGER

TRAVELERS' TALES

SAN FRANCISCO

Cover and interior design by Judy Anderson, Susan Bailey, and Kathryn Heflin
Cover photograph: © Craig Lovell/Eagle Visions Photography—A rafter enjoys the tranquil waters and beautiful rapids on the Colorado River in the bottom of the Grand Canyon.
Engravings courtesy of U.S. Geological Survey.
Maps by Keith Granger
Page layout by Patty Holden using the fonts Bembo and Boulevard

Distributed by: Publisher's Group West, 1700 Fourth Street, Berkeley, CA 94710.

Library of Congress Cataloging-in-Publication Data
    The Grand Canyon: true stories of life below the rim/collected and
    edited by Sean O'Reilly, James O'Reilly, and Larry Habegger.
    p. cm.— (Travelers' Tales guides)
    Includes index.
    ISBN 1-885211-34-1
    1. Grand Canyon (Ariz.)—Description and travel. 2. Colorado River
    (Colo.–Mexico)—Description and travel. 3. Travelers' writings, American—
    Arizona—Grand Canyon. I. O'Reilly, Sean. II. O'Reilly, James.
    III. Habegger, Larry. IV. Series.
F788.G756   1999   99-26917
917.91'320453—dc21   CIP

First Edition
Printed in the United States of America
10 9 8 7 6 5 4 3 2

All this is the music of waters.

—MAJOR JOHN WESLEY POWELL

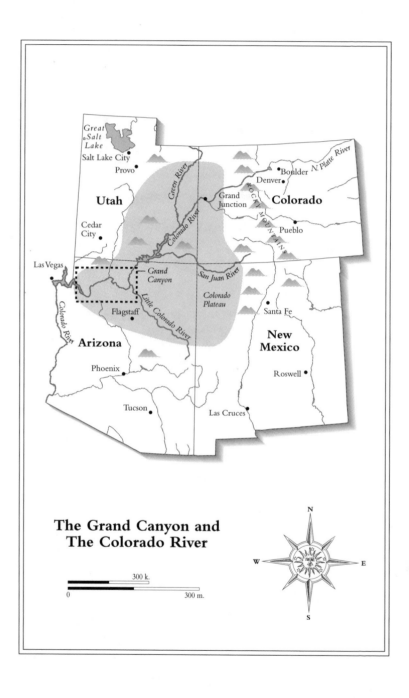

**The Grand Canyon and
The Colorado River**

300 k.

0   300 m.

Table of Contents

Regional Map .... *viii*

Detail Map .... *xiv–xv*

Geologic Cross Section .... *xvi*

Introduction .... *xvii*

Part One
ESSENCE OF THE GRAND CANYON

Beneath the Rim 3
SCOTT THYBONY

Nankoweap 6
GAIL DUDLEY

Gone Back into the Earth 14
BARRY LOPEZ

Revelation 25
PAGE STEGNER

Stone Creek Woman 35
TERRY TEMPEST WILLIAMS

The Green Room 40
MICHAEL P. GHIGLIERI

The Midnight Crack 44
JOHN ANNERINO

Bats Are Welcome 59
PETER ALESHIRE

Whitewater 63
PATRICIA C. McCAIREN

Part Two
SOME THINGS TO DO

Cape Solitude   81
  LARRY WINTER

Travertine Grotto   86
  SUSAN ZWINGER

Over the Edge   92
  DON KARDONG

Thunder   102
  MICHAEL P. GHIGLIERI

Wild and Free   110
  STEWART UDALL

Riders to the Rim   115
  SEAN O'REILLY

Legends of the Lost   119
  DEAN SMITH

Fishing Eagles   125
  ANN HAYMOND ZWINGER

Part Three
GOING YOUR OWN WAY

Shamans' Gallery   137
  SCOTT THYBONY

The Journey's End   142
  WILLIAM HAFFORD

G. B. and the Rangers   152
  CHARLOTTE MADISON AND NANA COOK

The Turbulent Times   157
  PAUL RICHFIELD

Women in the Canyon   161
  LOUISE TEAL

Trinitarian Thoughts   169
  W. PAUL JONES

Havasu   175
  EDWARD ABBEY

Transition   187
  COLIN FLETCHER

Part Four
IN THE SHADOWS

Flash Flood   203
  TOM JANECEK

Under Lava   211
  GAIL GOLDBERGER

Jackass Canyon   220
  MICHAEL P. GHIGLIERI

Blacktail Ghost   225
  CHRISTA SADLER

From Anasazi to Aircraft   229
  JEREMY SCHMIDT

Let the River Run Through It   240
  DAVID R. BROWER

Part Five
THE LAST WORD

Temples to Water   249
  JEREMY SCHMIDT

THE NEXT STEP

What You Need to Know   255
  Weather, permits, health, the works

Important Contacts   264
  Tourist Information

Fun Things to Do   265

Grand Canyon Online   267
Giving Back   268
Recommended Reading   269
Index   273
Index of Contributors   275
Acknowledgements   277

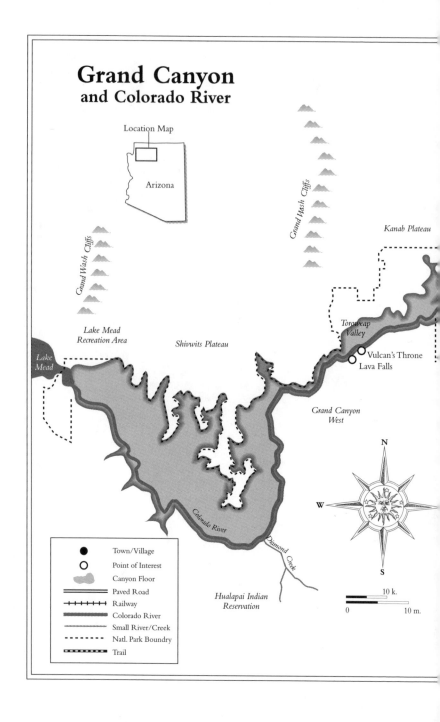

Grand Canyon
and Colorado River

Location Map

Arizona

Grand Wash Cliffs

Grand Wash Cliffs

Kanab Plateau

Lake Mead
Recreation Area

Shivwits Plateau

Toroweap
Valley

Vulcan's Throne
Lava Falls

Lake
Mead

Grand Canyon
West

Colorado River

Diamond Creek

N

W

S

Town/Village
Point of Interest
Canyon Floor
Paved Road
Railway
Colorado River
Small River/Creek
Natl. Park Boundry
Trail

Hualapai Indian
Reservation

10 k.

0   10 m.

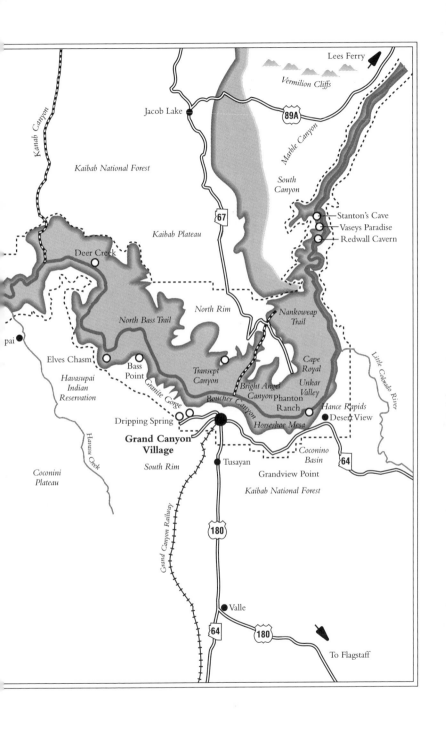

Lees Ferry

Vermilion Cliffs

89A

Jacob Lake

Kanab Canyon

Kaibab National Forest

Marble Canyon

South Canyon

67

Kaibab Plateau

Stanton's Cave
Vaseys Paradise
Redwall Cavern

Deer Creek

North Rim

Nankoweap Trail

North Bass Trail

Little Colorado River

pai

Elves Chasm

Bass Point

Transept Canyon

Cape Royal

Havasupai Indian Reservation

Granite Gorge

Boucher Canyon

Bright Angel Canyon

Unkar Valley

Phanton Ranch

Hance Rapids

Dripping Spring

Grand Canyon Village

Horseshoe Mesa

Desert View

Havasu Creek

South Rim

Tusayan

Coconino Basin

64

Coconini Plateau

Grandview Point

Kaibab National Forest

Grand Canyon Railway

180

Valle

64

180

To Flagstaff

Geologic Cross Section of the Grand Canyon

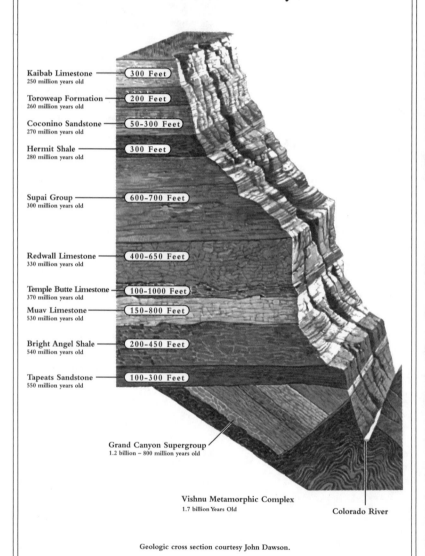

Kaibab Limestone
250 million years old — 300 Feet

Toroweap Formation
260 million years old — 200 Feet

Coconino Sandstone
270 million years old — 50-300 Feet

Hermit Shale
280 million years old — 300 Feet

Supai Group
300 million years old — 600-700 Feet

Redwall Limestone
330 million years old — 400-650 Feet

Temple Butte Limestone
370 million years old — 100-1000 Feet

Muav Limestone
530 million years old — 150-800 Feet

Bright Angel Shale
540 million years old — 200-450 Feet

Tapeats Sandstone
550 million years old — 100-300 Feet

Grand Canyon Supergroup
1.2 billion – 800 million years old

Vishnu Metamorphic Complex
1.7 billion Years Old

Colorado River

Geologic cross section courtesy John Dawson.

Grand Canyon: An Introduction

The Grand Canyon is not a place in the ordinary sense of the word. Upon gazing into the Canyon for the first time, one is left groping for words to describe the vast avenues and seemingly otherworldly ruins that appear to stretch in all directions, inclining both feet and heart to adventure. Instead, the Grand Canyon might best be described as a world of tiers. At roughly two hundred and eighty miles long and up to seventeen and a half miles wide, there are more side canyons and vistas than one can imagine.

If you took yourself upon the Colorado River in the Canyon's depths, you could stop every mile and visit a different beckoning arroyo, butte, and grotto, or you could take a hike to the startlingly eroded rock monoliths reverently referred to as temples. Had the ancient Egyptians lived in the Grand Canyon, they might have gone mad. They could have carved for a thousand years and not covered the endless walls that were already ancient while the Nile was still young.

If the idea of a world of tiers seems abstruse, think of the Grand Canyon as a pocket universe with six contiguous plateaus of differing elevation: the Marble Platform, the Kaibab, the Kanab, Uinkaret, Shivwits and Hualapai Plateaus. When you add in streams such as the Little Colorado River, Bright Angel Creek, Nankoweap Creek, Kanab Creek, Shinumo Creek, Havasu Creek, and many others, the plateaus and side canyons have a bewildering array of geologic features, guaranteed to widen the eyes of the most experienced traveler, to instill awe and reverence into even a jaded spirit.

The Colorado River runs its course from an average of 3,500 feet below the rim of the Canyon to a maximum depth of nearly

6,000 feet. There are more than 150 rapids which provide river-runners with not only world-class whitewater but an endless geology lesson. If you are one of the lucky ones to boat down the Colorado, among the wonders you will see by day are 1.7 billion-year-old Vishnu schist, pink-veined Zoroaster granite, the Great Unconformity, Redwall limestone, Hermit shale, and the fossil-filled Kaibab formation, which you will see as you gaze seemingly endlessly upward toward the rim. By night you will sleep under ancient cliffs and listen to vast silences that will echo in your mind long afterwards. On day hikes you may well find fossils and petroglyphs in side canyons.

The Grand Canyon is crisscrossed by old Indian and mining trails, which allow a wide range of access. Bright Angel Trail, which begins at the South Rim near the grand old El Tovar Hotel, is probably the most accessible. You can hike from there ten miles to the bottom or take a variety of shorter descents. All are rewarding, all are very serious walks. For those who wish to explore further on foot, there are four major hiking loops in the Grand Canyon: Phantom Creek/Crystal Creek Loop; Tuna Creek/Shinumo Creek Loop; Shinumo Creek/Tapeats Creek Loop, and Tapeats Creek/Kanab Creek Loop. Of these, the Tapeat/Kanab loop connects with three wonderful destinations within the Grand Canyon: Thunder River, Deer Creek, and Kanab Canyon. Each one of these loops is a six- to nine-day hike depending on which one you choose, your conditioning, and of course the weather.

The Colorado River runs through this canyon universe officially starting at Lees Ferry, which is just below Lake Powell, the town of Page, and the drowned-but-yet-gorgeous Glen Canyon. Glen Canyon opens onto Marble Canyon, which runs roughly 61 miles from Lees Ferry to the body of the Grand Canyon Gorge, which runs yet another 226 miles down to Lake Mead and Hoover Dam. It is this middle part of the Canyon that most people visit when they go to the South Rim. Smaller numbers of visitors go to the North Rim, as it is several hours farther to the north via a roundabout road link. (Of course if you want to hike or run across to the North Rim from the South Rim—assuming you are in fabulous shape—it is a good forty-one and a half miles round trip!)

The West Rim, an hour and a half drive west of Flagstaff and a two and a half hour drive from Las Vegas, is owned by the Hualapai Indians. It is the least visited of the three major viewing areas of North Rim, South Rim, and West Rim. This is a shame because the West Rim is as yet largely unspoiled by commercial ventures and gives you a taste of how the Canyon looked before the coming of the white man. Indeed, Guano Point on the West Rim has one of the most stunning of all views of the Colorado.

Many visitors to the Grand Canyon National Park are under the misconception that the entire Grand Canyon is administered and owned by the U.S. Park Service, but this is not the case. The Hualapai Indians own 108 miles of Grand Canyon riverfront and close to one million acres of land at the Western end of the Canyon. The Havasupai Indians also own the land of Havasu Canyon, which is surely one of the loveliest spots in the Canyon. The Park Service has no official authority in these areas.

No Canyon visit, is complete however, without visiting all three rims, hiking some of the shorter trails, and finally, enjoying the great water pilgrimage, a journey down the Colorado River into the heart of the Canyon. Many of the stories in this book concern themselves with life below the rim. You will discover what it is like to explore, live, play, dream, and work in a pocket universe of tiers that just happens to have a river running through it. The Grand Canyon, a national and world treasure, has provided enormous pleasure to millions of visitors and will continue to do so as long we thoughtfully prepare for the countless visitors yet to come. As wild as it is, this great chasm in the earth, it is also a managed ecosystem that requires wise custodianship. If you've been there once or twice and think you have seen it all, rest assured that you haven't. Come again and then again, and do your part to spread the word that this is indeed a holy and wondrous place.

—SEAN O'REILLY, JAMES O'REILLY, AND LARRY HABEGGER

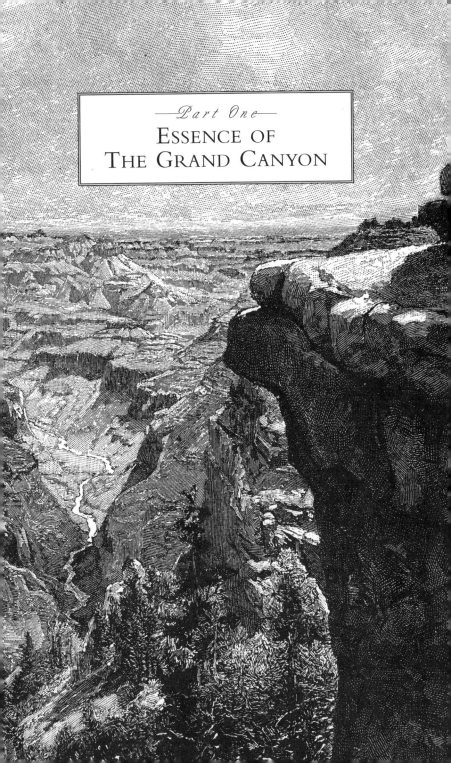

Part One
Essence of
The Grand Canyon

SCOTT THYBONY

Beneath the Rim

Something happens to you down there.

NIGHT ON THE TONTO, A PLATEAU SUNK DEEP WITHIN THE GRAND Canyon. I lie awake inside a thin bivouac sack with my pack over me for warmth and my boots for a pillow. On my back, I watch starlight above the highest rim, piercing the inner canyon. Pure brilliance. I shift position in the cold light, trying to get warm, drifting in and out of sleep. The star field spreads above the broken cliff line to the east, arches across the dark sky, and descends toward the Western Rim, half a mile above.

I set out this morning with no destination in mind, only with the idea to hike until midday before turning back, but I'm not surprised to find myself bedded down here on the Tonto at the end of the day. The Canyon has a way of drawing you into it. Once you start, it's hard to turn back. Knowing it's possible to get carried away, I always carry a bivy sack for day hikes that don't end. Years ago, when I began guiding in the Canyon, I knew where I wanted to go—always someplace more remote, more pristine. But where I end up doesn't matter so much anymore.

Part of my reason for returning to the depths of the Canyon is the physical push itself, the need to come into direct contact with the rough texture of the place. Another is to sink below the surface of things, to be contained for a time by vertical rock and sky.

Having covered 30 miles on a cross-canyon trail, I'm stretched out flat, stiff and tired. The Tonto will do for now. About two-thirds of the way between the outer rim and the Colorado River, it's the broadest step in the Canyon stairway, hanging above the Inner Gorge—a steep, 1,500-foot, V-cut trench that lies at the very bottom of the Canyon.

My starting point on the South Rim lies thousands of vertical feet above. Its dark outline appears close but is four miles away by trail. I've learned not to trust appearances in this place, where the scale of things is so vast, in a Canyon system 1 mile deep and 10 wide, cutting through the high-plateau country for almost 280 miles. Geologist Clarence Dutton wrestled with these immensities when he undertook a classic study of the Grand Canyon region more than a hundred years ago. "Things are not what they seem," he wrote, "and the perceptions cannot tell us what they are."

Centuries earlier, Spanish explorers had faced the same problem. When the conquistadors reached the great Canyon in 1540, three men scrambled into the gorge, trying to get to the Colorado River. They made it only a third of the way down before dragging themselves back to the rim. The scouts reported finding rocks, thought to be the size of a man when seen from above, standing taller than the 185-foot tower of Seville.

More than two centuries passed before the next European saw the Grand Canyon. Now, each year nearly five million people make their way to the classic lookouts. Nine out of ten see the Canyon from the South Rim, many pausing only for a quick look.

Peering into it from the rim, you take in what's not there—the great empty space. Then the eye sorts out the massive rock forms and the tangle of gorges. But the vast distances absorb the details, and it's in the details that another world opens up.

From above, you might glimpse a river threading far below, a trail scar, a clump of green trees. These only hint at what lies hidden beneath the rim—the waterfalls and the turquoise streams, the old mining camps and the Indian ruins, the mule trains winding up the trail and the rafts running the powerful rapids. Standing on one of the Canyon overlooks, you overlook more than you realize. A mountain-bike trip along the rim helps; a mule ride down the Bright Angel Trail gives you a taste. But a hike into the gorge lets your feet prove how wrong your eyes can be.

Scott Thybony writes books for the National Geographic Society, guidebooks to historical and natural areas, and essays. A resident of Flagstaff, Arizona, he has lived with indigenous peoples in the Canadian Arctic and the American Southwest. His travels through western North America have resulted in award-winning articles in Smithsonian Magazine *and* National Geographic Traveler *and contributions to other national magazines.*

✷

I'm not sure why I find the Tonto Platform so appealing. Perhaps it has something to do with openness. When it comes right down to it, other areas within the Upper Sonoran Zone are much more interesting in a biologic sense. Above the Tonto are found chaparral, mountain scrub, and pinyon-juniper woodland; these three often occur together or adjacent to one another and support a bigger variety of plants and animals, especially birds, than any place on the Tonto.

I once camped in an area of mixed chaparral, pinyon, and juniper beneath the North Rim. The night was quiet, and I slept like a stone, completely unaware of the mountain lion that came past in the dark. The next morning, I found clear tracks just yards from where I'd been sleeping. I followed them for about a half mile until they disappeared on slickrock. Through binoculars, from a high point, I spent an hour looking for that lion. I thought he'd be dozing somewhere, lying out on a sunny ledge. I never saw him, but knowing he was there made a big difference in the way I felt about the place. Lions are more appealing than the scorpions that capture my attention on the Tonto.

—Jeremy Schmidt, *A Natural History Guide:
Grand Canyon National Park*

GAIL DUDLEY

Nankoweap

It's a long way to the bottom.

ON MY LEFT, THE CANYON WALL JUTS UPWARD, A WIND-POLISHED
sheet of rock. There are no jagged outcroppings, no sturdy trees or
bushes that might serve as handholds if I begin to fall. There is only
a smooth-as-plaster surface reaching above me and before me as far
as I can see.

The sun reflecting off the rock sears my face and burns my eyes.
If I gaze at it too long, I become dizzy. This is the last thing I want
because of what is on my right: a sheer drop of at least 200 feet.
One misstep, one careless bump against the Canyon wall could send
me falling toward eternity. I dare not even look because I know I
will be overcome with fear. My legs tremble, and a hard lump forms
in my throat.

"Not now," I tell myself. "You've got to pull yourself together."

On this narrow trail there is no turning back. Somehow I have
to keep moving forward. I cannot focus on the deep chasm below
me or the vast emptiness that seems to be engulfing me.

Instead, I focus on my feet.

I devote every ounce of my attention to the aching flesh and
bone stuffed inside a pair of sweat-soaked woolen socks and cum-
bersome, size-eight hiking boots. My feet are dangerously close

positioned on a thin rock ledge along the canyon wall. I set them down carefully, one in front of the other, feeling for loose bits of stone or dirt that might cause me to slip.

In spots, the trail is less than three feet wide. There is barely enough room to place my feet side by side. Whether I can maintain my balance now is a matter of life or death.

I pretend I am walking a tightrope. Poking with my hiking stick like a cautious praying mantis, I move slowly. Heel-to-toe. Heel-to-toe. I arch my back and curve my shoulders to keep my 40-pound pack centered. One swing to either side could send me over the edge.

Poke. Poke. Heel-to-toe. I make tedious progress along the treacherous trail. Ahead of me, I see a wide spot with several welcoming benchlike rock formations and scrubby vegetation. Like Columbus reaching out toward a new continent, I concentrate my efforts on getting to this haven. It appears to be much closer than it actually is. Perspiration trickles from my forehead down the bridge of my nose. It creeps across my parched lips and into my mouth, leaving a briny taste.

"Steady, steady," I whisper in a shaky voice that does not seem to be my own. "You're almost there."

My pack grazes the canyon wall and sends a cascade of tiny rock fragments down behind me. I watch as they bounce and tumble into the abyss. Everything is moving in slow motion.

"Easy," I tell myself as I twist my right foot back and forth on top of the loose granite. "Don't panic." Gradually the crumbled rock packs down. I realize I have been holding my breath. For how long, I do not know. I exhale and place most of my weight on my right foot. It holds. Relieved, I move forward once again. Poke. Poke. Heel-to-toe.

Occasionally I hear the solid thud of photographer Rick Danley's footsteps behind me. I am not alone, I remind myself. However, on this dangerous passage, I might as well be. If I were to fall, there is nothing my companion could do to save me.

"He would just call in a helicopter to pick up the remains," I find myself thinking. Worse yet, what if Rick were to stumble and slide over the edge? A seasoned hiker and physically fit Grand Canyon ranger, he is much less likely to fall than I am. However, he is weighed down by heavy camera equipment. Anything can happen. "Would he scream?" I wonder. "What sound would he make when he hit the bottom?"

I cannot even think of trying to make it out of this canyon alone, bearing the horrible news. But I do not dare to look back to make certain Rick is all right. "Too risky," I tell myself. His footsteps tell me he is still there, and I must move forward. Most importantly, I must quit conjuring up terrifying images and think only of the wide spot ahead.

Poke. Poke. Heel-to-toe. Less than fifteen feet to safety. Poke. Poke. Heel-to-toe. I reach the wide spot after an eternity. My legs turn to rubber, and I slump down onto a broad slab of rock.

"You made it!" Rick yells. "That's the point where the Sierra Club turned back."

While we planned this trip, Rick had told me about the hiking expedition that was aborted when the group approached this dangerous point on the Nankoweap Trail. This and other stories about the adventurers who suddenly lost their zeal to explore are passed along as part of unwritten Grand Canyon legend.

In fact, these stories are the reason I am here. I am not a daredevil or an ardent canyon

---

The Nankoweap is a Wilderness Trail. Washouts and rockfall require some route-finding skills. One of the Canyon's most strenuous trails. Not recommended for inexperienced or solo hikers.

In 1882, Canyon explorer and geologist John Wesley Powell directed the building of a trail into Nankoweap Valley that followed a Paiute route. His colleague, geologist Charles Walcott, used it to reach isolated rock formations in the eastern Grand Canyon.

Kolb Arch, the largest natural bridge in the Canyon, is found in an upper arm of Nankoweap Canyon below Woolsey Point.

◆

—Scott Thybony, *Official Guide to Hiking the Grand Canyon*

hiker. I do not like steep or narrow places. I am not even well-conditioned enough to be attempting this arduous hike even though I walk an average of three miles a day. However, I *am* a sucker for a challenge. When one of our readers wrote that *Arizona Highways* should do a story on the Nankoweap if we wanted to feature the most difficult trail in the Grand Canyon, and when my editor asked if I would like to write that story, I simply said, "Sure."

Now, as I try to still my wobbly knees and calm my throbbing heart, I would like to meet that reader. I also would like to say a few words to my editor. Unfortunately these matters will have to wait. I take a deep swig of water from my canteen, unwrap a banana-flavored PowerBar, and laugh.

"I didn't want to say anything to you before we got here," Rick says. "I was hoping you wouldn't realize this is the most dangerous part of the trail until we were already past it. Did I succeed?"

"Yes," I answer humbly, unwilling to admit to the frightening thoughts that raced through my mind only moments ago.

"Shall we move on?" Rick asks.

"Okay," I respond with as much enthusiasm as I can muster.

It is midafternoon on the first day of our six-day hike. Already I am exhausted. The first three miles of the trek, down Forest Service Trail 57 to the Nankoweap trailhead, had not been difficult. A wide, shaley uphill road gave way to a flat stretch covered with a soft, yellow blanket of pin oak leaves.

I fell face forward once and lay spraddle-legged beneath my pack like a beached turtle. Flailing my arms and legs, I was unable to right myself. While in this grossly unflattering position, I decided to make some changes. I set down my pack, peeled off a few layers of clothing, and unloaded about ten pounds of nonessential items and food. After stuffing this excess weight into a plastic garbage bag, I hung it high in the thicket near the trailhead. I hoped it would be there when we got back.

Now I wish I had left another ten pounds behind. Weighing in at about 107, I had been foolish to try to pack so much.

"A common mistake," Rick tells me. "Sometimes people tend to overprepare. They want to be ready for any possible disaster."

With temperatures soaring to the mid-70s during the day and plunging to 10 degrees Fahrenheit at night, it is hard to decide what to take and what to leave behind. Unaccustomed to the heavy load, my shoulders and lower back are already getting sore. However, just when I am about to tell Rick I am turning back, that this is a big mistake, I gaze out across the canyon. I am captured by the majesty of its red walls, by its overwhelming beauty and mystery. A cool breeze blows through my hair, and a raven soars effortlessly overhead.

Croak. Croak. The great bird seems to beckon us to move.

I have had my first lesson in the deceptive nature of the Nankoweap. Its inviting beauty does not always prepare you for its extremities. The breeze blows through the canyon, giving it an aura of gentleness. In reality, this is a harsh and cruel land. The twisted junipers and bayberry testify to its rugged character. The raven is one of the few living creatures we encounter on this trek.

Near dusk, we reach Marion Point, where we will spend this first night. The lower level of the campground is barely large enough to accommodate two or three people. Rick climbs to a boulder-strewn lookout where he prefers to sleep. I unroll my sleeping bag in a narrow clearing just off the trail, remove my boots, and spread my sweaty socks on a rock to dry. My shoulders throb and my knees ache. I decide to eat my dinner of Lipton noodles and crawl into my bag before the sun goes down. Warmed by its last rays, I may be able to make it through the night without freezing.

The last thing I see is Mount Hayden, jutting up from the entrails of the canyon like a bright-orange thumb. I will become accustomed to its presence because it is visible from most vantage points along Nankoweap. It will become a familiar sentinel as I toil along the trail and as I drift into sleep.

Tonight, beneath a charcoal sky sprinkled with stars, I think of all those I love and pray I will see them again. Then I close my eyes and dream that things are falling helter-skelter from my pack and over the canyon's edge. My compass is the last object to disappear into the dark hole, and then I am lost and alone. I awaken abruptly, check to make sure my pack is still intact, and listen for signs of life.

The only sound I hear is the soft scrabble of mice searching for food on the rock floor.

The next morning, after a hearty breakfast, we set out for Tilted Mesa. The trail is more difficult than what we experienced yesterday. There are numerous rockslides, almost obliterating the narrow path. I have trouble balancing my pack while climbing through the boulders. At one point, I decide to straddle a tall rock. I put my right foot down, and my pack shifts sharply to the right. Suddenly, I am down, wedged between two sharp rocks. I struggle to get back up. Finally, I succeed by hugging one of the rocks and pushing down on my knees with all my might.

There is a soft throbbing below my right knee. I recognize it as the beginning of a large bruise. My right ankle is beginning to puff up. I am constantly thirsty, consuming much more water than I had anticipated. Still, my lips are cracked, and my tongue is swelling.

We emerge from the rockslides only to hit slippery patches of shale. Even in boots with deep-treaded soles, it is difficult to get a grip. I feel my way cautiously but still slip—often stopping just short of the trail's edge. I shudder to think of falling again.

With about a mile to go until we reach Tilted Mesa, we round a turn and catch our first glimpse of Nankoweap Creek. It glistens like a strip of tinsel in the morning sun, lined on both sides by lush green. This and the constant hum of airplanes and helicopters overhead are the only reminders that there is a more bountiful life beyond these desolate canyon walls.

> *A*t the very bottom of the Canyon you seldom hear aircraft noise. Helicopter access is strictly controlled and limited. Other aircraft may fly over the canyon but not into it.
>
> ◆
>
> —SO'R, JO'R, and LH

By noon, we reach our lunch stop. It took four hours to travel three miles. Tilted Mesa is exactly what its name suggests—a broad, angled slab of rock dotted with scrub. The distorted juniper, tortured agave, and yellow-blooming thistle look barely alive.

As we sit down to eat, I realize that Rick is growing happier and stronger with each step along the Nankoweap. He dances between the rocks like a mountain goat, moving quickly and assuredly. Rarely stumbling and never falling, he is in his element.

By contrast, I am becoming weaker and more tense. I now travel like an old woman, humped over my walking stick for support. Every muscle in my body is tight and sore. By now, my ankle is pulsing, and I do not remove my boot for fear I will not be able to get it back on.

We are only three miles from the silvery waters of Nankoweap Creek and the well-preserved ruins of the Indian granaries built near its banks centuries ago. This is our final destination. However, Rick has told me this will be the toughest part of our journey. We will need to descend a steep drop of about 3,000 feet, sitting down on the shale at certain points and sliding with our packs.

I believe I can make it down, but I am not certain about the climb back up. I am not comfortable on shale, especially on a slope. Even though I yearn to explore the granaries and swim in the refreshing waters of Nankoweap Creek, I have reached a moment of reckoning.

"I can't go any farther," I tell Rick. "I'm afraid I won't be able to climb back up on the shale."

Although I expect him to be angry, Rick responds positively. He knows I have reached my limit.

"You made it past the point where the Sierra Club turned back," he says. "This morning you also made it beyond a spot where I once met a severely dehydrated hiker and another with a big gash on his head. You made it farther than some people have—and you should be proud of yourself."

Although he is a man of few words, Rick offered some encouragement I will carry the rest of my life. My verbal backpack now includes well-earned reminders to admit my weaknesses and always walk with pride. After a good night's sleep, we head back up the Nankoweap Trail. I negotiate those tough eight miles much better than I did on the way down.

Gail Dudley is preparing herself to return and finish the trek. She currently lives in Cave Creek, Arizona.

✳

There is nothing else quite like it— a deeply entrenched water corridor 280 miles long through a desert wilderness of almost overwhelming beauty. No other American river offers, in one unbroken stretch, as great an aggregation of rapids. Contact with nature is direct and powerful. Nor is the encounter limited to water situations. Side canyons, some attainable by trail and some not, offer unexpected plunge pools, waterfalls, banks of ferns, brilliant flowers. One can swim, hike, climb, fish, take pictures, hunt for ancient Indian petroglyphs, study botany or geology in what has been called the world's greatest open textbook, or just sit still, watching small creatures go about their business while the variegated cliffs take on the rich hues of sunset.

Blue haze sinking past purpling walls to mingle with last streaks of light on the darkening river: it is a good moment to recall those who went before, to heed the Chinese saying, "When drinking the water, remember who dug the well."

—David Lavender, *River Runners of the Grand Canyon*

Gone Back into the Earth

The Canyon becomes music for the spirit.

I AM UP TO MY WAIST IN A BASIN OF COOL, ACID-CLEAR WATER, AT the head of a box canyon some 600 feet above the Colorado River. I place my outstretched hands flat against a terminal wall of dark limestone, which rises more than 100 feet above me, and down which a sheet of water falls—the thin creek in whose pooled waters I now stand. The water splits at my fingertips into wild threads; higher up, a warm canyon wind lifts water off the limestone in a fine spray; these droplets intercept and shatter sunlight. Down, down another four waterfalls and fern-shrouded pools below, the water spills into an eddy of the Colorado River, in the shadow of a huge boulder. Our boat is tied there.

This lush crease in the surface of the earth is a cleft in the precipitous desert walls of Arizona's Grand Canyon. Its smooth outcrops of purple-tinged travertine stone, its heavy air rolled in the languid perfume of columbine, struck by the sharp notes of a water ouzel, the thrill of a disturbed black phoebe—all this has a name: Elves Chasm.

A few feet to my right, a preacher from Maryland is staring up at the blue sky, straining to see what flowers those are that nod at the top of the falls. To my left, a freelance automobile mechanic from Colorado sits with an impish smile by helleborine orchids. Behind, another man, a builder and sometime record producer from New York, who comes as often as he can to camp and hike in the Southwest, stands immobile at the pool's edge.

Sprawled shirtless on a rock is our boatman. He has led twelve or fifteen of us on the climb up from the river. The Colorado entrances him. He has a well-honed sense of the ridiculous, brought on, one believes, by so much time in the extreme remove of this canyon.

In our descent, we meet others in our group who stopped climbing at one of the lower pools. At the second to the last waterfall, a young woman with short hair and dazzling blue eyes walks with me back into the canyon's narrowing V. We wade into a still pool, swim a few strokes to its head, climb over a boulder, swim across a second pool, and then stand together, giddy, in the press of limestone, beneath the deafening cascade—filled with euphoria.

One at a time, we bolt and glide, fishlike, back across the pool, grounding in fine white gravel. We wade the second pool and continue our descent, stopping to marvel at the strategy of a barrel cactus and at the pale shading of color in the ledges to which we cling. We share few words. We know hardly anything of each other. We share the country.

The group of us who have made this morning climb are in the middle of a ten-day trip down the Colorado River. Each day we are upended, if not by some element of the landscape itself then by what the landscape does, visibly, to each of us. It has snapped us like fresh-laundered sheets.

After lunch, we reboard three large rubber rafts and enter the Colorado's quick, high flow. The river has not been this high or fast since Glen Canyon Dam—135 miles above Elves Chasm, 17 miles above our starting point at Lees Ferry—was closed in 1963. Jumping out ahead of us, with its single oarsman and three passengers, is our fourth craft, a twelve-foot rubber boat, like a water strider with a steel frame. In Sockdolager Rapid the day before, one of its welds burst, and the steel pieces were bent apart. (Sockdolager:

a nineteenth-century colloquialism for knockout punch.)

Such groups as ours, the members all but unknown to each other on the first day, almost always grow close, solicitous of each other, during their time together. They develop a humor that informs similar journeys everywhere, a humor founded in tomfoolery, in punning, in a continuous parody of the life-in-civilization all have so recently (and gleefully) left. Such humor depends on context, on an accretion of small, shared events; it seems silly to those who are not there. It is not, of course. Any more than that moment of fumbling awe one feels on seeing the Brahma schist at the dead bottom of the Canyon's Inner Gorge. Your fingertips graze the 1.9-billion-year-old stone as the boat drifts slowly past.

With the loss of self-consciousness, the landscape opens.

There are forty-one of us, counting a crew of six. An actor from Florida, now living in Los Angeles. A medical student and his wife. A supervisor from Virginia's Department of Motor Vehicles. A health-store owner from Chicago. An editor from New York and his young son.

That kind of diversity seems normal in groups that seek such vacations—to trek in the Himalayas, to dive in the Sea of Cortez, to go birding in the Arctic. We are together for two reasons: to run the Colorado River and to participate with jazz musician Paul Winter, who initiated the trip, in a music workshop.

Winter is an innovator and a listener. He had thought for years about coming to the Grand Canyon, about creating music here in response to this particular landscape—collared lizards and prickly pear cactus, Anasazi Indian ruins and stifling heat. But most especially, he wanted music evoked by the river and the walls that flew from its banks—Coconino sandstone on top of Hermit shale on top of the Supai formations, stone exposed to sunlight, a bloom of photons that lifted colors—saffron and ochre, apricot, madder orange, pearl- and gray-green, copper reds, umber and terra-cotta browns—and left them floating in the air.

Winter was searching for a reintegration of music, landscape, and people. For resonance. Three or four times during the trip, he would find it for sustained periods: drifting on a quiet stretch of water below Bass Rapids with oboist Nancy Rumbel and cellist David Darling; in a natural amphitheater high in the Muav limestone of Matkatameba Canyon; on the night of a full June moon with euphonium player Larry Roark in Blacktail Canyon.

Winter's energy and passion, and the strains of solo and ensemble music, were sewn into the trip like prevailing winds, like the canyon wren's clear, whistled, descending notes, his glissando— seemingly present, close by, or at a distance, whenever someone stopped to listen.

But we came and went, too, like the swallows and swifts that flicked over the water ahead of the boats, intent on private thoughts.

On the second day of the trip we stopped at Redwall Cavern, an undercut recess that spans a beach of fine sand, perhaps 500 feet wide and 150 feet deep. Winter intends to record here, but the sand absorbs too much sound. Unfazed, the others toss a Frisbee, practice tai chi, jog, meditate, play records, and read novels.

No other animal but the human would bring to bear so many activities, from so many different cultures and levels of society, with so much energy, so suddenly in a new place. And no other animal, the individuals so entirely unknown to each other, would chance together something so unknown as this river journey. In this frenetic activity and

*C*hip a piece of the Redwall, and you will see that it is not red at all, except at the surface, which has been stained by the iron oxide leached down from above. It is, instead, a blueish-gray limestone, very fine, uniform, and abounding in seashells as well as in the remains of other forms of ocean life. It belongs to the period the geologists call the Mississippian, during which great coal deposits were made in warm, swampy areas in some parts of the world, though there are no such beds here.

◆

—Joseph Wood Krutch, *Grand Canyon: Today and All Its Yesterdays*

difference seems a suggestion of human evolution and genuine
adventure. We are not the first down this river, but in the slooshing
of human hands at the water's edge, the swanlike notes of an oboe,
the occasional hugs among those most afraid of the rapids, there *is*
exploration.

Each day, we see or hear something that astounds us. The thou-
sand-year-old remains of an Anasazi footbridge, hanging in twilight
shadow high in the canyon wall above Harding Rapid. Deer Creek
Falls, where we stand knee-deep in turquoise water encircled by a
rainbow. Havasu Canyon, wild with grapevines, cottonwoods and
velvet ash, speckled dace and mule deer, wild grasses and crimson
monkey flowers. Each evening, we enjoy the vespers: cicadas and
crickets, mourning doves, vermilion flycatchers. And the wind, for
which chimes are hung in a salt cedar. These notes leap above the
splash and rattle, the grinding of water and the roar of rapids.

The narrow, damp, hidden worlds of the side canyons, with their
scattered shards of Indian pottery and ghost imprints of 400-mil-
lion-year-old nautiloids, open onto the larger world of the
Colorado River itself; but nothing conveys to us how far into the
earth's surface we have come. Occasionally we glimpse the South
Rim, four or five thousand feet above. From the rims, the canyon
seems oceanic; at the surface of the river, the feeling is intimate. To
someone up there with binoculars, we seem utterly remote down
here. It is this known dimension of distance and time and the per-
plexing question posed by the canyon itself—What is consequen-
tial? (in one's life, in the life of human beings, in the life of a planet)—
that reverberate constantly and make the human inclination to
judge (another person, another kind of thought) seem so eerie.

Two kinds of time pass here: sitting at the edge of a sun-warmed
pool watching blue dragonflies and black tadpoles. And the rapids:
down the glassy-smooth tongue into a yawning trench, climb a
ten-foot wall of standing water and fall into boiling, ferocious
hydraulics, sucking whirlpools, drowned voices, stopped hearts.
Rapids can fold and shatter boats and take lives if the boatman
enters at the wrong point or at the wrong angle.

Some rapids, like one called Hermit, seem more dangerous than they are and give us great roller-coaster rides. Others—Hance, Crystal, Upset—seem less spectacular, but are technically difficult. At Crystal, our boat screeches and twists against its frame. Its nose crumples like cardboard in the trough; our boatman makes the critical move to the right with split-second timing, and we are over a standing wave and into the haystacks of white water, safely into trail waves. The boatman's eyes cease to blaze.

The first few rapids—Badger Creek and Soap Creek—do not overwhelm us. When we hit the Inner Gorge—Granite Falls, Unkar Rapid, Horn Creek Rapid—some grip the boat, rigid and silent. (On the ninth day, when we are about to run perhaps the most formidable rapid, Lava Falls, the one among us who has had the greatest fear is calm, almost serene. In the last days, it is hard to overestimate what the river and the music and the unvoiced concerns for each other have washed out.)

There are threats to this separate world of the Inner

*T*here are, however, a few distinctive features that even the C-student can't forget if he wishes to locate himself on a visual ascent from river to rim. The ancient Vishnu schist of the Inner Gorge is impossible to forget. It's nearly black, and if you're down there on the river floating past it, it gives you the creeps. The broad benchland called the Tonto Plateau just above the Inner Gore consists of a dark-brown sandstone called Tapeats, which gives way, as one moves back from the gorge, to a slope of greenish, Bright Angel shale. Both are easy to recognize topographically. And about midway up the Canyon walls, the sheer, five- to six-hundred-foot cliff that is visible throughout the Grand Canyon is Redwall limestone, impossible to mistake because it is so massive and so…red, stained that color by the formations above it. The whitish- or cream-colored cap that forms the rim of this entire aggregation is Kaibab limestone. You can't mistake it because there isn't anything above it.

◆

—Page Stegner, *Grand Canyon: The Great Abyss*

Gorge. Down inside it, one struggles to maintain a sense of what they are, how they impinge.

In 1963, Glen Canyon Dam cut off the Canyon's natural flow of water. Spring runoffs of more than 200,000 cubic feet per second ceased to roar through the gorge, clearing the main channel of rock and stones washed down from the side canyons. Fed now from the bottom of Lake Powell backed up behind the dam, the river is no longer a warm, silt-laden habitat for Colorado squawfish, razorback sucker, and several kinds of chub, but a cold, clear habitat for trout. With no annual scouring and a subsequent deposition of fresh sand, the beaches show the evidence of continuous human use: they are eroding. The postflood eddies where squawfish bred have disappeared. Tamarisk (salt cedar) and camel thorn, both exotic plants formerly washed out with the spring floods, have gained an apparently permanent foothold. At the high-water mark, catclaw acacia, mesquite, and Apache plume are no longer watered and are dying out.

On the rim, far removed above, such evidence of human tampering seems, and perhaps is, pernicious. From the river, another change is more wrenching. It floods the system with a kind of panic that in other animals induces nausea and the sudden evacuation of the bowels: it is the descent of helicopters. Their sudden arrival in the Canyon evokes not jeers but staring. The violence is brutal, an intrusion as criminal and as random as rape. When the helicopter departs, its rotor-wind walloping against the stone walls, I want to wash the sound off my skin.

The Canyon finally absorbs the intrusion. I focus quietly each day on the stone, the breathing of time locked up here, back to the Proterozoic, before there were seashells. Look up to wisps of high cirrus overhead, the hint of a mare's tail sky. Close my eyes: tappet of water against the boat, sound of an Anasazi's six-hole flute. And I watch the bank for beaver tracks, for any movement.

The canyon seems like a grandfather.

One evening, Winter and perhaps half the group carry instruments and recording gear back into Blacktail Canyon to a spot sound engineer Mickey Houlihan says is good for recording.

Winter likes to quote from Thoreau: "The woods would be very silent if no birds sang except those that sing best." The remark seems not only to underscore the ephemeral nature of human evolution but the necessity in evaluating any phenomenon—a canyon, a life, a song—of providing for change.

After several improvisations dominated by acappella voice and percussion, Winter asks Larry Roark to try something on the euphonium; he and Rumbel and Darling will then come up around him. Roark is silent. Moonlight glows on the canyon's lips. There is the sound of gurgling water. After a word of encouragement, feeling shrouded in anonymous darkness like the rest of us, Larry puts his mouth to the horn.

For awhile he is alone. God knows what visions of waterfalls or wrens, of boats in the rapids, of Bach or Mozart, are in his head, in his fingers, to send forth notes. The whine of the soprano sax finds him. And the flutter of the oboe. And the rumbling of the choral cello. The exchange lasts perhaps twenty minutes. Furious and sweet, anxious, rolling, delicate and raw. The last six or eight hanging notes are Larry's. Then there is a long silence. Winter finally says, "My God."

I feel, sitting in the wet dark in bathing suit and sneakers and t-shirt, that my fingers have brushed one of life's deep, coursing threads. Like so much else in the Canyon, it is left alone. Speak, even notice it, and it would disappear.

I had come to the Canyon with expectations. I had wanted to see snowy egrets flying against the black schist at dusk; I saw blue-winged teal against the deep, green waters at dawn. I had wanted to hear thunder rolling in the thousand-foot depths; I heard Winter's soprano sax resonating in Matkatameba Canyon, with the guttural caws of four ravens which circled above him. I had wanted to watch rattlesnakes; I saw in an abandoned copper mine, in the beam of my flashlight, a wall of copper sulphate that looked like a wall of turquoise. I rose each morning at dawn and washed in the cold river. I went to sleep each night listening to the cicadas, the pencil-ticking sound of some other insect, the soughing of river

waves in tamarisk roots, and watching bats plunge and turn, looking like leaves blown against the sky. What any of us had come to
see or do fell away. We found ourselves at each turn with what we
had not imagined.

The last evening it rained. We had left the Canyon and been carried far out onto Lake Mead by the river's current. But we stood
staring backward, at the point where the Canyon had so obviously
and abruptly ended.

A thought that stayed with me was that I had entered a private
place in the earth. I had seen exposed nearly its oldest part. I had
lost my sense of what people were, clambering to gain access to
high waterfalls where we washed our hair together; and a sense of
our endless struggle as a species to understand time and to estimate
the consequences of our acts.

It rained the last evening. But before it did, Nancy Rumbel
moved to the highest point on Scorpion Island in Lake Mead and
played her oboe before a storm we could see hanging over Nevada.
Sterling Smyth, who would return to programming computers in
twenty-four hours, created a twelve-string imitation of the canyon
wren, a long guitar solo. David Darling, revealed suddenly stark,
again and then again, against a white-lightning sky, bowed furiously in homage to a now-overhanging cumulonimbus.

In the morning, we touched the far shore of Lake Mead, boarded a bus and headed for Las Vegas Airport. We were still wrapped
in the journey, as though it were a Navajo blanket. We departed on
various planes and arrived home in various cities and towns, and at
some point the world entered again, and the hardest thing, the
translation of what we touched, began.

I sat in the airport in San Francisco, waiting for a connecting
flight to Oregon, dwelling on one image. At the mouth of
Nankoweap Canyon, the river makes a broad turn, and it is possible
to see high in the orange rock what seem to be four small windows.
They are entrances to granaries, built by the Anasazi who dwelled
in the Canyon a thousand years ago. This was provision against
famine, to ensure people would survive.

I do not know, really, how we will survive without places like the Inner Gorge of the Grand Canyon to visit. Once in a lifetime, even, is enough. To feel the stripping down, an ebb of the press of conventional time, a radical change of proportion, an unspoken respect for others that elicits keen emotional pleasure, a quick, intimate pounding of the heart.

Some parts of the trip will emerge one day on an album. Others will be found in a gesture of friendship to some stranger in an airport, in a letter of outrage to a planner of dams, in a note of gratitude to nameless faces in the Park Service, in wondering at the relatives of the ubiquitous wren, in the belief, passed on in whatever fashion—a photograph, a chord, a sketch—that nature can heal.

The living of life, any life, involves great and private pain, much of which we share with no one. In such places as the Inner Gorge, the pain trails away from us. It is not so quiet there or so removed that you can hear yourself think, that you would even wish to; that comes later. You can hear your heart beat. That comes first.

Barry Lopez was born in Port Chester, New York, in 1945. He is the author of Arctic Dreams, Of Wolves and Men, *and* Crossing Open Ground, *from which this story was excerpted, along with several collections of fiction, including* Winter Count *and* River Notes. *A contributing editor to* Harper's *and* North American Review, *he has received an Award in Literature from the American Academy and Institute of Arts and Letters, the American Book Award, and the John Burroughs Medal, among other honors. He now lives in Oregon.*

✳

We paused for lunch in Elves Chasm. The cave is not visible from the river, and it is masked by trees that have evidently grown there in the last fifty years. Before we came to this point, we noticed that the left wall of the Inner Gorge had at one time been covered by lava flowing into the canyon. Because we had almost passed out of the schists, the lava covered the brown sandstone that formed the rim farther up the canyon and here almost reached the water's edge. In many places, the lava resembled giant drapes billowing over the sandstone. Flowing down the canyon in which Elves Chasm is located is a delightful stream that forms large pools. We, of course, plunged into one to cool off and then went into the cave for lunch. The stream is Royal Arch Creek, rising in the Aztec Amphitheater between Point Quetzal and Point Centeotl. From Elves Chasm, we could look across to the large formation known as Explorer's Monument, which stands rather isolated at the foot of Marcos Terrace. The river at this point veers north, and we could see far up Stephen's Aisle.

—Barry M. Goldwater, *Delightful Journey:
Down the Green and Colorado Rivers*

Revelation

*It has never been easy to grasp the
immensity of the Grand Canyon.*

IT HAS BEEN PRAISED AS THE MOST "SUBLIME SPECTACLE" IN THE
world and condemned as the most "profitless locality" on earth.
Some have peered into it with a sense of oppression and horror;
others have been moved to great acts of creative expression and a
sense of profound spiritual identification. It has inspired agony and
ecstasy in thousands of photographers trying to deal with its
changing light; it has moved poets and writers to absolute excesses
of purple (and sometimes indecipherable) prose. There is, after all,
nothing quite like this Canyon anywhere else on the face of the earth.

Many of us, particularly those whose aesthetic sensibilities have
been trained by pastoral hills, blue lakes, verdant meadows, and
contented cows, don't quite know what to make of the Grand
Canyon—at least not at first. I can think of nobody who put the
problem more succinctly than Clarence Dutton, the man who led
the first U.S. Geological Survey expedition into the region in 1880.
"Great innovations," he said, "whether in art or literature, in science
or in nature, seldom take the world by storm. They must be understood before they can be estimated, and must be cultivated before
they can be understood."

So let's get some of the clinical factoids out of the way right up front. The Grand Canyon region extends, east to west, from the Echo Cliffs near Lees Ferry to the Grand Wash Cliffs near Lake Mead. On the north, it is bordered by the Kaibab, Kanab, Uinkaret, and Shivwits plateaus, and on the south by the Coconino Plateau. The elevation of the North Rim at Grand Canyon Lodge is 8,200 feet; the South Rim at Grand Canyon is 6,965 feet. The highest juncture within the park boundaries is Point Imperial on the North Rim at 8,801 feet; Yaki Point on the South Rim is about 1,500 feet lower, at 7,262 feet.

The Colorado River drops 10,000 feet from its Green River headwaters in Wyoming's Wind River Range to its outlet in the Gulf of California (actually it never quite makes it all the way, dying in the sands of Laguna Salada a few miles short of the gulf.) In total, it is about 1,700 miles long, and it is the drainage system for nearly 250,000 square miles—an area encompassing a significant portion of seven western states. Its Grand Canyon section, between Lees Ferry and the Grand Wash Cliffs, is 277 miles long—though the last 40 miles now lie beneath the waters of Lake Mead. The river through the Canyon descends a total of 1,900 feet, or approximately 7.8 feet per mile. Its flow is controlled by Glen Canyon Dam and currently varies between a high of 20,000 cfs (cubic feet per second) and a low of 5,000 cfs. It carries a canyon-scouring sediment load of about 40,000 tons a day—a small fraction of its predam burden of 380,000 to 500,000 tons per day.

The Canyon area contained within the national park itself encompasses about 1,900 square miles. Its depth varies from less than 1,000 feet downstream from Lees Ferry in the upper sections of Marble Canyon to 6,000 at its deepest point in Granite Gorge. It varies in width from less than 1 mile to 17.5 miles from rim to rim.

Now that the data gods have been temporarily appeased, we can get more personal. I first encountered all of the above more than 50 years ago. In 1944, after a 6-year sojourn among the diminutive hills and hummocks of New England, my parents, both Westerners by nature and training, packed up their worldly possessions, tied them all on top of our Ford station wagon, and moved from

Massachusetts to California. They took the southern route, old Highway 66, through St. Louis, Oklahoma City, across the Texas panhandle, and into New Mexico and Arizona.

I was six or seven at the time, and half a century has cleared my memory of much of that midsummer odyssey, though a few imagistic scraps and one king-sized revelation still remain. For scraps, there is the overloaded, overheating Ford station wagon in which we motored sedately away from the lush greenery of the eastern United States and into the parched, uncharted wastelands beyond the hundredth meridian. There is a leaking, canvas water bag that hung from the hood ornament, and a cylindrical "air cooler" that attached to the driver's seat window like a food tray at a drive-in restaurant. It failed to perform any cooling, though it did humidify—a particularly jolly feature through the damp heat of the East and Midwest.

For revelation, there is…the revelation. That is what the British novelist J. B. Priestley called the Grand Canyon—"not a show place, a beauty spot, but a revelation," a place indescribable in "pigments or words." He said he had heard rumors there were those who were disappointed by the spectacle, but he opined that such people would be disappointed by the Day of Judgment. "In fact," he mused, "the Grand Canyon is a sort of *landscape* Day of Judgment" (italics mine).

A must-read for anyone whose imagination is fired by exploration: *Beyond the Hundredth Meridian: John Wesley Powell and the Second Opening of the West*, by Wallace Stegner (Page Stegner's father), in which he tells the story of the distinguished ethnologist and geologist who explored the Colorado River, the Grand Canyon, and the Indian lands of the Southwest.

◆

—SO'R, JO'R, and LH

My revelation was somewhat different from the one experienced by Mr. Priestley, and perhaps it might be worth stepping back in time here for a moment to review it. I should like to film this ret-

rospective from an elevated perspective, however. I no longer wish
to be too closely identified with its author.

Let us imagine we are looking down into the rear seat of a Ford
station wagon as it travels along Highway 66 east of Tucumcari,
New Mexico, circa 1944. A snuffling preadolescent is expressing his
lack of enthusiasm for cross-country expeditions in a tedious litany
of toneless, monosyllabic questions: "Are we there yet? When are
we gonna be there? How much farther?"

Trying to cheer the lout, his father begins to tell him fanciful
tales about the wild and woolly West, promising encounters with
cowboys and Indians, rattlesnakes, scorpions, Gila monsters, and the
most horrible creature in the northern hemisphere, the "so terrible
to look on it gives me the fantods just to think about it" saber-
toothed jackalope.

No response.

"This thing is all teeth and hair. It can run eighty miles an hour
and jump forty feet in the air, and it devours side-hill cowgits in a
single bite. Of course, the cowgit is somewhat at a disadvantage,
what with its uphill legs being shorter and all—fine for grazing on
steep slopes, but hell on flat ground."

"How far is it?"

"When we get to Arizona."

The desert rolls on, rises slowly up to low juniper-piñon woodland, then to pine forest as they climb toward the San Francisco
Peaks. Dim recollection here of fry bread, or maybe Navajo taco,
then more desert, and father's voice saying, "Well, this is it, bub,
jackalope country." Car stopping. Young Fauntleroy, groggy from
his postprandial nap in the back seat, told to climb out. Peevishly
complies. Is led stumbling across an asphalt parking lot past a sign
announcing Yavapai Point. Hands placed on iron pipe railing at
the edge of a rocky precipice. Where he stands blinking out
across…the revelation.

Revelation? He sees flat rock, red ledges, a void, an emptiness,
nothing, an ensemble of dumb space and fractured horizons, hazy
silence, collapsed perspectives. (I'm afraid we may have here one of
those people about whom Mr. Priestley heard rumors.) He looks up

and down, left and right, scans from rim to layered rim, begins to understand that he's been duped, bamboozled, gypped, swindled. He's been had. Sputtering disappointment, he turns and wails, "The jackalopes. Where are the jackalopes?"

It has been about 50 years since this time-lapsed simulation, but I have to confess I still feel as if I'm looking for jackalopes when I stand on the rim of the Grand Canyon, staring out over a 5-to-12-mile-wide gap, 200 miles long and 6,000 feet deep, with a river at the bottom the great environmentalist David Brower once described as the carotid artery of the intermountain West, and exposed rocks down there 1.7 billion years old. I possess the information. I understand that the geological history of the world is laid out before me. But it's too much. Really. I can't process it.

The truth is that a lot of people have trouble processing it—as any afternoon spent observing the sightseers at Yaki, Mather, Yavapai, and Hopi points will demonstrate. Some simply have no information about what is out there in front of their eyes, and after a few obligatory snapshots for the folks back at home, head for the snack bar. Others may simply find the spectacle unnerving. The southwestern writer Haniel Long said the Grand Canyon gave him a kind of "cosmic vertigo" and made him feel seasick and sleepless. Irvin Cobb of the *Saturday Evening Post* wrote, "You stand there gazing down the raw, red gullet of that great gosh-awful gorge, and you feel your self-importance shriveling up to nothing inside you." Even Clarence Dutton, the topographical engineer with the Powell survey in 1880, and a man who processed geological information better than almost anybody, used words like "awe," "dread," "shock," "oppression," "horror" to describe the initial sensation of gazing out over the sudden void, that saber-toothed jackalope of the mind.

We can only speculate what the first white men to encounter the Grand Canyon thought about their discovery. None of them got exactly lyrical. A group of Coronado's men under Don García López de Cárdenas reached the South Rim in 1540, where they spent three days looking for a way to descend to the river. Unable to get more than a third of the way down, and depleted of their water supply, they retraced their steps east to the Hopi villages from whence they had come. Having nothing remotely analogous in their experience against which to make comparisons, they reported that some of the rocks in the Canyon were "bigger than the great tower of Seville."

Over 200 years later, in 1776, Fray Francisco Garces, a Franciscan missionary and colleague of Juan Baptista de Anza, strayed into the region of Aubrey Cliffs, where he met a band of Havasupai and spent an unsuccessful week trying to convert them at their village in Cataract Creek. Garces stolidly described the Canyon as "profound" and remarked in his diary that he was "astonished by the roughness of this country, and at the barrier which nature has fixed therein." Beyond that, he seemed to have little to say. That same year, the famous Dominguez/Escalante party, trying to return to Santa Fe from the Great Basin, wandered around lost for several weeks in a maze of side canyons before eventually discovering a way to cross the Colorado, near the present site of Lees Ferry. Escalante's account of this ordeal, like those of his predecessors, wastes little time in florid admiration of the scenery.

And during the first half of the 19th century, there were a small number of Americans who penetrated the canyon region of southern Utah and northern Arizona—fur trappers like William Ashley and James Ohio Pattie and the Mormon colonizer Jacob Hamblin, who was sent out during the 1850s by Brigham Young to establish settlements at Moab, Lees Ferry, and St. George. But no systematic exploration of the canyon of the Colorado occurred until 1857, when the

---

*D*uring the late 19th century, prospectors, cattlemen, and scientists improved the old footpaths for horse and burro. Today a widespread network of trails, many abandoned more than half a century ago, crisscross the park. They range from faint traces to broad, well-maintained thoroughfares—but no trail is easy.

◆

—Scott Thybony, *Official Guide to Hiking the Grand Canyon*

United States War Department ordered Lieutenant Joseph Christmas Ives to attempt to navigate the river from its mouth near Fort Yuma to the Mormon settlements in Utah. A 58-foot, steel-hulled steamboat was built in Philadelphia, dismantled and shipped around the horn to San Francisco, carried overland in wagons to the Gulf of California, and reassembled. On January 11, Ives and a company of 24 men departed Fort Yuma and steamed north in the newly christened *Explorer*. And immediately ran aground.

It was a bad omen. For the next 150 miles, the steamboat repeatedly encountered shoal waters, sunken rocks, and rapids. She ran aground a half dozen times and then finally suffered a horrendous wreck that flung everybody near the bow into the drink and nearly tore the stem clear out of the boat. Ives knew that he had gone as far by water as he was going to go, and if the mission was to succeed, it would have to continue on foot.

The company marched north and then east as far as Cataract Canyon (now called Havasu) and the village of the Havasupai Indians—a point that on today's maps would lie roughly midway between Lake Mead and Lake Powell and nearly opposite the great canyon of Kanab Creek. Ives mistakenly identified Kanab Canyon as the main branch of the Colorado and, being unable to cross the river and venture into it, decided he had now gone on *foot* as far as he was going to go, and turned back.

Not that this seemed to make him all that unhappy. From the tone of voice evident in his 1861 *Report Upon the Colorado River of the West*, Lieutenant Ives appears to have seen enough: "The region last explored is, of course, altogether valueless. It can be approached only from the south, and after entering it there is nothing to do but leave. Ours has been the first, and will doubtless be the last, party of whites to visit this profitless locality. It seems intended by nature that the Colorado River, along the greater portion of its lonely and majestic way, shall be forever unvisited and undisturbed."

As a lot of people have observed, Ives was a lousy prophet. In 1993, nearly 5 million people visited the two rims of the Grand Canyon, and over 1 million actually ventured down into it either by mule or shank's mare. Twenty thousand people floated the river on rafting trips. Another 800,000 viewed the park from one of the nonstop "scenic air tours" (primarily helicopter overflights) that rattle the Canyon's solitude more than 70 percent of the time. In fact, Grand Canyon Airport is the busiest airport in Arizona, except for Phoenix, and daytime conversations in Tusayan are conducted in short bursts between the racket of helicopter departures and landings.

During the summer months, up to 6,000 cars a day were observed endlessly circling Grand Canyon Village, fighting for fewer than 2,500 parking spaces, and over 100 bus tours a day, on average, rolled through the park. *The Colorado Plateau Advocate*, a publication of the conservation organization the Grand Canyon Trust, observed that during July of 1993 "more than 231,000 vehicles carried over 800,000 people into the park. Another 14,000 visitors arrived by train, and approximately 30,000 people roared over the Canyon in 10,000 separate air tours."

The "profitless locality" is not only massively visited, it is massively affected and disrupted in other critical ways, the most obvious of these being air pollution. Smog from Phoenix, Los Angeles, and the coal-fired power plants of Page, Arizona, and Four Corners, New Mexico, cuts visibility by an annual average of 30 percent.

But the major challenge that the National Park Service (NPS) faces today at Grand Canyon is how to manage a volume of visitors that already vastly exceeds the park's infrastructure, and that is projected to increase to 7 million annual visitations. As far back as 1978, then–Superintendent Merle Stitt acknowledged that the NPS mandate to manage the parks "by such a means as will leave them unimpaired for the enjoyment of future generations" was an unattainable goal at Grand Canyon. He simply did not have the staff or the budget to do it. And in 1978, Stitt was only trying to accommodate 3 million visitors.

It is hoped that the updated Grand Canyon Management Plan will seriously address the need for establishing limits. The time has come. Obviously there is a real need to restrict private automobile access to the South Rim in general and to continue to develop shuttle bus transit [and light rail] along East and West Rim roads. We are, as historian Roderick Nash and others have long argued, loving our parks and wild areas to death. The biggest threat to wilderness used to be from grazing, mining, and timber harvesting; now it's from what one cynical wag referred to as industrial-strength tourism.

Perhaps there is no solution to this phenomenon, short of wrapping the whole Kaibab Upwarp in concertina wire and running people off with packs of rabid dogs. Or perhaps the solution is very simple. We stop the tour buses 20 miles short of the rim and usher people into a warehouse-size cinema, where they'll have a quick and easy virtual reality tour of the park. In fact, the prototype is already in place in Tusayan, where the IMAX Theater presents, in six-track Dolby and on a screen 70 feet high, *Grand Canyon—The Hidden Secrets*. We won't close the Canyon—we'll just insist that anybody who wants to see the real McCoy walks. Like Cárdenas, Father Garces, Dominguez and Escalante, and Lieutenant Joseph Christmas Ives.

he national parks are, in truth, not a system so much as an aggregate of baronies; the political philosophy is feudal, with each park administered by a superintendent possessed of great latitude; the director of the National Park Service is no more than a medieval monarch, accepting symbolic expressions of fealty and offering thaumaturgical services in return. Superintendents can ignore national directives with relative impunity. By contrast, the national forests are a federal system, and no amount of local discretion is allowed to defy a national policy.

◆

—Stephen J. Pyne, *Fire on the Rim: A Firefighter's Season at the Grand Canyon*

Page Stegner is an award-winning author who was first introduced to the Grand Canyon by his father, Pulitzer Prize winning writer Wallace Stegner. He received his Ph.D. in American Literature from Stanford University and served as professor of literature and creative writing at the University of California, Santa Cruz. He explores and enjoys the outdoors along with his

wife, Lynn, and daughter, Allison. This story was excerpted from his book
Grand Canyon: The Great Abyss.

★

The Iron Gates of the Danube and the river gorges of the Caucasus might be multiplied a hundred times, and they could be buried in one side gorge of this king of gorges. Careful estimates show that the main Canyon with its tributaries, if placed in one continuous length, would reach over twenty thousand miles, and any mile of this distance would far surpass any mountain gorge to be found in England, Scotland, Ireland, or Wales.

My camp at the Canyon is in the sweep of a vast amphitheater. It extends from "cusp to cusp," over 60 miles. It is from 6,000 to 7,000 feet deep. From the rim to the wild river which turbulently dashes through its inner gorge of granite it is about seven miles. In other words, it is from twelve to fifteen miles, in a straight line across the Canyon, from rim to rim, at any point in this amphitheater.

Make, in imagination, a real theater of this vast space. Allowing twice as much room for the seat of each person as is given in the most comfortable theater in existence, you could seat here an audience of 250 millions of people. And these would all be in the stalls on this side. An orchestra of 100 million pieces and a chorus of 150 million voices could be placed very comfortably on the opposite side. Is it in the power of the unaided imagination to conceive such a scene?

If the waters of the Thames, Severn, Trent, Ouse, Tyne, Tay, and Clyde were all massed together, they would flow in the dark depths of the inner gorge, and one standing on the rim and looking down upon the rapidly flowing waves would see only a silvery ribbon, here and there glistening in the brilliant Arizona sunlight.

—G. Wharton James (1909)

Stone Creek Woman

It's not often you meet a Goddess.

FEW KNOW HER, BUT SHE IS ALWAYS THERE—STONE CREEK Woman—watching over the Colorado River.

Over the years, I have made pilgrimages to her, descending into the Grand Canyon, passing through geological layers with names like Kayenta, Moenave, Chinle, Shinarump, Toroweap, Coconino, and Supai to guide me down the stone staircase of time. It is always a pleasant journey downriver to Mile 132—Stone Creek, a small tributary that flows into the Colorado. We secure our boats and meander up the side canyon where the heat of the day seeps into our skin, threatens to boil our blood, and we can imagine ourselves as lizards pushing up and down on the hot, coral sand. They watch us step from stone to stone along the streambed. The lizards vanish, and then we see her. Stone Creek Woman: guardian of the desert with her redrock face, maidenhair ferns, and waterfall of expression. Moss, the color of emeralds, drapes across her breasts.

I discovered her by accident. My husband, Brooke, and I were with a group on a river trip. It was high noon in June. Twice that morning the boatman had mentioned Stone Creek and what a refuge it would be: the waterfall, the shade-filled canyon; the constant breeze; the deep, green pool. Searing heat inspired many of us to jump off the boats before they had been tied down. The group ran up Stone Creek in search of the enchanted pool at the base of the waterfall, leaving me behind.

I sauntered up Stone Creek. Sweat pouring off my forehead, and I savored the salt on my lips. The dry heat reverberated off the canyon's narrow walls. I relished the sensation of being baked. I walked even more slowly, aware of the cicadas, their drone that held the pulse of the desert. An evening primrose bloomed. I knelt down and peeked inside yellow petals. The pistil and stamens resembled stars. My index finger brushed them, gently, and I inhaled pollen. No act seemed too extravagant in these extreme temperatures. Even the canyon wren's joyous anthem, each falling note, was slow, full, and luxurious. In this heat, nothing was rushed.

Except humans.

Up ahead, I heard laughter, splashing, and the raucous play of friends. I turned the corner and found them bathing, swimming, and sunning. It was a kaleidoscope of color. Lycra bodies, some fat, some thin, sunburned, forgetting all manner of self-consciousness. They were drunk with pleasure.

I sat on a slab of sandstone near the edge of the pool with my knees pulled up to my chest and watched, mesmerized by the throbbing waterfall of Stone Creek, its sudden surges of energy, how the moss anchored on the redrock cliff became neon in sunlight, how the long green strands resembled hair, how the fine sprays rising from the water nurtured rainbows.

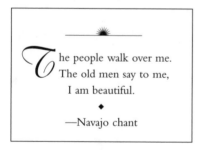

*The people walk over me.
The old men say to me,
I am beautiful.*

◆

—Navajo chant

I eventually outwaited everyone. As Brooke led them back to the boats, the glance we exchanged told me I had a few precious moments I could steal for myself. And in that time, I shed my clothing like snakeskin. I swam beneath the waterfall, felt its pelting massage on my back, stood up behind it, turned and touched the moss, the ferns, the slippery rock wall. No place else to be.

I sank into the pool and floated momentarily on my back. The waterfall became my focus once again. Suddenly, I began to see a face emerging from behind the veil of water. Stone Creek Woman. I stood. I listened to her voice.

Since that hot June day, I have made a commitment to visit Stone Creek Woman as often as I can. I believe she monitors the floods and the droughts of the Colorado Plateau, and I believe she can remind us that water in the West is never to be taken for granted. When the water flows over the sandstone wall, through the moss and the ferns, she reveals herself. When there is no water, she disappears.

For more than five million years, the Colorado River has been sculpting the Grand Canyon. Stone Creek, as a small tributary to the Colorado, plays its own role in this geological scheme. The formation I know as Stone Creek Woman has witnessed these changes. The Colorado River, once in the soul-service of cutting through rocks, is now truncated by ten major dams generating twelve million kilowatts of electricity each year. Red water once blessed with sediments from Glen Canyon is now sterile and blue. Cows drink it. We drink it. And crops must be watered. By the time twenty million people in seven western states quench their individual thirsts and hose down two million acres of farm-land for their food, the Colorado River barely trickles into the Gulf of California.

If at all.

Water in the American West is blood. River, streams, creeks, become arteries, veins, capillaries. Dam, dike, or drain any of them and somewhere, silence prevails. No water: no fish. No water: no plants. No water: no life. Nothing breathes. The land-body becomes a corpse. Stone Creek Woman crumbles and blows away.

Deserts are defined by their dryness, heat, and austerity of form. It is a landscape best described not by what it is, but by what it is not.

It is not green.

It is not lush.

It is not habitable.

Stone Creek Woman knows otherwise. Where there is water, the desert is verdant. Hanging gardens on slickrock walls weep generously with columbines, monkey flowers, and merensia. A thunderstorm begins to drum. Lightning dances above the mesa. Clouds split. Surging rain scours canyons in a flash of flood. An hour later, there is a clearing. Potholes in the sandstone become basins to drink from. Creature—coyote, kit fox, rattlesnake, mule deer—adapted to the call of aridity, drink freely, filling themselves from this temporary abundance. Stone Creek Woman begins to dance.

I want to join them.

Wallace Stegner, in his book *The Sound of Mountain Water*, says, "In this country you cannot raise your eyes without looking a hundred miles. You can hear coyotes who have somehow escaped the air-dropped poison baits designed to exterminate them. You can see in every sandy pocket the pug tracks of wildcats, and every water pocket in the rock will give you a look backward into geological time, for every such hole swarms with triangular crablike creatures locally called tadpoles but actually first cousins to the trilobites who left their fossil skeletons in the Paleozoic."

And here stands Stone Creek Woman, guardian and gauge of the desert, overlooking the Colorado River, with her redrock face, her maidenhair ferns, and waterfall of expression. I have found a handful of people who have seen her. There may be more. Some say she cannot speak. Others will tell you she is only to be imagined. But in the solitude of that side canyon where I swam at her feet, she reminds me we must stand vigilant.

With her first book, Refuge: An Unnatural History of Family and Place, *Terry Tempest Williams won an immediate reputation as an eloquent and impassioned naturalist-writer in the traditions of John Muir, Rachel Carson, and Wallace Stegner. Her books since then have included* Pieces of White Shell: A Journey to Navajoland, Coyote's Canyon, *and* An Unspoken Hunger: Stories from the Field, *from which this story was excerpted. She lives in Salt Lake City with her husband, Brooke.*

✳

As we walked along a dirt road by her home in northern New Mexico, she told me about one of her trips.

"It was sort of a vision-quest charter," she said. "One night we were going to have a whole evening of 'celebrating womanhood.' Before we started, a bunch of women from twenty-five to seventy years old were taking a bath at Fern Glen. We had walked to the other end of camp. All the guys were back cooking dinner.

"So we're all taking baths, and for one, I thought it was amazing. How few times have I just been naked running around the planet? I mean, not very many times for being thirty-seven years old. But I looked around and saw that most of those ladies had never stood on the earth without any clothes on. And here these woman were all just going nuts. They didn't care about how they looked or if they had fat asses or big bellies. They were all just having the greatest time running around naked. In fact, they were having so much fun, I got them to have this peeing contest. And here were these women lined up—I mean, women like your mother—lined up on the beach with their legs spread like this, seeing how far they could pee. It was great!"

—Louise Teal, *Breaking into the Current: Boatwomen of the Grand Canyon*

MICHAEL P. GHIGLIERI

The Green Room

Don't even think about doing this.

I SHIPPED MY OARS FOR A MOMENT. FROM THE COLORADO RIVER, the confluence of Havasu is obvious if you know the geography, but pulling out of the mainstream into the narrow mouth of Havasu Canyon still requires stopping on a dime. Neophytes often see it too late to stop. Now I rowed so close to the polished, fluted wall of dark-gray limestone that our stern seemed in danger of being sliced to ribbons. I pulled on my upstream oar just before reaching the mouth to tug my boat into the small eddy…on that dime. Behind me, spaced at long intervals, four boats followed. The strangely blue-green waters of the little eddy here were empty; Havasu was ours.

After rigging the boats to the cliff face to withstand a flash flood disgorging from the narrow slice of bedrock funneling Havasu into the Colorado, we ascended ledges of Muav and followed a narrow trail into the mouth. We passed a solitary ocotillo (Spanish for "little torch"), a spiny octopoid of a plant waving crimson-tipped blossoms ten feet in the air as if announcing, "Welcome to the Lower Sonoran Life Zone."

The immense, U-shaped canyon was still in shade. I led everyone across the turquoise creek where it is less than waist deep. Later we followed a path worn a foot deep into the hardpacked sand and flanked by grass so lush that every step is caressed by greenery. Ahead, two western whiptail lizards rushed before me frantically. Tiny dinosaurs fleeing in terror from a voracious *Tyrannosaurus rex*…me. The forest of grass along the path is so impenetrable that the frantic lizards jetting through the dust found no exit route to escape me, so they fled along the path, my footfalls even with their pace and hot on their tails, which were dragging lines in the fine sand. One hesitated. I slowed down to avoid stepping on it. Finally, they located an exit and dived from the trail to rustle through dry leaves. As soon as they vanished into safety, they were replaced by new whiptails who began fleeing ahead of me in a panicked search for an exit off the trail. And so on.

The morning was so peaceful that no one uttered a word. As if on a holy pilgrimage, we trekked purposefully upstream past deep, inviting pools created by the travertine cementing of logjams, along a trail winding through acre after acre of native wild grapes, tall grass, scattered groves of mesquite and catclaw, and through thick stands of velvet ash, willows, and old cottonwoods gnawed by beavers. I scanned for bighorn sheep and spotted several prince's plumes, concentrations of which indicate uranium in the soil.

Our destination was Beaver Falls, four miles from the Colorado. Beaver is a paradise within a paradise. Tandem twenty-foot falls feed one wide, deep pool, then another and another; some are fifty yards long and twenty feet deep. These swimming holes exceed all specifications for Paradise. At the base of the lower falls is an optional excursion into the limits of one's courage—or faith. It is called the Green Room. And I definitely do not recommend it.

The Green Room is under a split between the two main

The National Park Service doesn't make reservations or issue hiking permits for the Havasupai Indian Reservation. These must be obtained by calling Havasupai Tribal Enterprises, at 520-448-2121.

◆

—SO'R, JO'R, and LH

streamers of the lower falls, perhaps six to eight feet directly upstream behind the wall of travertine behind the falls. To enter it one must jump into the boiling pool between the streamers, swim to the wall, and, as water pounds on one's head, locate the base of the apron of the travertine about four feet underwater, then inhale a very large breath of air and dive. That's the easy part. Next, after diving about four feet straight down, one must swim underwater directly under the falls and the rock, away from the atmosphere, the sunlight, and everything that makes life possible, for about eight feet. To surface too soon during this swim is to collide head first with the sharp ceiling of travertine, airless and dark and suddenly evil, an easy place in which to drown. One must swim those eight feet horizontally and then surface with one hand placed on one's head to prevent lacerations by stalactites. When that hand breaks into the air, it's time to surface. Carefully. If the sun is shining on the pool outside, this tiny cave hidden beneath the falls will glow a soft, radiant green.

On my last hike to Beaver Falls, I was leading twenty main players in the Hollywood movie industry. It was an afternoon hike, and the sun had already fled from the pool and the falls leading to the Green Room. Only one person was interested in exploring it, Hollywood superstar Tom Cruise.

I explained to Tom exactly how to get in. Then I leapt into the pool between the pounding streamers to lead the way. He plunged in behind me but then gave me fifteen seconds lead time. I swam through the murky water, not quite jet black but too dark to see even my own hands. You've got to be nuts to do this in the dark, I thought, or you must have faith in your comrades. After a year or so, my hand finally felt air. I surfaced, then turned quickly to watch for Tom. On anyone's first excursion in here, it is impossible to know when to surface. I would guide his head with my hand.

But, with sunlight gone from the pool, the light was too dim. Was that him? It suddenly struck me: here was a guy with a face worth at least 100 million dollars swimming face first in the dark into a black room where everything but me was sharp. Tom Cruise was currently the hottest, most valuable property in Hollywood, and despite this he was a good man: generous, humble, with a great sense of humor, a positive attitude, and the mental and physical self-discipline to accomplish his goals. I liked him. I had just sold him on a risky experience that might rearrange his face.

I reached deep into the water. That had to be his head. I grabbed his hair as if he were just about to be swept over Niagara Falls and tugged him into the safe zone. Clean, not a rock grazed in passing. Relief.

Ignoring my iron-gripped panic, he grinned that 100-million-dollar grin and said, "This is *great*, Doc!" as he studied the not-so-Green Room. We were surrounded by stalactites clustered like the teeth of Monstro the Whale swallowing Pinocchio. Our pool was apparently bottomless, but we barely had head room. "You can't even hear the falls," Tom whispered, almost in awe. Suddenly I respected him even more. And I knew that I need not worry about his roaring exit through the falls to the outside world. He had what it took.

Michael Ghiglieri holds a Ph.D. in biological ecology from the University of California, Davis, and is a professional river guide. His books include The Chimpanzees of Kibale Forest, East of the Mountains of the Moon, The Dark Side, *and* Canyon, *from which this story was excerpted.*

※

The side canyons are worlds unto themselves. We had stopped at a waterfall and after taking a cold plunge were refreshed enough to consider climbing the adjacent walls. As soon as we picked our way to the top, we discovered a trail. A series of travertine basins filled with water and lined with reeds led gently upwards towards what could only be described as Shangri La. The cliffs seemed to recede into a blue haze in a series of stairs—cliff upon cliff, sky-woven. I could barely tear my eyes from the view. I wanted to just forget about my river companions and the rafts waiting below and hike until I dropped. Regretfully, I turned back, glancing frequently over my shoulder, wondering if I'd made the right decision.

—Sean O'Reilly, "Canyon Light"

The Midnight Crack

An extreme runner gets another extreme idea.

IT IS MAY. THE HOUR IS LATE. SNOW HAS BEGUN TO FALL, AND THE wind will not let up. We have come prepared for the heat, the kind of skull-numbing heat that sweeps over the inner canyon this time of year like a simmering mirage, not the last vestiges of a brutal winter still frothing down off the alpine heights of the North Rim.

Standing there shivering on a small ledge, 4,370-odd feet above the muddy Colorado River, I have to make a decision: continue climbing for the summit in hopes of finding enough firewood to survive a freezing bivouac at 7,123 feet or attempt a long and dangerous retreat down the Southwest Face of Zoroaster Temple in the dead of night. That's where the three of us are perched now, on a majestic sandstone temple in the heart of the Grand Canyon, and we're burning what little daylight remains. Worse, we are anchored to a confusion of nylon rope, our teeth are chattering from the cold, and we are hopping in place like old men on a blustery winter night.

I look at my partners.

Dave Ganci, the bearded pioneer among us, had been here two decades earlier, when he and Rick Tidrick pulled off the audacious first ascent of Zoroaster Temple. In the process, Dave and Tidrick not only climbed what is arguably the most magnificent temple in the Grand Canyon but also proved that rock climbing techniques pioneered by John Salathé during the golden age of climbing in Yosemite Valley could be used to climb what were once considered the Canyon's unscalable summits below the rim. So a first ascent of the Southwest Face wouldn't be as important to Dave as it was to me—even if he hadn't been doubled over from the debilitating effects of giardia.

George Bain, my other partner, was a Colorado River boatman and a veteran Grand Canyon climber with an enviable list of Canyon ascents to his credit, including a new route up Zoroaster's north side the year before. If push came to shove, he could live with that for another year or so.

Me, I'd never climbed anything as mesmerizing as Zoroaster before, except in conversation over a brew with these two lads. But having been touched by the magic of a temple named for the Persian deity of Zoroastrianism, I am now drawn to its summit like a moth to a flame and little else seems to matter—with the exception of the safety of my partners.

That's why I'm fretfully trying to sort out the pros and cons of continuing, given that I personally have a lot riding on Zoroaster. It's the first difficult new route I've attempted since my fall, and I knew that if my ankle could stand the rigors of the rugged, two-day approach to Zoroaster I could at least entertain the possibilities of a career of Himalayan climbing. But if my ankle fell apart en route to the climb, I always had running, running wild, I thought. But shortly after crawling out of the Galiuro Mountain fastness of the Aravaipa Apache, I had doubts as to whether I'd be able to take running wild to the limits I'd first imagined. Tossing and turning around the dying embers of that lonely Galiuro bivouac fire, my ankle had been seized with such pain I felt like I was back on Squaw Peak with crutches. Come daybreak, I needed an agave stalk to hobble another dozen miles out to my rendezvous with Chris on Aravaipa Creek. The Galiuro run had driven me to a troubling crossroads in my life, and by climbing the Southwest Face, I hoped to be able to determine the path, I was truly destined for: Himalayan climbing or running wild—I couldn't master both.

If I decided to push on, the three of us would be drawn into another dangerous race, a race against darkness. We'd already lost the first race with our dwindling water supply. Natural springs and perennial streams are as scarce in the Grand Canyon as they are difficult to reach; so most of the water we needed for this weeklong adventure had to be carried: a gallon a day per head, eight and a half pounds a gallon. Combined with enough climbing gear, ropes, and food to attempt an ascent of what had repulsed several other strong parties, the staggering weight and unwieldiness of water sloshing around in our packs made our knees buckle—and my ankle scream. Even so, we knew three gallons of water each wouldn't be enough to reach Zoroaster, do the climb, and descend all the way back to Phantom Ranch at the confluence of Bright Angel Creek and the Colorado River. So once we established an advance camp at the base of Zoroaster, we replenished our marginal supply with water George had cached above the Redwall formation the year before and water Dave and I collected from a *tinaja*, "rain pocket," below neighboring Brahma Temple. But when Dave pressed his lips to that shallow water pocket, he sucked out a nasty intestinal amoeba called giardia, and it dogged him like a marked man throughout the day.

We'd been on Zoroaster Temple since sunup, slowly and methodically free-climbing our way five rope lengths up of this monolithic rock pinnacle. At high noon, the fossilized sand of the Southwest Face absorbed the warm rays of the Canyon sun like an unended beach. We stripped down to our t-shirts and savored each airy pitch, because we were climbing in a great inverted mountain range that stunned us with its scale and thousands of feet of heart-stopping exposure. But none of us had had any water since noon, and that had only been a few mouthfuls each. It is now 5:28 p.m., and the severe fluid deficit is beginning to take its toll.

But the dark pall of night is my biggest worry now, never mind my fear that these wind-whipped snow flurries might turn into a merciless storm that could bury us on our perch. If night lies down on us before we reach the Toroweap summit blocks, neither George nor I will be any more fit to lead than Dave is now. I wasn't sure about George, but up until now night climbing had not been my specialty.

George and Dave wait silently for my decision; their eyes say everything: they can go either way. Just make the call. But I'm tired and distracted, and precious minutes tick by as I'm held rapt by the scene before us. Staring back across the immense gulf of the inner canyon like an awestruck tourist, I can see the imposing escarpment of the 7,000-foot Coconino Plateau; it tumbles off the South Rim like a tsunami of rainbow-hued rock collapsing en masse atop the thin silver strand of the Colorado River a vertical mile below. As heavily laden as we'd been during the approach, it had taken a full day to reach the river from the South Rim through that brink, through the declivitous South Kaibab Trail provided the quickest route through the Toroweap, Coconino sandstone, and continuum of Neapolitan rock walls that would have otherwise proved insurmountable. But once we headed north from Phantom Ranch, we had had to rely on Dave's and George's recall of a route that ascended the glass-black Vishnu schist, the rotten Redwall limestone and the bloodstained Hermit shale. In the process, we had climbed nearly a vertical mile to reach the foot of this magnificent, flat-topped horn of Coconino sandstone. Yet, Zoroaster Temple was not the only temple of the Grand Canyon lost to the modern world; before us and all around us stood dozens of other supernal spires and buttes that also resembled the dwelling places of deities. Part of the allure and fascination of climbing in this stupendous gorge was that many of its temples had been named by geologist and cartographer Clarence E. Dutton after temples he'd visited in the Orient during the 1800's; they were too sublime to be named after mere mortals, Dutton had rightly concluded. Better to name them Tower of Ra, Angel's Gate, Confucius, Buddha....

"Annerino! What do you want to do?"

Startled from my twilight reverie, I turn back and ask George if he has any matches. I know he does, but I just want some reassurance that if we manage to climb to the summit in the dark we can at least build a bivouac fire.

"Yeah," George says. The word hangs there momentarily, before being swept into the depths of the canyon by a chill wind.

"All right, I'll make you a deal," I tell him.

"What's that?" George yells above a gust of wind.

"You lead that," I say, pointing to a dangerous pitch looming above, "and I'll lead that."

His orange parka flapping wildly in the wind, George eyes the two tomb-sized blocks we'd seen earlier, it doesn't look like it'd take much to dislodge them and squash us like roadkill. Faced with such a prospect, I have no illusions about trying to make the delicate nerve-jangling moves around them myself. George isn't enchanted with the prospect either, because, if he blows a move on this pitch and doesn't dislodge those blocks, he will take a bone-crushing pendulum against the opposite rock wall. A long fall down a smooth rock face or a screaming bounce into an overhang were acceptable risks I was willing to take, but the throbbing pain in my ankle was a potent reminder to avoid unprotectable leads above ledges and such.

Having apparently worked

---

*O*f the 120-odd named temples within the Grand Canyon, few are more striking than Zoroaster or Brahma. Comprised largely of Coconino sandstone and Kaibab limestone, these spectacular monoliths occupy a singular arm of Hermit shale that extends southward from the North Rim into the heart of the Grand Canyon. Named after the Persian deity of Zoroastrianism, 7,123-foot-high Zoroaster Temple is a flat-topped pyramid with imposing walls of buff-colored sandstone more than 500 feet high. Brahma Temple, at 7,551 feet high, was named after the Hindus' Supreme Creator. While it overshadows neighboring Zoroaster in sheer mass and height, its walls are largely broken on its northern half, offering easier ascents for nonclimbing canyoneers. Unexplored till December 1957, Zoroaster and Brahma are now seen by more than four million visitors each year.

◆

—John Annerino, *Adventuring in Arizona: The Sierra Club Travel Guide to the Grand Canyon State* out the sequence of delicate moves in his head, George peered beyond his lead into mine. "You want it bad enough to lead that, in the dark?" he asks me.

"I'd rather climb at night than rappel at night," I tell him, and as soon as I do, I realize there isn't any other option; if we're going to survive the night without caving in to hypothermia, we have to climb. Our hand has been forced. Unlike climbing, which ideally melds mind and body to rock in a series of fluid movements, rappeling requires a climber to rely almost entirely on the mechanics of rope anchors and a rappel harness. And the history of mountaineering and rock climbing has been tragically marked with the corpses of world-class climbers who, at one distracted moment, fell screaming to their deaths because they'd accidentally unclipped the wrong carabiner while rappeling.

"You lead the traverse, George. I'll do the rest," I tell him.

Each of us holds the key for the other; without them both, the door to the summit will remain locked, and the three of us will be forced to rappel one frightening rope length after another into the dark and who knew what kind of fatal mistake awaiting below. Clad in flimsy parkas and heavy sweaters, we are too cold to remain at an impasse. Buffeted by strong, erratic gusts of wind, George starts up. Snow pelts his thick red beard, and his gold earring swings back and forth like a soundless wind chime.

"You got me, Annerino?"

"I got ya, George!"…

A nerve-rattling half hour later, George is on the crux. If he makes the moves across wafer-thin footholds, we'll gain a stance at the bottom of the final pitch; if not, he'll take a shocking 60-foot fall, pendulum into the wall, and probably dislodge those two huge blocks above us.

I'm scared. Dave gives me one of those what'd–we–get–ourselves-into looks. We both remember the 25-foot lead fall George took earlier in the day; the force of it jerked up in the air so violently, it nearly uprooted the three bushes Dave and I were anchored to. It was a thin line between survival and hurtling into the yawning drop, all roped together, toward our water cache in Summer

Wash 3,000 feet below. A masonry bolt would have prevented that near disaster, but we were trying to climb clean.

"You got me, Annerino?" George screams again.

"I got ya, George!"…

In the falling snow and failing light, I can barely discern the dark image of George as he stretches across the crux. It's an awkward and desperate move. The key handhold must be just out of reach, maybe an inch, maybe two. Dave and I can't see clearly. But George pauses for a moment, steeling himself against the fear of not putting the delicate moves together. There won't be a second chance. At that moment, I try to detach myself from the reality of a long lead fall; if he takes one, there's nothing I can do except hold on and pray none of us is killed. Dave seems equally resigned at the moment. As for George, I can feel the tension of his right leg resonate down the length of rope into my cold hands. Or maybe it's simply the wind trying to dislodge the human spider tenuously clinging to the wall above.

George has to make the move now, before he's overcome with fear. As if prompted by some atavistic cue, George stretches farther across the wall and grasps the hold to make sure it won't slough off in his cold fingers. When he knows it is sound, I can feel the relief reverberate back down the length of rope. He steps across the dark heavens and screams, "Yowwweee!!!" He's done it. He's crossed the Twilight Traverse, and he was the only one among us who could have put those desperate moves together tonight.

"Guess it's my turn," I tell Dave. He nods silently, still doubled over with cramps.

George ties off and puts me on belay. I start climbing up his perilous vertical puzzle, confident I'm safeguarded by his taut rope above. With night almost upon us, there is no time to remove the anchors George had carefully placed on this difficult stretch. So, I climb past each dangling nut and make the crotch-ripping stretch beneath the two huge blocks. I grasp what remains of the gear rack from George and sling it around my neck and shoulder.

"Your turn," George says, puffing on his stogie.

"Glad I didn't lead that," I tell him, half hoping he'll be swept away by the camaraderie and volunteer to lead my pitch as well. But George has earned his stogie-lit perch; I, alone, have to earn mine high above.

"Wait till you see the off-width," he says, trying to laugh off the last of his fears and rush of adrenaline.

"I don't want to look at it till I get there," I tell him. George laughs again, and we wait, ritually passing the stogie back and forth between us, the brightness of the burning red ember a gauge to measure the depth of the darkness and the cold that will dictate my own movements above.

It's nearly midnight when Dave finally reaches us. The wind is still blowing, dusting our legs and eyelashes with dry spindrift, a promising sign that we may have escaped hell's fury. Dave ties off next to George. Based on how long it's taken him to jumar and clean the pitch, I assume giardia has left him weak so I don't broach the subject of his leading the last pitch.

I grab the plastic flashlight and stick in my mouth. It's my lead, Dave's belay. There is no time for backslapping. Darkness had already beaten us to this perch, and we are losing a grim third race to cold and fatigue. George has since climbed out of the blowing snow and crawled lizard like between two boulders. He knows I won't sprint up the "Midnight crack." Tentatively, I start up. The small battery-powered beam shines the way, but I don't need the light to know I'm groping through a layer of Permian sea sludge that forms the mortar between the Coconino sandstone and the Toroweap limestone; it is too soft and crumbly to permit a solid purchase with my fingers or slick-soled climbing boots. The sharp steel ice hammers and rigid twelve-point crampons of an alpine climber would have been more suitable for this appalling layer, but who could have guessed that while viewing the Southwest Face from the distant South Rim vista four days earlier? We hadn't. So I take the climbing a foot at a time, aware that Dave may be dozing on and off, unable to stave off the irresistible pull of sleep.

Carefully removing my right hand from the crumbly hold, I take the light out of my mouth and shout into the black void below.

"Dave!…Hey, Dave!…You awake?!"

"...huh...yeah, I gotcha!"

I tug at the rope and continue groping, as though I'm spelunking out of a dark, muddy cavern. Fatigue is enveloping me in a deadly embrace, and it feels like I'm on the edge of the world and about to tumble into an endless free fall through black space. I have to stay awake long enough to finish the lead. I mouth my upper lip between my eyeteeth and the flashlight; whenever fatigue darts in from its ominous orb, I bite down until I can feel the pain, the salty trickle of my own blood. I am climbing for my life.

With each grungy foot I gain, I yell back down to Dave, flashlight in mouth: "Dave!...Hey, Dave, you awake?"

But it always takes the second or third cry to get a response out of him:"

"Yeah...yeah, I gotcha."

I'm not sure how much rope I've run out, but once I climb over the crumbly edge of mud, I arrive at the base of a chimney and decide to place a bolt; under normal, daylight conditions, it wouldn't be necessary, but fear has me on a tight leash. I'm high above my sleeping belayer with no reliable anchors between us. I fumble for the bolt driver and commence hammering, occasionally hitting my left hand instead of the aluminum drill, but it is too cold to feel the steel hammerhead bruising my bare knuckles. The bolt placed, I clip into it and fight my way into the base of the chimney. I'm safe in here, I think to myself once inside; there's no exposure. There's no exposure at night, anyway, so what are you thinking? I'm getting groggier; I bite down on my lip again. With my knees and the palms of my hands pressed against the wall in front of me and my heels, buttocks, and shoulders wedged behind me, I shinny up. Wriggling awkwardly, it feels like I'm going to be spit out of the crack at any moment because, for every difficult foot I gain, I slip a half foot back.

Temporarily wedged, I shine the light at the black catacomb above and see several sinister-looking chockstones that look like they're going to fall on me. But as I struggle through this natural bomb bay, I carefully thread each of those chockstones with nylon webbing and clip my carabiners and rope to them, wondering how much of a fall it would take to avalanche them on top of me.

Cursing and grunting, I struggle upward a few inches at a time, knowing I wouldn't fall far before the chockstones permanently wedged my broken legs and back between the narrow walls of this tomb.

If I'm lucky, the chimney will widen above and end in a womblike cave leading to the summit blocks. I follow it, hoping this fantasy will play out. But the higher I climb, the more disoriented I become. It's so dark, I have no real sense of up-or down; I only know this is the way I entered the chimney, so that's the way I continue struggling against gravity—headfirst, until I smash my helmet on the pointed ceiling. When I do, my worst fears are confirmed: dead end. Fear races me back down thirty feet of the most desperate climbing I've done. As long as I control my breathing, though, I don't have to down-climb; my body, pulsating like a snail in its shell, prevents me from falling.

I can see nothing below me except the black hole I once knew as the Grand Canyon; I can see nothing above me except blackness. If I'm about to die, I want to do it climbing as I never have before. Above me, I know, is the off-width George laughed off earlier. Too narrow to chimney in with my body and too wide to jam-climb with my hands and feet, it is the crux of the Midnight Crack, and it defies me to climb it.

Convinced I'm about to take a killer fall, I thread the last chockstone with a nylon runner, insert my left hand and arm into the overhanging fissure, and contort them until it feels like a ten penny nail is sticking in my shoulder. I try to focus all my energy in my pain-racked left arm, and when I pull down on it with everything I've got, it feels like I'm going to pull Zoroaster down on top of me. When I realize the temple is not going to tumble, I stem my right leg against the wall in front of me, but I repeatedly miss the crucial nubbin with my quivering right foot. I begin shaking all over. My left arm feels like it's going to dislocate, and I feel myself start to slip. I scream and begin sobbing until the pitiful cries stop as quickly as they'd begun.

"I gotcha, John!"

"Get us off here, Annerino!"

But their voices are from another world, both of them straining to see that which they cannot: a fading pinprick of light crawling toward the dark, starless heavens.

I never could do a one-arm pull-up, so I take in a deep breath and grab my left forearm with my free hand to prevent my shoulder from dislocating. Hanging by my fist, I relax my right leg as best I can under the torque and strain, then point the toe of my boot at the small nubbin of rock, now dimly lit by the small flickering beam of light. The batteries are starting to fade, and I can taste the salt trickling out of the side of my mouth. My leg quivers like a wand bending in the breeze, but my boot kisses the nubbin. Once, twice, I can feel it, and when the light comes back on, I can see it again. I press against the nubbin, caressing it to make sure it won't flake off; slowly it takes the pressure of my weight. I stand up on it and relieve the torturous strain on my twisted arm

Peace surges through me like a warm, gentle wave when I realize I'm negotiating a crux I could never really see; but I rein in this small feeling of pleasure before it leaves me stranded 30 feet below the summit. I dig furiously into the crack above with both arms. I brace my bruised left knee below, push off with my right leg, and move up again. Just a few more feet and it's over....

When I crawl over the edge of the summit block, I spit the flashlight out of my mouth and collapse. I fall into a fitful doze. I don't think about freezing to death in my sleep; it's just that it seems so passive in the cold, and I welcome the rest, at long last.

"Annerino!...Hey, Annerino! You awake?!"

I hear voices. Someone's calling me from my dreams: I blink my eyes, but I still can't see anything. It's suddenly bitterly cold and voices are screaming.

"Annerino!...Hey, Annerino! You awake?!"

I draw up my left leg, which had been dangling over the edge, crawl on my hands and knees to the nearest bush, and anchor the rope. I remember wiping blood off the side of my mouth before yelling into the center of the earth: "All right, we're up!"

We are lost in the steel-gray mist of first light, three small figures huddled next to the damp, smoldering coals of a dying fire. We are anxious. At any moment, the sun is going to erupt out of the Desert Facade far to the east…when it does, it shrouds us in an ethereal orange mist that stirs the drifting smoke of our fire as if we've been seated around a magic lantern all night. We are groggy, and our bodies feel cold and burnt—burned on the front side from restocking the fire through the waning hours of night, bone chilled on the backside from the force of the wind. We are stiff, sore, hungry, and thirsty. And my ankle feels as if a wolf's been gnawing on it all night in hopes of crunching through the leg bone for the sweet marrow within. But we are alive atop majestic Zoroaster Temple, and we are suddenly enveloped by the spherical prism of the rising sun, and it feels like we're being projected through a holograph where time, distance, and pain are temporarily suspended.

Levitating in the middle of this canyon sea until its fleeting visual magic dissipates, the sun slowly bakes the deep chill out of our haggard bodies, and I drift back into the last burning embers of our fire while Dave and George rustle from their own half sleep. I've been dreaming, the fire off and on throughout the night, and in its burning-red core, I've seen a recurring image: a man, running alone, half-naked through the Grand Canyon. I'm not sure who it was; it was just a figure running through the dancing red-and-orange flames as my head drooped on and off my chest. But he—it—was running east to west through the canyon as far as I can now see, through the clouds that part as if a curtain has been rolled back to reveal a colossal amphitheater. From the mouth of the Little Colorado River Gorge, where it spills its cerulean blue waters into the muddy Colorado River, the tiny figure ran west along the broad, undulating platform of the Tonto formation, 150 stories above the turgid river…and he didn't stop until he reached the tier of turquoise waterfalls spewing out of Havasupai at the other end of the canyon.

That's all it was, an image of a man running through a canyon dreamscape, any man, everyman, and it stays with me as the three of us rope off the backside of Zoroaster like three thieves who have just pulled off the heist of their lives. But as soon as I shoulder my heavy pack at the foot of Zoroaster, I know who that figure is, because my ankle starts screaming at me like an old fishwife. It's an argument I've lost before, and this time it lasts the two days it takes us to stagger back out of the South Rim under heavy loads. En route, however, I'm too leery to mention my dream to Dave or George, or even to Chris, who'd kept the vigil of a one-woman support crew and expedition photographer at our base camp throughout the night. The idea is too preposterous: running end to end through some place I am having a difficult time just trying to crawl out of?

I wait until I return to Prescott, where I am soothed by the warm winds of summer blowing through the pines outside my Groom Creek cabin, before I phone Tim Ganey. He will tell me I've gone off the deep end, or if there is the remotest possibility that somebody, anybody, could run the length of the Grand Canyon.

I first met Tim in high school when a beautiful lass named Kathleen Jowdy hog-tied both our hearts. Kathleen had long, brown hair she sometimes festooned with ribbons at the ends of her wavy locks, a warm smile that made your knees weak, and class that overshadowed her peers. But Tim had the schoolboy charm and Redford good looks, and he won Kathleen's heart hands down. Instead of butting heads over Kathleen or even drifting apart, though, Tim and I grew closer, drawn together by the same unending flow of adolescent dreams and ideas. But there was another force at work between Tim and me, too; more often than not, each of us

> *T*he Mojave Indians of the lower Colorado River put all the energy they gave to aesthetic and religious affairs into the recitation of long poetic narratives. Some of the epics are remarkably precise in describing the details of the vast basin and range deserts of the Southwest, but the raconteurs held that they were all learned in dreams.
>
> ◆
>
> —Gary Snyder, *A Place in Space: Ethics, Aesthetics, and Watersheds*

already knew what the other was thinking without having mentioned it. And I came to trust Tim's perspective and judgment implicitly. If anybody could realistically grasp the concept of a man running through the Grand Canyon, Tim could. I ring him up.

"What do you think, honestly, Tim?"

"I think it's a great idea."

"But nobody's ever done it before," I protest.

"John,"—Tim always used your first name like an exclamation point if he wanted your undivided attention—"that's exactly why we should do it."

John Annerino is a photojournalist whose work has been published in Life, Time, Newsweek, *and* The New York Times Magazine. *He is the author and photographer of five books, including* High Risk Photography: The Adventure Behind the Image. *He went on to run through the Grand Canyon, a journey he recounts in* Running Wild: Through the Grand Canyon on the Ancient Path.

⁜

The Grand Canyon has been called an inverted mountain range. In fact, a mountaineering term has been adapted to describe the combination of trekking, scrambling, and rock climbing necessary to explore the great chasm's backcountry: "canyoneering." The goals of many canyoneers are the "temples" that rise from the depths of the canyon.

Zoroaster Temple and its close neighbor Brahma are among the most photographed landforms in the Grand Canyon. They are part of the backdrop in most tourist photos taken in front of Bright Angel Lodge on the South Rim. Millions of people see them every year, but few visit them. The reasons are obvious: you cannot drive there, and there is no trail.

The round-trip to Zoroaster involves a trek of more than 30 miles, gaining and losing a total of more than 20,000 feet in elevation.

Zoroaster Temple's namesake was a Persian prophet, born circa 660 B.C., who founded a religion we know today as Zoroastrianism. Adopted by the emperors of Persia, it dominated the Near East until it was displaced during the Moslem conquest in the 6th century. Its revolutionary tenet was "ethical duality," meaning that one's spiritual destiny is determined by the choices between good and evil made during life. At death the soul must pass over the Chinvat Bridge, which narrows to a sword edge in the middle. For the righteous, the sword presents its broad side and passage into heaven, but the wicked soul is cut on the sharp sword edge and falls into hell. Zoroastrianism was influential among the Greeks and Romans and long persisted as a powerful secret society in the Roman army.

—Bob Kerry, "A Pilgrimage to Zoroaster,"
Arizona Highways

PETER ALESHIRE

Bats Are Welcome

*Ecological consciousness rises
as the sun sets.*

I LAY ON A FLOOD-POLISHED ROCK BESIDE THE COLORADO RIVER in the depths of the Grand Canyon and watched as the first stars glimmered in the violet sky.

The river murmured to itself as darkness seeped from the rearing canyon walls. I surrendered myself to the sound of the river, the spell of the breeze, and the seamless expanse of the gathering night.

Suddenly, a small shape hurtled past just above me. A bat. Startled by the flutter of sound, I sat up abruptly on the rock, which lay on the downstream edge of the bench that had become that night's safe harbor for our little party of researchers charting the extinction of the Colorado's native fish.

Another bat swooped past, dipping in its erratic quest for flying insects. I could just make out the bats' shapes in the lingering shreds of twilight. Furry daredevils, they veered to the rolling surface of the river, slipped into a near barrel roll, careened to the side, and pulled up an instant before slamming into the unyielding two-billion-year-old schists that form the sides of the armored gorge through which the river plunges at this point.

Fascinated, I watched their aerobatics until the moonless night made it impossible. Then I reclined again on the rock, straining to hear their frail flutter, now and then glimpsing their tiny forms as they flitted past the growing brilliance of the stars. It dawned on me that these flying creatures with eerily human faces inhabit the world of night—a country irrevocably foreign to me.

I know this seems obvious, hardly worth noting. But I never really understood the concept of night until that night at the edge of the river while the stars wheeled past overhead. Suddenly it seems miraculous that these peerless hunters of insects could maneuver unerringly in the dark, guided by the echoes of squeaks inaudible to my ear. I couldn't see the river. Could barely discern the pale outline of my hand before my face. But the bats hunted all through the warm night, part of life's remarkable improvisation aimed at filling every niche.

I've always admired the bat, a creature that can inspire dread, and superstition, and screams in the dark. Bats come in 900 species, from the fruit-eating flying fox with its five-foot wingspan to the bumblebee-size Kitti's hog-nosed bat of Thailand. Guided by high-frequency echoes, many find and eat their own weight in insects each night. Others thrive on fruit and pollen, helping ensure the survival of giant plants like the saguaro cactus. Some even sip blood from cattle. They creep across the ground and open a small bovine vein with a quick slash of razor teeth, before lapping up a teaspoon of blood.

Some hibernate, some seek food year-round. Some migrate; some return each morning to the same cave for twenty years. Some gather in coed colonies in the millions. Some keep males and females segregated, coming together only in great mating migrations that would strike dumb the most fulsome poet.

They've survived for millions upon millions of years. So far, they've even survived us, although human beings have proven adept at destroying their roosting sites, spreading pesticides throughout the food chain, and evincing so mindless a malice that many experts say key bat populations have slid into deep declines. Some experts believe the declines have hindered the reproduction of the saguaro, which would then affect an array of species downstream ecologically.

All this I knew. But until I lay on that rock in the utter dark, I didn't truly understand how utterly different bats are from we creatures of the day. It's not just bats, of course. Nature divides the world into two shifts. The brilliant-emerald-green swifts harry the insects through the air above the river day by day then yield to the bats seeking a whole new cast of insects by night. The gleaming trout lurking behind rocks waiting for floating insect larvae by day give way to the whiskered catfishes patrolling along the bottom for nighttime prey. The wheeling peregrines, with their binocular eyes and their 220-mile-per-hour death dives, surrender the night skies to the great horned owls with their stereo ears and sound-baffled wings.

The realization that I sat, blind, on the edge of an alien world imparted a strange sense of belonging. You see, I'd been five days on a river trip. We lit no lanterns but retreated to our thoughts and our sleeping bags with the dark. That's the way the Indians lived when they told stories in which the animals were indistinguishable ethically from the people. They, no doubt, rose and fell with the sun, as linked to their half of the cycle as the peregrine, the swift, and the trout. Our modern lights have banished the night. Now we don't go to bed until *Nightline* has finished its final minute of airtime.

But on the river, the ancient rhythm of light and dark reasserted itself. And so, for the first time, I could see the world of the night

> *A* newly minted sandbar shortly below Bat Cave at Mile 267 serves as last camp. Bat Cave was mined for guano from the late 1940s to the early 1950s; the guano was taken by tram across the river to Quartermaster Point, 2,600 feet above, and trucked out. Like most of the commercial mining adventures along the river, it petered out, leaving a trace of failure in the air and debris on the Canyon wall.
>
> ◆
>
> —Ann Haymond Zwinger,
> *Downcanyon: A Naturalist*
> *Explores the Colorado River*
> *Through the Grand Canyon*

because I had rediscovered the boundary of my own world. It made me love the bat. And the daylight. And the feel of the rock in the alien dark.

Peter Aleshire wrote this story for Arizona Highways.

✳

When the scarlet luminescent moments of twilight fade to black, we are greeted by a Milky Way airbrushed across the dark heavens like sparkler smoke, fireballs of shooting stars trailing streamers of fluorescent silver contrails, and tiny white satellites whirling at distant corners of our little piece of the universe, as if they've been fired out of puny earthborne BB guns. For the next eight hours, our synaptic reverie will be played and replayed against this celestial cyclorama; tenuously perched as we are, we don't dare close our eyes any more than the Havasupai had, who, according to ethnographer A. F. Whiting, viewed Orion's belt as *amu'u'*, "flock of bighorn sheep...being ambushed by the star Rigel, who was known as Wolf Man (Hatakwila)."

—John Annerino, *Running Wild: Through the
Grand Canyon on the Ancient Path*

PATRICIA C. McCAIREN

Whitewater

*A solo rafter finds her home
on the Colorado River.*

THE CANYON IS ALIVE WITH CREATURES: LIZARDS, SCORPIONS, rattlesnakes, deer, coyotes, bighorn sheep, ringtail cats, skunks, and mice. Most I'll never see, some will leave only their tracks, and some, like the two quivering, gray-brown mice trapped at the bottom of a five-gallon bucket this morning, plead with huge eyes for mercy. Bewildered by their predicament and terrified by my presence, the mice press tightly against each other, head to tail, as if by the sheer force of compressing themselves together they can vanish. "This is what curiosity will get you," I advise them. "In the future stay away from buckets. Next time you might fall into soapy dishwater and drown." Their quivering intensifies. I carry the bucket away from the kitchen and turn it on its side. Two gray streaks disappear into a tangle of tamarisk roots.

I return to the kitchen aware that the trip is changing once again. Today's energy is different from yesterday's. It's a subtle yet strong perception, like knowing someone is watching you before you actually see them. I'll be alone again. My solitary passage won't be interrupted. I welcome it....

Solitude's biggest physical challenge commences at my doorstep in rapids that come one right after another. Big, difficult, scary rapids. From Granite, whose rumble I can hear from camp, to Hermit, one-and-a-half miles downstream, through Boucher, Crystal, the Jewels—Agate, Sapphire, Turquoise, Ruby—and others before and after them. Combined, they form the most difficult obstacle of my trip: more than eleven chances to mess up, to flip, to be thrown out of my boat, or to succeed and feel wonderful.

The Colorado is a typical desert river with a negligible gradient that drops eight feet per mile through the length of Grand Canyon, yet it contains some of the biggest rapids in North America. Unlike the steep gradient of mountain rivers, where water crashes through a narrow passageway over and around rocks, creating a technical obstacle course, the Colorado heaves itself into towering waves or powerful hydraulics that form holes, reveals, boils, whirlpools, and turbulent eddy fences. Voluminous amounts of water course through the bottom of the Canyon. While mountain streams often flow at one or two thousand cubic feet per second, the Colorado River is considered low at levels below ten thousand cfs. As volume grows, so does velocity and power.

Between each big drop, the Colorado River pools out, sometimes for less than a mile, more frequently for a distance of two to five miles and occasionally for more than twenty miles. The topography of the Canyon determines where rapids occur. Adjacent to every drop on the Colorado lies the inevitable side canyon. A build-up of cumulus clouds over a particular drainage sends a heavy rainfall down a dry wash, turning it into a raging turmoil. As a flash flood gains momentum, rocks and boulders are spewed into the river, forcing it into a narrower space. If the flash flood is small, an inconsequential riffle is formed. But when a major storm drives huge boulders and tons of mud down a side drainage into the river, a rapid is born.

For many years, whitewater was considered unrunnable. During his trips of 1869 and 1872, Major Powell portaged or lined his boats around most of the Canyon's big drops. He was an explorer and a scientist, not a whitewater boatman. But as time passed and interest grew, river runners developed techniques for navigating rapids, and a new sport was born.

A myth existed for many years, and lingers still, that maintains it takes a large, powerful man to row a boat through whitewater. The truth is, it takes brains to run a rapid—not brawn. The key to a flawless run is understanding the dynamics of a river. The direction and velocity of the current, the power of a hydraulic and the force of a cresting wave deliver specific messages to be read and examined closely, like important documents. I take it seriously. This chronicle could save my life.

Learning to maneuver a boat was a challenge, full of mistakes and triumphs. But when my heavy oars finally felt light, when my awkward strokes evolved into fluid motion, and when I learned to read the complex language of a rapid, I gave myself a gift of exhilaration and vitality that transcended ordinary experience. And for every year I row, the joy of running rivers increases.

> *W*ell I honestly thought I would not come out of the Canyons alive. But down in those immense gorges it came over me how really small and insignificant a man is. Then it did not seem to matter so much. The river, the rapids, the cnayon walls, stars and moon, took on real friendly personalities.
>
> ◆
>
> —Buzz Holmstrom, quoted in *The Doing of the Thing: The Brief Brilliant Whitewater Career of Buzz Holmstrom* by Vince Welch, Cort Conley, and Brad Dimock

I walk along the narrow pathways that meander between the tamarisks to scout Granite Rapid. At the mouth of Monument Creek, the jungle of feathery branches ends, cut off as abruptly as a sharp knife cuts off the head of a fish. The massive boulder garden that once barreled down the side canyon wiped out the trees. I step carefully over the boulders looking for a good vantage point.

A boulder garden on the left pushes most of the current to the right against a sheer wall, resulting in ten-foot, curling waves that rebound off the wall at a 45-degree angle to the main current. Meanwhile, other curlers angle off the first, creating an upside down **V**. It's an ugly hydraulic, for it's often difficult, if not impossible, to keep a boat from turning sideways to one or another of the waves. As a result, runs through Granite are often wildly out of control. And there's no easy way to avoid the right run, for the left passage is blocked by two unrunnable holes, one at the top of the rapid and the other in the center.

I like holes as much as a cat likes a bath. They're dangerous and unpredictable. From exploding monsters that curl back upstream to quiet "keepers" filled with white, foaming, aerated water, holes always pose a problem. When water pours over a rock that is fairly close to the surface, it dives to the bottom of the river leaving a "hole" that must be filled in. The filling takes place when the surface of the river reverses itself into a backflow. Rowing a raft into a hole is akin to riding a bicycle at high speed into a pothole.

If a rock is very close to the surface or partially exposed, the hole behind it appears flat as water rushes back upstream toward the rock. The hole is called a "keeper" when it stops a raft cold and holds it in the bubbling froth where the backwash meets the downstream rush of water. I've had intimate rendezvous with keeper holes, and they've all been terrifying.

When a raft slips over the brink into one of these killers, it is pounded, spun around, and shaken. Gear can be ripped off the raft, a frame bent, a seat snapped in two. During frantic seconds that seem like hours, as you try to keep the raft from flipping and from falling in the hole yourself, you search for a downstream current to grab with an oar in order to pull the boat out of the hole's grasp. If the hole is large enough, the downstream current is far out of reach, and you remain stuck, looking into the face of death while recirculating around the hole until it decides to release you—usually after the raft is full of water.

It's easy enough to keep away from Granite's holes. The challenge lies in staying upright in the **V**-waves and missing a large swirling eddy at the bottom right of the rapid. The force of the water going downstream against the surge of the water traveling upstream forms the eddy fence, a fluvial barrier sometimes strong enough to flip a raft. Many, such as the one at the bottom of Granite

Rapid, are powerful enough to make it extremely difficult, if not impossible, to cross in order to rejoin the main current.

I scout large rapids, reading them from the bottom up. I note each obstacle, its location, and relationship to the main current. I have to: once I start my run I'm committed, and if a hole or rock is in my path, I might need to take strokes away from it long before I actually reach it.

I push off from shore and pull hard on the oars, using my entire body to row the boat across the width of the river. My race with the current is a close one, and at the last moment, I slip to the right of the hole and drop over the lip into the rapid. I point *Sunshine Lady*'s bow into the apex of a curling V and begin a wild ride up the side of one wave and down another. At the end of the rapid, the boat is brimming with water. I turn and look upstream. The rapid graces the brown river with a beautiful white bodice of froth. Seconds later, the river carries me around a bend, and Granite is out of sight. As I float in the calm stretch between Granite and Hermit Rapids, I bail gallons of water out of the raft.

When a rapid is entirely visible from above and easy to run, I don't scout from shore. Instead, I look the rapid over from my raft, gaining about three feet in height by standing on the ammo boxes tied in front of my seat. It usually works, except for the time when I should have scouted but didn't, and ended up in the wrong place at the wrong time.

On the tenth day of a thirty-day trip, with Hance and lunch behind us, the group of twelve people and five boats floated into the Inner Gorge toward a cataract appropriately named Sockdolager. Like a lioness stalking her prey, the river flows downward into a glassy tongue until, in one swift, violent motion, it erupts into a curling reversed V—waves that tower fifteen to twenty feet— exploding and crashing down upon themselves. I was an overenthusiastic neophyte rowing *Sunshine Lady* for the first time in the Canyon, and I knew I should scout. But the others did not stop, and since I had no idea where to find a vantage point, I followed the leader.

We slid down the tongue in formation. The first raft disappeared in the apex of the V and was buried beneath crashing whitewater. "Oh shit!" I muttered, not bothering to watch what happened to the second raft. Frantically, I pulled on my oars. "Hang on," I shouted to my passenger Jeff as I pointed the raft's bow into the left side of the V. I threw my strength against the oars and felt the raft shudder as she met the wall of water and slid up the face of the wave. It was the right thing to do, the wrong place to do it. Hidden behind the back side of the wave was another wave, perpendicular to the first. I looked up and knew we were doomed.

Green, swirling water blotted out the day, tossing me around like clothes in a washing machine. I surfaced into dim light, the top of my head bumping against the thwart. I quickly ducked my head under the tubes and a moment later bobbed up next to the upside-down raft. Jeff's head surfaced near mine, his knuckles white from his death grip on the raft, his face twisted in fear. Wave after wave buried me, leaving me gasping for air, then coughing and choking. "Jeff, help me," I yelled, while I struggled vainly, again and again, to pull myself up the slippery tubes to the floor of the boat, "I can't," he screamed, "I'm tangled in the bowline." A chill, worse than the 50-degree temperature of the river, ran through me. Then, without warning, the raft swung around and launched us toward a glistening black wall. I raised my feet in a futile attempt to keep from being crushed, when just as suddenly the boat twirled away from the rock. Prodded by fear, I grappled with the raft until I found a foothold on a submerged oar and heaved myself on top. I crawled to Jeff, still struggling to untangle himself, and with more strength than I thought possible, pulled him up on the bottom of the boat with me.

Relief brushed over me with a comforting hand as the first boat tossed us a line. Securing my raft to his, Stewart pulled hard into an eddy. "We're safe," I said, and Jeff smiled. Safe until the D ring on Stewart's boat tore loose, releasing us to the current. Clinging to the underside of the boat, shivering uncontrollably in the first stages of hypothermia, we drifted into a small rapid. *What's next?* I wondered, but that was answered when the river calmed and Jeff tossed the line back to Stewart. A moment later, we swirled around an eddy, five rafts and two kayaks, an adrenaline-charged flotilla.

With my boat hemmed in securely by the others, I abandoned it and jumped across the tubes toward a thermos of hot chocolate. While Jeff and I sat sipping the scalding liquid, Stewart leaped on my overturned raft and attached a flip line to the frame. "C'mon guys," he yelled, "let's get this over with." With a laugh and a shout, the others joined him. The boat rose out of the water, like the trapdoor of a storm cellar, as their weight pushed one side down while they pulled the opposite side up. The raft was perpendicular when Stewart announced, "You know this means we're all going to get wet!" A moment later five people disappeared in the river, and *Sunshine Lady* floated upright.

I glanced over my load. It was tied as firmly as it had been that morning, cleaner and wetter, but nothing lost—a consolation prize to soften the embarrassment of the flip. I looked away, then spread myself out on a slab of schist like a pagan sacrifice to the gods, soaking in solar radiation.

"Well, Patch, you've crossed the line."

"How's that, Stewart?"

"When it comes to flips, there's only two kinds of people: those who have and those who will."

Hermit Rapid, with its symmetrical waves and straightforward chute, is one of the prettiest rapids in the Canyon. Beginning with a wave about seven feet tall, each succeeding wave is taller, until the fifth one, which often reaches a height of twenty feet. Then in orderly fashion, the waves diminish in the same way they built up. They resemble ocean breakers in size and form, with one important difference: in the ocean, the waves move while the water remains stationary; on a river, the waves are stationary while the river moves.

Smoothly, effortlessly, I slide down the tongue, the bow of the raft descending at a sharp angle into the glossy trough. Magnetically, the wave draws me to itself as illusion and reality blend and entwine. Briefly, the raft stalls, then mounts the face, kissing the foam-tipped haystack before gliding down the back side. One wave

follows another, a ride of rhythm and motion, dancing and sway-
ing, rising and falling. The fifth wave holds itself erect like a soldier
proud of her bearing. We mount the steep face and hang on top,
suspended on the curling crest. A scream ascends above the roar of
the rapid. A long, high-pitched wail, seemingly distant and apart
from myself, but coming from some unknown place within me,
simultaneously connecting me to and releasing me from the river,
the Canyon, myself.

The rapid is over, I bail the knee-deep water out of the raft.

I pass Boucher Rapid.

I bail.

In the distance, against a black wall darkened by its own shadow,
a fine, almost imperceptible mist ascends out of the river. Far above
the mist and the occasional splash of water leaping high into the air,
far above the sound that resembles the roar of fans in a stadium, I
pull _Sunshine Lady_ over to the right shore. Involuntarily, my stomach muscles tighten.

The rapid that causes the mist to hang heavy in the air is a legend. A Sagittarius with a reputation. Before December 7, 1966,
she contained burbles and bubbles and not much more. Then a
heavy storm moved over the North Rim and dropped fourteen
inches of rain within a 36-hour period, turning the side canyon
into a raging monster. The flood wiped out pueblo sites that had
existed for 900 years and washed a fan of boulders into the river,
giving birth to a wild child known as Crystal Rapid.

Crystal's fame grew, and for more than sixteen years she terrified
boaters with a nightmarish hole and a rock garden. The hole snug-
gled against the left wall just below the mouth of Slate Creek, ran-
domly mushrooming twenty feet above its trough before crashing
in upon itself like an explosion gone awry. The rock garden, downstream from the hole, loomed in the center of the river with naked
fangs of granite and schist.

As if dissatisfied with her notoriety, in 1983 she expanded to
awesome proportions. That summer, the Colorado River peaked at
92,000 cfs. Giant boulders rumbled beneath the raging waters, and

a new hole, rising to heights of 40 feet, formed a barrier across the gateway of the rapid. Within a week, Crystal demolished seven 33-foot pontoon motor rigs and killed one person. More than 100 had to be evacuated from the Canyon by helicopter.

Boatmen and -women prayed for the flood to transform Crystal. Their prayers were answered. When the high water subsided, the old hole was gone, replaced by a solid wall of water at her entrance that can lead straight to hell.

Once upon another time, on a trip before the 1983 transformation, I scouted Crystal with a group who had a lot of experience on other rivers but very little in the Canyon. While the rest of the party discussed a jarring run through smaller holes to the right of Crystal Hole, I fixed my gaze on the Highway, an unruffled ribbon of current, perhaps eight to ten feet wide, slicing between the hole and the right run. The big guy's run, the run that required precise timing and nerves of steel. The run that combined the irresistible with the terrifying.

For a long time the group was silent, then Mark declared, "The only run is far right. Anything else is suicide."

"Yeah," Larry agreed, "I don't want to be anywhere near the hole."

"What about the Highway?" I asked. Eleven pairs of eyes examined me as if I'd just arrived from outer space.

"You want to go over there, we'll watch from shore," Mark said.

"Ha! Trash City. Let me get my camera," Larry snorted.

"Don't try it, Patch," Greg said. "I'm not going to do it."

I wondered what that had to do with me. I studied the Highway again.

"Where exactly are you planning to go?" my passenger Lisa asked. Our life jackets bumped up against each other.

I pointed out the route. "I'm sure I can do it. As long as we don't get into the haystacks above the hole, we should be okay." I bit my lip. "I did it last year with no trouble."

"I believe you," she said, and cast her big brown eyes up at me. "But please don't miss."

"I'll do my best."

"I'm ready," I said to the rest of the group.

"You going for it?" Greg asked. I knew he was genuinely concerned. I nodded.

"Want me to be the lead boat?" This would put him in a rescue position should I flip.

I nodded again.

The others looked at me in disbelief. "We'll stay here and watch the show," Mark smirked.

I marched back to my boat, my stomach overrun with butterflies, my mouth laden with cotton fluff. I tied up the bowline and handed it to Lisa, then climbed over the gear to my seat. Sitting still, I closed my eyes, took a number of slow, deep breaths and said a silent prayer to the spirit of the river.

Greg waved and rowed away from shore. When he was thirty or forty feet ahead of me, I pulled evenly on both oars, rowing *Sunshine Lady* to the middle of the river. Then, with a double-oar pivot, I turned the boat 180 degrees, facing the boat's stern toward the right side of the tongue. I would row hard to gain momentum, break through two or three small holes, pivot the bow downstream, and allow the Highway to carry me past Crystal Hole, giving her right edge a kiss as I went by.

It was a good plan, and it went like clockwork. I was exactly where I was supposed to be. I powered through the small holes. I relaxed. I allowed the bow of the boat to turn slightly downstream toward a cauldron of exploding waves. Something was wrong. Things didn't look right. In less than a fraction of a second, I recognized everything. I was too far left— on top of the current that went directly into Crystal Hole.

Sheer panic churned my brain to mush. Sprouting wings seemed the only escape. Instinctively, I pivoted the raft, turning the bow directly downstream, and lay every ounce of my 150 pounds hard against the oars. *Sunshine Lady* responded, gliding up and over one haystack, then another, until we slid down the back of the final wave into the yawning curve of the Hole, which opened wide like a mythical monster and swallowed us whole.

Tons of water buried us in a liquid night, buried us with a force that shook *Sunshine Lady* to her thwarts and ripped the oars from my hands. I waited for the surge of water that would flip us, waited helplessly in the belly of the whale until slowly, very slowly, she regurgitated us to the topside of the hole. An eternity passed up there in the rarefied air on the crest of a wave that surged beneath us. Then, with the power of a shotput, she catapulted us downstream.

Lisa and I remained motionless for what seemed a lifetime. Then her scream pierced the air. *"We ran Crystal Hole!! We did it!! We did it!!"* She danced in waist-deep water, laughing and screaming.

I lunged for my oars, then sat on my rowing seat trembling until a scream was wrenched from my throat, and I joined her in announcing our feat to the world. "We did it, we did it, we ran Crystal Hole!"

After the worst of the waves subsided, Lisa and I hugged in ecstatic joy. Then I glanced upstream. No, Lady, we didn't run you. You were kind and forgave our absolute audacity. Still, I laughed. "Bail!" I yelled. "Bail."

Now I face other challenges: the stark emptiness of solitude and a vulnerability greater than the perils of flipping or dying. I'm more alone than I have ever been before. On previous trips, I had someone else with whom to confer and share the excitement and apprehension. Which leaves me in a unique situation: I'm alone, and I'm not going to wait for someone else to show up.

Fear erupts like the exploding waves in a rapid; rowing Crystal is suddenly unthinkable. My shoes are lead weights, affixed to this rock I'm standing on. Stuck once again. What difference does it make where it happens or what causes it? Fear is a prison door waiting to confine me when I give in to it. All my fears congregate, each one clamoring for attention. Fear of being confined and losing my freedom. Fear of loving, fear of being intimate and exposing myself to another. Fear of rejection. Fear of being dependent on another. Fear of leaving a job I hate because it provides security. Fears that cause me to create excuses for my contradictory behavior, to spend months searching for an ideal, then run from it as soon as it is within my grasp.

I've tried burying my fears in the sand and writing them on a piece of paper to be thrown into a fire. These symbolic acts struck me as a beautiful way to rid myself of my fears so I could be free. But my fears returned, stronger than they were before. All the running and burying and denying and excuses have not worked. Once again I'm plagued with fear and self-doubt as I stand above Crystal.

A sensible side of myself provides an excuse. A certain amount of fear can serve a purpose, honing me to a razor's edge so that I am keen and sharp and able to make fast, decisive moves. The secret is knowing whether I have crossed the thin line between having just enough apprehension to see danger clearly and being so overwhelmed by fear that I'm paralyzed. I think back to the first time I rowed Lava Falls. I was overcome with fear, until a friend told me to turn my negative energy positive by putting my fear into the river and not allowing it to disarm me of my power. My run through Lava that day was excellent.

Your fear has very little to do with my ferocity, Crystal declares. The hole is no longer than it was when you went through it years ago. It's your emotions you're afraid of, not me.

I nod. Her truth is too penetrating to ignore.

aniel Long once wrote: "If a person does not fear to look into the Canyon and see distance such as he has never seen elsewhere, depth such as he has never dreamt of, and if he becomes lost in shades of gentian and cherry and troutlike silver, watches the unceasing change of hue and form in depth, distance, and color, he will have feelings that do not well go into words and are perhaps more real on that account."

◆

—John Annerino, *Running Wild: Through the Grand Canyon on the Ancient Path*

My emotional fears may not be as tangible as her rocks or holes, and they may be easier to deny, but by not dealing with them, I'm running the same rapid over and over, going into the same holes that continually tear me apart. I'm repeating mistakes by not looking at myself and accepting the fears that are part of me. They need to be acknowledged in the same way that the river's obstacles require attention. Fears must be embraced, treated like friends instead of enemies, acknowledged in the same way I respond to whitewater—with reverence and respect.

I watch the river roll by, and as I study Crystal, my perspective changes. I've stopped coming apart. She is steadying me, bringing me back to reality and away from the illusory world of fear.

When I first met Mother River, I realized immediately that she was a source of knowledge for me. As a beginner, I'd sit in an eddy behind a boulder in the middle of a rapid, fascinated by the water's motion. I wanted to learn to row well, and as I learned, I gained a sense that if I managed my life the same way I guided a raft through a rapid, I would be very successful. When I rowed too hard and fought the current, I usually didn't get where I wanted to go. Or worse, I might be thrown out of the boat into the river, where I was truly helpless. If I let the boat go without guidance, I was no better off. As my rowing improved, I came to understand that using the river's strength, direction, and flow helped me more than absolute control or total passivity.

I uproot my feet and walk along the edge of the river, studying the rapid, picking out a particular curl of a wave, a pillow of water as it flows up on a rock. I examine each subtlety until it is established firmly in my memory, and there is no chance I will get lost when I begin my run.

Back at *Sunshine Lady*, I tuck things away, untie and gently shove off. I float slowly downstream, holding the raft just outside the eddy that hugs the right shoreline. As I near the head of the rapid, I pivot the raft, turning the stern downstream at a 45-degree angle to the current, which gives me additional power when I pull on the oars. It is at this moment, on the edge of the rapid, that everything else disappears. I am totally focused—nothing else matters, nothing else exists. Everything blends together: even *Sunshine Lady* no longer exists of her own entirety, but instead becomes part of me, and the two of us together become part of the rapid.

I hug the right shoreline, skirting smooth stones and small holes, neither pushing the river nor allowing her to sweep me away. I pass by Crystal Hole with more than a boat-length to spare, awed by her power and majesty. Maybe I have finally learned to acknowledge and accept my fears, learned that they are more like a collection of rapids than the monsters I make them out to be. If I can deal with them as I do rapids, I may even learn something about my own vulnerability.

At the bottom of the rapid I catch an eddy and look back upstream. This river is my mother and she loves me. I'm certain of that.

The Jewels glimmer and gleam, boil and roll between schist and granite walls rising straight out of the river. There's Agate, Sapphire, Turquoise, Ruby, and Serpentine—boisterous, churning scamps who would be given more respect if they were situated at the beginning of the Canyon instead of coming as they do after Crystal. Crystal diminishes them, unjustly so, though they might actually be easier to run after encountering that great lady.

When the Jewels and I part company, I row for Lower Bass Camp, named after William Bass, one of Grand Canyon's eccentrics, who operated a tourist camp in the early decades of this century. It is a spacious place to stay, lying at the base of an open arena where the Grand Canyon series of rocks is exposed for a short distance, along with a fault zone that tears open the impassable walls.

At the last possible moment, I catch the eddy and slide toward a grove of tamarisk trees that grow directly in front of the landing site. Behind the trees, the camp opens up, first as small, secluded areas surrounded by low walls of schist, then into a wide expanse with terraced spots overlooking the river. With more time and energy, I'd hike the trail that leads up to a saddle, then down the other side to Shinumo Creek, where a natural rock alcove houses relics from Bass's original camp.

Thousands of stars, acting as handmaidens to a full moon, entice me to eat a leisurely dinner and relax beneath the celestial magnificence. I untie and carry the usual paraphernalia to the beach, glance over the menu, then spread out my ground cloth, pad, and sleeping bag and fall onto them like a rag doll.

Patricia C. McCairen left her native New York City when she discovered white-water rafting on a trip down the Colorado River through the Grand Canyon. She has been rafting for more than twenty years, worked as a guide for five years, and has visited all seven continents. She is the author of River Runners' Recipes *and* Canyon Solitude: A Woman's Solo River Journey Through Grand Canyon, *from which this story was excerpted.*

✳

To many river runners, floating into the Grand Canyon for the first time feels like coming home. But for some newcomers, it seems just the opposite. As one boatwoman describes it, "You truly walk through the door into a different reality. The place is such an assault on your senses—the massive cliffs, the strange plants, the shrill cicadas, the intense heat, and the swirling water. But you're held up because the intensity of everything buoys you up."

—Louise Teal, Boatwomen of the Grand Canyon:
Breaking into the Current

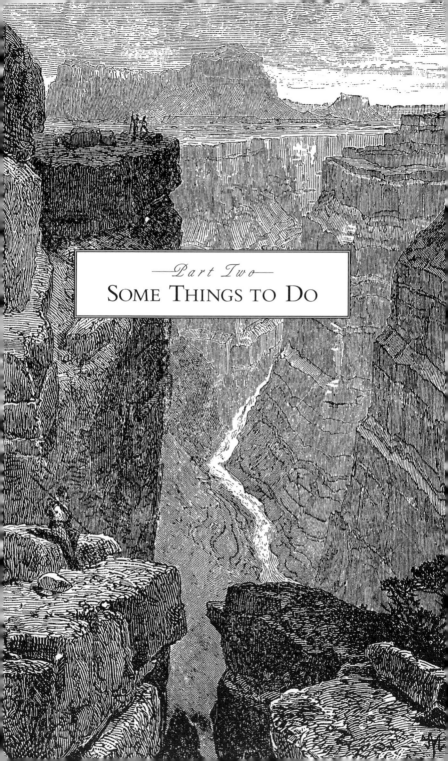

—*Part Two*—
SOME THINGS TO DO

Cape Solitude

A family takes the hard way.

NO ONE DESIGNED THE ROAD TO CAPE SOLITUDE; NO ONE MAIN-
tains it. On the contrary, the road evolved over a few decades to fit
the special needs of Navajo shepherds and others who occasionally
require a lot of space. There's room to spare at Cape Solitude.

It is the farthest buttress of the Palisades of the Desert, the great
sandstone wall on the South Rim of the Grand Canyon that sepa-
rates the Canyon from the Painted Desert to the east.

In almost every direction from Cape Solitude, you can see a
hundred miles and a hundred wonders. Look straight down, and a
mile below, you can see the confluence of the Little Colorado and
the Colorado rivers.

The prudent never go there. Of the four million who visit
Grand Canyon National Park each year, fewer than a hundred find
their way to the Cape.

The reason is the road. Its surface is littered with every variety
of lethal rock, and it traverses slopes at angles more appropriate to
cartoons than to cars. Moreover, since the road is fifteen miles long
and lonely, a miscalculation—or just plain bad luck—can entail a
long walk out.

So, it's hard to explain why my wife, our eight-year-old son and six-year-old daughter, and I, an otherwise sensible family, forced our way to Cape Solitude one stormy day in April.

The facts, as I know them, are these: we started the drive innocently—no road, we believed, could stay as bad as this one is initially—then we got stubborn, dug ourselves in deep, and before long it was as easy, and more rewarding, to go forward as to turn back.

When we left the tourist center at Desert View, we were well equipped. We had a reliable spare tire (two would have been even better), plenty of water and food, and a truck we could beat up. Four-wheel drive and high clearance are required for this trip.

Furthermore, we had obtained good directions; the way was clear, and the basic rule of driving to Cape Solitude—head north and always turn left—never failed us. All we had to do was stay attached to the road.

Less than a mile east of the East Entrance Ranger Station, I turned (left) onto a heavily rutted dirt road. No sign marked the way, we just took the first track that looked likely. "Likely" is a relative term.

During the winter, some desperate soul had really churned up this stretch of road. Axle-deep ruts swerved across the red dirt for hundreds of yards, testimony to an epic struggle to reach pavement. But in spring with the ground firm, we easily spanned the ruts, and for that one mile, we cruised the juniper forest like idle tourists.

Soon, however, the road turned rocky. When we came to a set of tight switchbacks, I put the truck in first gear, and we began inching down the slopes of the east Kaibab Monocline, a hillside of surpassing age and steepness. For the next five or six miles, we never got above second gear.

As we descended and the junipers thinned, the Vermilion Cliffs and Navajo Mountain appeared in the distance at the far edge of the Kaibab and Kaibito plateaus. Nearer, Cedar Mountain, covered almost to its flat top with juniper, dominated the view east. Beyond lay the tableland of the Painted Desert, its pastels muted by shadows of clouds, its flat expanse broken only by a dark seam marking the narrow gorge of the Little Colorado.

After the switchbacks came some narrow draws. The rocks

cemented in the bottoms of these draws, having stood the test of time, proved more than a match for our oil pan. When we began to bottom out repeatedly, my wife got out to scout obstructions.

For the next mile, she directed us around boulders when she could and moved them when she had to. And when that didn't work, she resorted to cursing those rocks in the same hopeless but skillful way a wrangler swears at mules.

Cursing doesn't work any better on rocks than it does on mules, so, in desperation, we adopted the radical strategy of steering directly over the worst rocks. It was that or the oil pan.

Our tires deformed sickeningly as they passed over horns of sharp rock, and, not for the last time, I wished we had another spare. On the way back, we would blow a tire in one of these draws, the sidewall torn out by an unseen blade of rock.

Even with seatbelts secured, we bounced in the cab like pips in a rattle. As we crept down scary ledges, I miscalculated a turn, and we dropped completely off one foot-high ledge, then crashed onto the next below. Net result: four

---

"*I*t's the place," Suzanne said softly. "It just wraps its arms around you." She reminisced about what she loves about the Grand Canyon—the aromatic scent of sand verbena, the smell of rain coming in the distance, the smell of silt in the mud water, the water ripples reflecting orange and purple at sunset, the moon casting a silhouette of the canyon rim on the opposite side of the river.

"The canyon is my sanity," she said. "It's a meditation that most people don't get in their lives. A Japanese man who spoke little English once told me, 'When I came on this trip I thought I was going to be really lonely. And you know, I *enjoy* being lonely, being alone sitting by the river just looking at the water. This is the Japanese way. For the first time in my life, I feel Japanese.'"

◆

—Louise Teal, *Breaking into the Current: Boatwomen of the Grand Canyon*

spines compressed several inches apiece, a loose tooth popped out from our six-year-old's mouth, and the truck's right rocker panel crushed.

Eleven miles into the ride, after we'd crossed a short section of the Navajo Reservation, we came to the crux, an open hill covered with loose sandstone shards. The angle would have deterred a mountaineer. At this point, my family got out and walked. Based on my recent form, I could hardly blame them.

On my first try, I started up the hill steady, confident, going fast for the conditions. About midway, a series of ruts and ridges stopped me cold. For a moment, the truck bucked in place, straining to jump one more ledge. But a decent respect for our tires and drivetrain—and the specter of a long walk out—made me back down. After three more tries, a couple of large-scale excavations, and a few false starts, I finally bounced the truck up and over the hill to the cheers of my family.

Through air redolent with the fragrance of sage, we rolled the last few miles across tableland on the western fringe of the Painted Desert.

Sticking close together, we tiptoed as close to the point of the cape as we dared. In the canyons, where roots of mountains grew out of the floors and shores of lost seas, the Little Colorado, stained by shades drained from the Painted Desert, flowed out of its own deep canyon to muddy the Colorado.

Balanced at the edge of canyons, desert, and sky, we held hands on the brink of the void at the end of the road to Cape Solitude.

Larry Winter, a mathematician and cabinet maker, lives in White Rock, New Mexico. He continues to explore the canyons of the Southwest by truck, boat and foot. A few things have changed since the trip to Cape Solitude recorded here. His truck, which is new with unblemished rocker panels, carries two spare tires. The other casualty of the trip, his daughter, is now a teenager with a full set of beautiful teeth.

★

The greatest tributes to the Grand Canyon have been paid by many whose words were never written. A sheik of Arabia, beturbaned and solemn, stood on the rim and for several minutes murmured to himself. To his guide, it sounded like a Moslem prayer. Thousands of ordinary people say nothing, and their silence is tribute enough. There is more than humor in the statement of a Midwestern farmer whose only comment was: "Heck of a place to lose a cow!" And there is deep meaning, too, in the way so many people exclaim "Gosh!" the first word that comes when the canyon appears before them. A president of the United States, William Howard Taft, a man who had seen much of the world, was more eloquent than he thought when his first exclamation, on seeing the Canyon, was heard by a guide and carefully remembered. President Taft said: "Golly, what a gully!"

—Raymond Carlson, "Golly, What a Gully,"
Arizona Highways Classics

Travertine Grotto

*A dory trip with the grand master
of the Colorado River.*

FOR THE FIRST TIME ON THE JOURNEY, WE FEEL URGENCY. WE MUST make it downriver to Travertine Falls before the crowds. Seven miles farther there is much cliff debris in the river, so the rafts must swing in first just above a rapid. Next come the dories.

This is the last full day of the nineteen-day trip, and my first day riding with Martin Litton, the Grand Old Man of the River. He has been saving the river since before I was born. Without him, the Grand Canyon would be just another slimy, trashed lake bottom above the proposed Marble Canyon dam site. How close we came to losing one of the most magnificent spots on Earth.

We tie up to Jeff's raft, and Lew Steiger helps Martin balance across the yellow tubes. The river roars directly underneath us toward the white water. I straddle the tubes with no grace, but the thought of body surfing these rapids holds no appeal. We scramble amid shed-sized hunks of limestone and schist tossed as if by an earthquake. Head down, I am admiring clear pools in pearly travertine basins formed when calcium carbonate precipitated out of limestone. Someone inevitably says, "Oh, schist!"

My head shoots up. Towering above us is orogeny with a sense of humor. Travertine Falls shoots out of solid rock hundreds of feet above us. I gaze in awe at the highly burnished Vishnu schist; black, metallic, scalloped bulges hump up the narrow chasm. A land of immense and regular flash floods.

I find a safer passage up near the canyon wall where the water has not scoured all the handholds out. Then standing below a seventeen-foot slick, vertical wall, I wait for my turn to use the stout rope a boatman has thrown down. I have good arm strength, but this leaning back into midair will take a leap of faith. To distract myself as I stand in line, I admire the whorls in the black stone which contrast the white travertine basins.

Michael flies up the wall on his spindle legs, then the rope is in my hands. I lean back and find I can "walk" up ten feet, then traverse a ledge which lands me at the second-level pool and waterfall. There is no rope to help me up to the third level, and after several moments of confusion, I discover the travertine is as gritty as a carbon grinding pad. Bracing with my sandals, I'm able to hoist myself up.

The next level lies only twelve feet up and into a slit solid rock where the water pounds. The sidewall next to the pouring water looks impassable to me, although Bonnie, Lili, and John are scrambling up it with ease. I pluck myself from the line of human ants and stand under the waterfall while hoping to become invisible.

Underneath is a satin tapestry of pale green and chartreuse moss, yellow algae, and gleaming white travertine. Over it all shimmer the electric threads of white water.

"Susan! The handholds are easy," snaps Shawn. Since I rode in his boat, listened to his stories, and sang with him last night, I am definitely not invisible to him. I watch as he glides up the twelve feet of black stone, finding substantial knobs, keels, and ridges with his hands. The slick stone seems to wrinkle into ledges under his feet.

I sail upward, finding it embarrassingly simple and infinitely pleasurable. I do not have even a moment to savor this climb, however. We shuffle down a dark corridor whose sides themselves are filled with grottos. After the heat of midday, the cool dampness massages our skin. Fifty feet back the slit opens up into a palatial womb where a forty-foot waterfall smashes down over a stone lip.

An even taller waterfall roars out of the heavens above that. The walls rise higher still to create a mysterious cylindrical room. Within it is an inner column of light where mist swirls in a microclimatic spiral.

Around the column stands a semicircle of drenched human beings—no, not merely drenched, but pouring off water, clothes flattened, hair parted to the point of baldness. Their grins are conspiratorial, I say to myself. Trouble.

"Get in the center," commands Bonnie. I crouch into the pounding waterfall like a timid animal, then back out. Suddenly, it dawns on me that, even with all this water power, there is no pain. I fling myself back inside with arms stretched wide open and head tilted back, right up into the central airhole. A thousand pulsating showerheads pound, thunder, hammer, thrum, and pulverize my head. My clothes are pummeled, my hair is pummeled. All the dirt, sweat, bug juice, sun grease, nose snot, heat rot, and smoke scum are hosed off my joyful skin; my soul is polished clean.

The downclimb goes smoothly now that I have dis-

---

*T*he bad rapid—
Lava Cliff—
that I had been looking for,
nearly a thousand miles,
with dread—
I thought:
once past there
my reward will begin,
but now everything ahead
seems kind of empty
and I find I have already had my
    reward,
in the doing of the thing.
The stars,
the cliffs
and canyons,
the roar of the rapids,
the moon,
the uncertainty and worry,
the relief when through each
    one—
the campfires at night,
the real respect of the rivermen
    I met
and others…

◆

—Buzz Holmstrom, quoted in
*The Doing of the Thing: The Brief
Brilliant Whitewater Career of
Buzz Holmstrom* by Vince Welch,
Cort Conley, and Brad Dimock

covered travertine is as rough as a rasp. At the second-level waterfall basin, I pause, waiting for the rope. Martin is down-climbing slowly, painfully over against the cliff. Since none of us can move past him, all eyes are glued to him, all our joints ache with each of his stiff joints, all our hearts are thumping with his. We are well aware of what a fall would mean to his fragile, eighty-year-old bones.

Yet there is not one of us who would deny him this challenge. We are all honored to have our tribal elder climbing with us, sharp as a tack, witty, loving life.

When I am finally handed the rope, I traverse and downclimb ahead of everyone else so that I may pee in peace. Crouching in the roaring mouth of Travertine Creek, I find pleasure in watching my body's chemicals mix into the Colorado. When I turn, three boatmen from the large tour company upriver have arrived and are staring at me.

"Hah!" I think. "This is how a *real* river woman lives. I bet none of your passengers loosen their decorum for their entire motorized, wimp-assed, two-day trip—even if they have to hold it in." What hubris I've gained from a little bit of rock climbing and nineteen days of freedom.

We clamber back into the boats and shoot out into the rapids. Lew, Martin's watchperson, takes another passenger, Don, into the *Sequoia's* bow and leaves me solo in the stern. He is coaching Don on how to trim, or balance, the lightweight dory so that it makes rowing easier for the eighty-year-old man.

Sadly, these are the very last of our rapids before the mighty Colorado is drowned, defrothed, and degraded into Lake Mead, and eventually into one wide mud slime down a Sonoran delta into the Sea of Cortez. Only a few rapids remain: Mile 231, Mile 232, Mile 234, and Bridge Canyon Rapids. Silenced is Gneiss Canyon Rapid and all the rapids below; Lake Mead has risen fifteen feet in this year alone. With joy and mourning, we enter these last rapids with Martin Litton. Martin sways us through the huge waves with the ease of an ice skater who, in midair, knows exactly how to land.

Pure, liquid beauty: an old man in a sea-blue hat, a bright-yellow life vest, red oar handles twirling under reddened, gnarled hands, a bright-turquoise dory, and white paddle blades dipping and gleaming. I attempt to reexperience the fear I felt a lifetime ago before the first rapids of this journey but cannot. I attempt to remember the cold, sodden misery of the first four April days of snow, sleet, and downpour but cannot. Instead, I balance high on the stern deck in sheer bliss.

Martin spins us around completely, and the *Sequoia* sweeps toward the muscular granite wall. I clutch the gunnels hard, praying, "Oh, no, not on your last rapids, Martin!"

As we pass within a few feet of the canyon wall and out of the rapid, Martin is saying, "You wouldn't believe it from today, but last year I flipped right here in this rapid. Was so confident all the hatches were open. We lost all our stuff, but floated on down the river.... I popped up next to the boat. It is very different at lower water levels. I once sat in a chair with Lana Turner." And he launches into a story about the movie stars he met while fighting to save the Grand Canyon.

Now I understand why caretaker Lew Steiger was uptight at the beginning of these rapids. These were the last of the substantial rapids. He stands and bows toward Martin with a huge shit-kickin' grin slicing his face. The Old Man has rowed almost the whole damned river at eighty. The all-time, Earth-wide, universal record. He has rowed it almost flawlessly with the precision timing of Itzhak Perlman, Bierstadt painting the waves. Lew clusters his fingertips, kisses them, and flicks them toward the sun.

"That was golden, Martin, absolutely golden."

Susan Zwinger was given the Governor's Writers Award for her book Stalking the Ice Dragon. *This story was excerpted from her book,* Writing Down the River: Into the Heart of the Grand Canyon. *She lives on Whidbey Island, Washington, and is the daughter of noted author Ann Haymond Zwinger, whose story "Fishing Eagles" also appears in Part Two.*

✳

And if you happen to be rowing a wooden boat, there is also a unique feeling of joy. When river guides describe a past rapid run, it doesn't take long before their eyes start sparkling, and they are back on the river. The listener becomes the vehicle they ride back to the water. But the women who row dories get more than a gleam in their eyes. They get special smiles, and then their voices actually take on a lyrical lilt, like a dory riding up and over the waves. Ellen was no different. At least, not after she got over her hesitancy to talk about how she felt about dories as compared to rafts. She didn't want to give the impression that she thought dory boatwomen were superior oarswomen. But dory guides definitely accomplish something each time they row their rigid, quarter-inch-plywood boats through the Grand Canyon in one piece, without crashing on a rock or flipping. It is what they refer to as a "golden trip."

—Louise Teal, *Breaking into the Current:*
Boatwomen of the Grand Canyon

DON KARDONG

Over the Edge

A run from rim to rim is not for the faint-hearted.

THIS WAS THE PROVERBIAL MOMENT OF TRUTH. A MOMENT OF TIME in this ancient Grand Canyon landscape as inconsequential as one drop of water in the river below us. But for me, it was the moment that mattered.

It was 3 p.m. I had been running, jogging, walking, and otherwise transversing the rocky path beneath my feet for eight and a half hours. From the interminable drop off the South Rim to the Colorado River, followed by the steady climb to the North Rim, and then the long trek back to the Colorado River. I had pattered along, determined to complete this 41.2-mile journey before sunset.

Since dawn, freezing weather had steadily warmed, and for the past two hours, conditions had flirted with hot. Dehydration was a worry. Blisters, too, were a concern, and I could feel their throbbing on my right heel and big toe. Mostly, though, it had been the steady thump down, and up, and down again, carving a visceral map of the Grand Canyon in my quads, that was making life difficult.

When my running partner for most of the day, Steve Utley, came skipping lightfooted past me at Phantom Ranch, I felt the way an old, lumbering plant-eater must have when *Tyrannosaurus rex* danced the two-step of death around it. I had no life in my legs to respond. I was unable to take another running step.

Now, crossing the suspension bridge, I could look down at the copper-brown rapids below me, or up at the cold, black rocks of the Grand Canyon's Inner Gorge, the top of a mountain range two billion years old. Either way, it was a scene without pity.

There at the nadir of my journey, I knew I had nearly three hours left. If I took longer, it would grow dark on this part of the earth. I was tired enough to wonder what the bottom line was on exhaustion in the bowels of the Grand Canyon. Overnight at the ranger station? A helicopter airlift?

Face it, though, I wasn't going to stop. There were many reasons, but one main one: back on the South Rim, my nine-year-old daughter, Kaitlin, and her grandmother were waiting. I imagined panic if I didn't show up.

"Where's Dad? Is he all right? Why isn't Dad back yet?"

I couldn't quit. And a little more than six miles from the finish, nearly a mile straight down in this majestic hole in the ground, there was only one way out. Left foot. Right foot. Up. Up.

I had heard about runners in the Grand Canyon, as long as fifteen years ago. Immediately, way back then, I felt inclined to join. There is something about the wonders of nature that elicit an instinctive human urge to wander, explore, assimilate. For many of us, that can mean only one thing—a good, long run.

The romanticism of the quest was severely strained, when I finally stood on the South Rim, I could see ten miles straight across to the North Rim, the halfway point, and could follow the trail as it wound down through yellow, orange, red, and purple cliffs, buttes, castles, and crags that define the landscape. It's a stunningly beautiful sight, but it was going to be a long, difficult "run."

This precipitous drop took my breath away. Could there be a reasonable trail down there? Could I manage this, or would my fear of heights turn to panic, leaving me a whimpering mess, clinging to a rock somewhere below? My fear was softened when I finally met my fellow travelers for dinner on the night before the run.

"This hardly qualifies as a trail run," said Ross Zimmerman, one of about twenty ultrarunners who would be making the trip. "It's more like a road."

Steve Corona nodded in agreement. Corona, already a veteran of nine Grand Canyon round-trips, was my advisor, so I paid attention to his nod. I found it comforting.

Still, these were ultrarunners, so their lack of intimidation was understandable. Used to 24-hour treks in rain, snow, burning daylight, and foggy darkness, traveling on narrow trails at high altitudes and through improbable territory, they develop a firm conviction that whatever will happen, will happen. And they will be ready for it because they have a couple of Band-Aids, a PowerBar, and a penlight in their fanny packs.

One of their ilk once did the rim to rim and back in 7 hours and 43 minutes. Others have managed a "double double," 82.4 miles, in one fell swoop. I love these people, with their sublime confidence, their steady yet intense eyes, their ultimate faith in themselves. They calm me.

Back in my room, however, I reread the visitor's guide. In bold print, it read: "Warning: Do not attempt to hike from the rim to the Colorado River and back in one day. Many people who attempt this have suffered serious illness or death." I took this warning seriously, knowing we would be going over three times that far.

I reviewed my fanny pack. Food bars, packets of replacement fluid, three water bottles, first-aid supplies. The pack was heavy, so I removed my flashlight. If I didn't make it back before dark, I would travel as ancient Canyon travelers did. By moonlight.

Dawn. "It can snow, it can rain, it can do anything," Corona had told me weeks earlier. When I awoke after an agitated, mostly sleepless night and looked outside, though, the ground was dry, the temperature was below freezing, and the stars were crackling.

I wanted Kaitlin to see these blazing desert stars sometime during our trip, but she was still asleep. I fidgeted with my pack, dressed and walked to the lodge to catch a ride to the trailhead.

A few minutes later, four of us stood at the top of the Kaibab Trail, waiting for first light. There were no timers, no starting

instructions, no crowd to cheer us on. This was a totally unstruc-
tured adventure. Some runners had already left, others would start
later. When it got light enough, we went.

I hadn't seen the Kaibab Trail before, and it was probably a good
thing. It may be a road to
some, but to me it was a slith-
ering serpent of a path,
marked by mule-hoof holes,
rocks set across the trail to
inhibit erosion, and a variety
of natural stumbling blocks.

It was a swift descent for
the first three miles down to
and across the crest of Cedar
Ridge. In places, the scenery
soared downward on both
sides, and I was glad to focus
on the trail to avoid flirting
with vertigo.

Zimmerman and Corona
had assured me that heat, not
cold, would be my Canyon
nemesis. Sure enough, after
only a few minutes, I began
peeling off windpants, windbreaker, and gloves, gear I
wouldn't need again that I
would have to carry for the
rest of the journey.

The previous evening,
Zimmerman had asked if I
had done any long, sustained
downhills and stared mutely
when I answered no. Now,
trying to skip as dexterously as
I could from spot to spot

*or the Paiutes, it was
an important summer
hunting ground. They called it
Kaiuw A-vwi, or "Mountain
Lying Down," perhaps because
instead of a distinct, craggy
summit, its recumbent heights
roll through a gentle landscape
of meadow and forest. White
settlers, when they arrived on
the scene, called it Buckskin
Mountain because its abundant
deer provided them with meat
and hides. The official name
today is the Kaibab Plateau. The
very opposite of a canyon, it
lies 8,000 to 9,000 feet high,
covered with snow in the winter
and fragrant with the smell of
mountain wildflowers in
summer. While the adjacent
desert shimmers beneath a hot
sun, and lizards in the Inner
Gorge go underground to escape
the heat, cool breezes sigh
through the forests of the plateau.

♦

—Jeremy Schmidt,
*A Natural History Guide:
Grand Canyon National Park*

down the trail, avoiding the brakes as much as possible, I appreciated the point of his question. I had tried to simulate jarring as much as possible in my training by running repeats down steps, but it hardly seemed to be making a difference. Neither that nor my longest training runs of eighteen miles were going to help much today.

Our group of four made no attempt to stay together but instead headed down following separate agendas, stopping to adjust packs, remove clothing, and take a swig or two of liquid. I was drinking Wild Bill's XXX Grand Canyon Mix, a high-energy concoction personalized for this occasion by an ultrarunner friend of mine.

It was incredible to imagine, but after an hour of steady downhill running, I still hadn't reached the bottom. I had descended through gold, orange, and red sediments deposited before the birth of dinosaurs, reached a plateau formed half a billion years before the land on this part of the continent began uplifting against the flow of the Colorado River, but I still hadn't bottomed out. From the Tonto Platform from where I now jogged, I was enjoying the dawn of one more day, the warmth of one more sunrise, the glow of one more morning deep in the Grand Canyon. And my quads hurt like hell.

Finally, trying in vain to buffer my ever-tightening muscles, I made the final descent down one last series of switchbacks into the Canyon's Inner Gorge and reached the Colorado River. After descending from 7,200 to 2,450 feet and completing perhaps one-tenth of my journey, I could already tell it was going to be a long day.

Steve Corona had warned me that there would only be two places on the trail that I could rely on for water. One was a spigot at Phantom Ranch, a hiking, riding, and overnight area on the north side of the river. Even there, the water supply was tenuous, though, due to a recent break in the pipe, and I was grateful to be able to refill my bottles.

A part of me wanted to stay at Phantom Ranch, where campers were frying bacon for breakfast while deer grazed nearby. I could dunk my feet in the creek, kick back for a few hours, have a meal, and join the run back up the Canyon in a few hours…Just a thought.

A minute later, I was back on the trail, winding up the dark, narrow gorge of Bright Angel Canyon, the handiwork of one of the many streams responsible for the extensive erosion that defines the Grand Canyon. Not much direct sunlight gets in here, and the granite walls are nearly vertical. I began to feel isolated, even lonely. I wondered where the other runners were.

A few miles later, I found out, as I caught up with three men, none of whom I had met before. Two of them, Irv Nielsen and Tom McFarland, were members of the Utah Symphony Choir and were singing a Mozart tune in honor of the scenery. The third, Steve Utley, seemed to be listening. I offered to sing something by Jim Morrison, and in spite of this, they allowed me to tag along.

All three had some experience with ultras, they seemed to be in no pressing hurry, and they were eager to share stories and information. Irv, a pharmacist and the trail supervisor at the Wasatch 100, had a good understanding of local vegetation and a seemingly endless supply of really bad jokes, which got even worse at higher elevations. In short, this was the perfect group to trudge along with to the top of the North Rim.

We reached the pump house near Roaring Springs, nearly nine moderately uphill miles from the Colorado River, without a whole lot of grief. The pump house caretaker, Bruce Aiken, spends his free time painting landscapes. He moved to this spot from Manhattan twenty years ago and raised a family here. He looked genuinely pleased to see us using the spigot in his front yard.

It would be nearly two hours, five miles, and 3,600 feet later that our gang of four would reach the North Rim. We could see it most of the time, but we didn't appear to be getting to it very quickly.

"Every time I look up there," observed Irv at one point, "it's farther away."

"Well then," scolded Tom, "stop looking up there."

I remember occasional running during this long uphill march, and lots of moments when I felt like Wile E. Coyote, standing on a trail carved precariously into a rock face, staring out past one long misstep to what could be a very nasty landing hundreds of feet below.

"Isn't it beautiful?" bellowed Utley as we skirted around one cliff. I was hugging the inside, though, averting my eyes. How was I going to get past this point, I wondered, coming back down? Eventually, though, the trail headed into the trees, and my fear passed. Around eleven, we began passing runners on their way back.

One woman, who must have been fifty, was beside herself with joy on her return. "Isn't this great?" she enthused, beaming.

I think most ultrarunners are like this. The only opponent on race day is the distance, and fellow runners are greeted with open hearts and honest enthusiasm. And their encouragement helped me reach the North Rim, finally, twenty minutes before noon.

As I stood munching a granola bar, I remembered something Steve Corona had said: "What people should do is come here in October, run to the North Rim one day, stay overnight, and run back to the South Rim the next day."

Good advice, I thought, as was the opinion of going just one direction during late spring or early fall, when weather conditions in the Grand Canyon are reasonably pleasant, and catching a ride back.

"Have you ever done that?" I asked Corona about his suggested overnight rest.

He just smiled, of course, as people do who never follow their own good advice.

Noon. By this time, our group was on the way back down. Given my skittishness coming up some of the dicier sections of this trail, I was amazed at how quick and panic-free the run back to Bruce Aiken's was. The tensest moment came a few hundred yards from his house, when we faced off with a mule deer on a rocky section of the trail. He finally blinked, turned, and clattered off.

Reaching Aiken's, we stopped for a rest, refill, and a tall glass of lemonade. I'd been running in t-shirt and shorts for most of the day, so I was surprised when a woman runner in tights and windbreaker stopped for water.

She introduced herself as Lorraine Gersitz, but I found myself over the next few miles trying to remember if she had said Eileen or Irene or Ellen, and was that Gershwitz or Dershwitz or something else? I recognized my confusion as the normal deterioration of the brain function in the latter stages of a long, long run.

I followed Gersitz down the next nine miles, still stunned that she was dressed so warmly while I was struggling more and more with dehydration. I was also amazed at her flowing ease down the trail, in comparison to my own fumble-footedness. After that second long downhill of the day off the North Rim, every small barrier had become a high hurdle.

The final stages of Bright Angel Canyon narrowed to the dark corridor I remembered from early that morning, but the trip seemed infinitely longer. At every turn, I expected to see Phantom Ranch, but every turn produced yet another dark corridor and yet another turn. My legs were really giving out now, as was my stomach, which finally rebelled against lemonade, warm weather, and perhaps the general human condition. I retched, paused for a minute, then continued.

"You all right, partner?" asked Steve Utley, who was running behind me. I was, but I was also promising myself, with the sincerest conviction, that I would never do this again.

By the time Steve and I reached Phantom Ranch, I realized I was within reach of my goal. Crossing the Colorado River, I vowed to put my head down and make it back to the South Rim before dark, before my young daughter could panic.

"The climb out is a real killer," Steve Corona had told me. "I call it the hardest 10k in the world."

It was also nearly a three-hour return to the present. From a landscape half as old as the planet itself, upward through geological layer after layer, winding between and among rocks chiseled and eroded by the elements over millions of years, I hiked as fast as I could, anxious to reach the top. Being in the Grand Canyon is a compelling reminder of how long the earth has been here, and how short our stay will be. It made me want to get back to the present, to family and friends, as soon as possible.

There were places on the upward journey where I could look straight across at some of the most impressive monuments in the Canyon, landforms that the first white explorers here named after ancient shrines and temples, which still inspire hushed reverence in visitors.

The Kaibab Trail had nowhere to refill my bottles, so I rationed water, rewarding myself for every ten-minute increment of time with a swallow of liquid. Ten minutes, drink. Ten minutes, drink. Steadily, my bottles became lighter, and I got closer to the top. If I stopped, my legs would cramp, so I kept moving. Steve promised me a cold beer on the top, and I began dreaming about it.

Coming around a bend in the trail halfway up, I startled two ravens the size of Labradors. They jumped off the cliff and floated away, soon becoming two whirling black dots in infinite space below.

Hikers began asking if we were the rim-to-rim runners, and I was proud that our fame had spread. We passed a sign advising, as had the visitor's guide, not to attempt to hike to the Colorado River and back in one day, and I enjoyed the irony. With only a mile or two left, a pale moon rose on the other side of the Canyon. The only sound, other than our own huffing and plodding was the breeze.

Looking out over several especially precipitous drops, Steve and I agreed that, no matter how tough this had been, tempting fate by riding down the Canyon on the back of a mule would have been worse.

On our own two feet then, finally, at 5:34 p.m., after more than eleven hours in the Grand Canyon, we reached the top. A few minutes later, the light began to dim.

Dusk. Back at the lodge, I reunited with Kaitlin and my mother-in-law, and we shared our day's adventures. They had gone horseback riding. I had gone for a long run. We were all glad to have ended the day alive and well and back together.

An informal gathering of Canyon runners scheduled for that evening didn't materialize, so I wasn't even sure how many runners there had been. Twenty? I ended up comparing notes, one-by-one, when I recognized someone I had seen along the trail. Some had taken a little over nine hours, others, like sixty-one-year-old Hal Winton, wasn't quite sure and didn't really care.

Still, without a ceremony or celebration of some kind, I was curious about how to put the day into perspective. Was this the hardest run I'd ever done? My legs felt as if someone had been beating on them with a hammer all day. My back was sore from the weight of the fanny pack. There was a fairly impressive blister on my right heel. Both feet were shriveled up like raisins.

I had no trophy to display for all this, just a couple of shoes caked with orange dust. And, of course, a whole lot of images to carry around in my head.

That night I lay down on my bed, overcome with fatigue. Quickly, I began fading toward sleep. Then I heard a voice.

"Dad?" said Kaitlin, her voice tinged with concern.

"Huh? What?"

"Are you okay? Your breathing is kind of weird."

"I'm fine Kaitlin," I answered, smiling in the dark. "Yeah, I'm fine."

Don Kardong is a longtime senior writer for Runner's World *magazine, the president of the Road Runners Club of America, and the founder of the Lilac Bloomsday Run in his hometown, Spokane, Washington. In 1976, he finished fourth in the Montreal Olympic Marathon.*

⁂

Children loved John Hance, and to them he always explained how the Canyon came into being. "I dug it," he would say simply. This story worked well for years until one little four-year-old girl asked seriously, "And where did you put the dirt?" Hance had no ready answer; he never used the story again. But it bothered him the rest of his life, and when he was dying he whispered to his waiting friends, "Where do you suppose I could have put that dirt?"

—Edwin Corle, *Listen, Bright Angel*

Thunder

*The secrets of the Canyon
are without number.*

IN THE GRAND CANYON, WHERE EVEN SUPERLATIVES FAIL TO match the real scale of things, it's hard to explain in mere words how and why a special place is special. Normal earthly experience does not prepare people to grasp the scope of things here without seeing them—and then attempting to climb them. Knowing this makes it even tougher. Even so, it is worth a try.

I have a favorite place in the Grand Canyon. It's not a secret place, although sometimes I wish it were. Anasazi Indians knew of it a thousand years ago. Hunters of the Desert Archaic probably were familiar with the region millennia earlier. People of both groups could descend into the canyon and hike to it along a route from what they today call Monument Point on the North Rim, a dozen miles from (and a mile above) the river. Paiutes followed the Puebloans several centuries later. Prospectors used the same route just a century ago but found no mineral wealth. The U.S. Forest Service improved parts of the trail in 1926. So, rather than being secret, my favorite place is more like Grand Central Station in slow motion. But it holds the most incredible collection of landscapes in Grand Canyon.

The route to it from the river begins at Tapeats Rapid (Mile 134) and circles above the roaring gulch of lower Tapeats Creek along a steep trail ascending a few hundred feet straight up to a bench atop the Diabase Sill, splitting the Bass limestone. This part of the trail is so steep that climbing it becomes an act of faith in the work ethic. Nothing this taxing could fail to earn a reward. And it does. The view is stunning. From up here, our boats look like yellow toys dinky enough to drop down the neck of a water bottle. And Tapeats Creek—at about 65 cfs the largest creek originating in the Grand Canyon and loaded with trout, the kind of creek that can knock people down when they misstep crossing it—seems a cellophane-thin trickle where it joins the implacable beast of the Colorado. From up here atop the Diabase Sill, it is a mere saunter (a careful one) along the bench descending gently inland to Tapeats Creek.

What lies ahead is hidden by a bend in the Canyon, but it is so huge that one can safely anticipate that something interesting awaits discovery up there. The question is, what? Here the hidden Canyon becomes an urgent mystery, a promise, a mysterious desert oasis concealing austere delights to make the senses whirl. Soon the route connects with the creek where it metamorphoses from a roaring gorge into a trout stream again, tumbling over waterfalls flanked by cottonwoods. It races to the Colorado as if the earth were about to end and it had to be there on time. The best crossing is located at a wide ford where no rope is necessary unless the creek is in spate. From here, the path snakes upstream between groves of succulent prickly pear cacti and junglelike thickets of bear grass hiding rattlesnakes, and over ledges perched above the rushing creek. Soon, it enters a wide canyon flanked by tall cliffs of Shinumo quartzite, cliffs of swirled maroon and purple and tan and cream.

In the Shinumo quartzite are sheer cliffs punctuated by ledges, niches, overhangs, benches, caves...and dozens of hidden granaries of the Anasazi. One, the Mystic Eye, is unique in Grand Canyon. It is constructed entirely of wattle and daub (straight sticks completely plastered with mortar) except for its threshold and door, which was a solid slab of quartzite. It is also perched high in a cliff face, in a niche better suited to a nesting peregrine falcon than a granary. Because of an exposure of from 30 to more than 100 feet of a free fall, the difficult friction traverse across the cliff face required to visit the Mystic Eye stops normal humans cold—even some abnormal ones. Boatmen have fallen from this cliff while attempting to traverse the quartzite, paying the price of trying to absorb a bit of magic in the Eye. Mystic Eye manna, at too high a price. But most Canyon boatmen do not even know where the Mystic Eye is, and it is far too dangerous to take clients there. So it remains somewhat of a secret. Another secret is how an Anasazi loaded with maize made this move across the cliff. Maybe they built ladders. The view from the eye is worth the risk—but only if you are very good on cliffs.

The path in the valley winds between these cliffs and passes several dwellings of the vanished Anasazi, but to the untrained eye most of these ruins are invisible. The Indians must have planted fields of maize, beans, and squash along the expanse of gentle slopes near the roaring creek. When I study the lay of the land here, I am forced to admit that agriculture would have been possible with more rain, but converting the boulder-strewn slopes to terraced fields would have been hellish work. Yet the Anasazi did just this.

Less than three miles from the Colorado, we abruptly abandon Tapeats Creek and the swirled cliffs to ascend a steep trail to the northwest—we are now traversing a slope parallel to the world's shortest river.

---

*T*he Havasupai Indians, a small tribe who dwell near the bottom of Grand Canyon, eat the berries of the Utah juniper as food…. These berries are collected after they have fallen to the ground, pulverized in a bedrock mortar, soaked in water, put into the mouth by the handful, and the juice sucked. The solid matter is then spat out…. At the Hopi pueblo of Hano, the young people and children eat the berries as a delicacy. They are considered more palatable if heated in an open pan. The Hopis of this same pueblo also chew the gum of the juniper with relish.

♦

—*The Best of Grand Canyon: Nature Notes 1926–1935*

Thunder River is a spiritual experience. No one who crawls up the switchbacks on that sun-baked slope, then suddenly beholds an entire river blasting forth from the dry face of the Redwall limestone fails to be moved. No matter that a half mile from this roaring spring and tumble of wild cascades, Thunder loses its identity by merging with Tapeats Creek (is this the only case of a river flowing into a creek?). Thunder River is unforgettable, and because of the struggle to reach it, precious.

The temperature among the cottonwoods along the falls a hundred feet below the source is perfect. Thunder River pours over mossy boulders and the twisted and gnarled roots of cottonwoods. Crimson monkey flowers form a foot-deep carpet flanking the flow. They are in turn bordered by lush maidenhair ferns, horsetails, then willows, grasses, and herbs. The place is a riotous jungle oasis perched on the face of a bone-dry cliff in a barren, sun-baked Canyon.

The water tastes pure and cold and seems a sacrament. A glance upward to the narrow slices in the limestone from which Thunder Spring blasts into the sunlight to become Thunder Falls and then Thunder River gives no hint, though, that through those narrow portals and within that massive cliff are underground falls and grottos, sluices and caves, rooms and auditoriums, rapids and lakes...and fear, in helpings not normally available in the outside world.

On my first hike up here in 1976, I climbed the cliff alone past several nasty exposures to gaze into the source of Thunder. I don't recommend it. The river blasts out of a four-foot-wide fissure with the speed of an F-16. Or so it seems. And to enter the cave, one must step over this Mach-1 blast of water onto a steep, wet wall only a few feet from the falls. The thought alone prompts panic. This move into Thunder Cave makes the friction traverse to the Mystic Eye seem like rocking on a front porch with a mint julep. A misstep would join you with Thunder Falls and spin you into a mix of air and falling water for a couple of seconds before you pound onto the rocks below. From there, you would rag-doll down one impressive and scenic set of falls to another. Altogether an unattractive prospect.

I gazed into the cave and felt fear prowl around in me like a loose tiger. I decided not to try that one step over Thunder River. Even so, I could not shake the conviction that the secrets of the universe were contained within the unattainable cavern. It bothered me for nine years, during most of which I led people on trip after trip up Tapeats Creek and up Thunder River to the falls below the source. The awe, joy, reverence, and appreciation people felt did not quite satisfy me. None of them imagined that a cave existed behind that cosmic fire hose in the cliff. But I knew, and it seemed to stare down at me in patient scorn: "I'm here."

Nor could I simply absent myself briefly from my group and hop up there with a flashlight and a rope to explore the cave in the mere hour or so we spent there. First of all, an hour is too little time. Second, someone would want to come with me. Taking any paying client up there would be potential manslaughter. Yet, although I don't recommend it to anyone, that hole in the cliff haunted me.

Finally in 1985, on a trip I was leading, Michael Boyle, Mike Anderson (our trainee), and I left our group early to hustle up to Thunder Springs, where we climbed the cliff face, slipped on wool shirts and headlamps, uncoiled our rope, belayed one another on the entry, and made that horrendous step across the rush of Thunder River. "One small step for man…" and one scary one. But with the rope for protection, it was easy. None of us slipped. We were inside Thunder Cave. Immediately at our backs an entire river shot into bright sunlight and thin air. We deroped ourselves. A slip here now would mean adios.

The long entry into Thunder Cave is merely a deep slit with a river rushing along the bottom. For the next half hour, each of us employed every bouldering trick we knew to straddle the flow as we traversed our way along the vertical Redwall limestone. Here, the rock was eroded into knife blades at nearly every edge. There was literally nothing in this cave that was smooth or rounded. Carefully, cautiously, and with the precision of diamond cutters, we examined the cliff walls for tiny cracks and nicks that would allow a hand- or foothold. It was as if we had a hundred-foot exposure below us rather than ten feet to a small river. Actually, we had both; one led to the next. Inch by inch and foot by foot, we penetrated the zone of mystery. Eventually, after several traverses, climbs and descents, chimney moves and crawls, we found sections where we could drop into the bed of the creek itself and walk or wade upstream. This was heaven.

Why do batteries always fade when you need them the most? Despite fading lamps, we pressed on through grottos and stream corridors. We paused at waterfalls that would have been scenic in the world behind us, then climbed up around them to continue. Would we discover something absolutely unbelievable beyond the next bend? A cavern large enough to support the last survivors of a nuclear holocaust? The skeleton of some antediluvian beast...a *Tyrannosaurus rex*? A portal through the fabric of time to the lost world of the Anasazi?

What we did find was grottos, some as big as auditoriums, alternating with narrow slits through which Thunder River raced. We found falls, walls, and dry "extinct" caves branching from this main channel and begging to be explored. We also found ourselves shivering.

Finally we came upon a silent lagoon, a wall-to-wall lake. Upstream, the roof of the cave dipped almost to the water. It did not look inviting. We were cold. But it did exert an irresistible magnetism. One after another, we slid into the water and swam upstream. We climbed up beyond the dip and, shivering, studied the lake. It continued for an unknown distance, hidden by the very low roof. We needed a small boat or an air mattress. Reluctant to leave but satisfied with our effort, we turned and retraced our steps. Our lamps were glowing only a dim yellow now.

We rounded one of the last sharp corners. Here we had to straddle the stream channel about six feet above it with hands and feet on each side. Boyle was just ahead. Anderson had fallen behind. I looked back and could not even see the glow from his lamp. I started worrying about him. I tried to find a more comfortable position in which to wait, but half-inch-wide nicks in the Redwall were all that was available. I finally spotted his lamp, then him. Then

I turned to follow Boyle. As my weight shifted, the tiny ledge of rock under the heel of my right hand broke off, and I suddenly lost that hold plus my other two contacts. Abruptly I free-fell into Thunder River in the dark. My knee jammed into the sharp point of a large boulder. It hurt. I climbed back out. In the dim glow of my lamp, blood flowed down my shin.

The sunlight beyond the opening of Thunder Spring seemed like the flash of an atomic explosion. Each of us had to avert his head for a moment for our pupils to adjust to the brightness. Three hours after our entry, we roped up on belay again and made that single step across Thunder to Grand Canyon. It was easier this time.

Everyone had gone. We descended the cliffs to the trail. I looked again at my knee. It was as swollen as a ripe peach. Then I looked back up at that enigmatic slit in the Redwall with the explosion of water bursting from it.

Thunder Spring is an amazing reality. It seems too improbable to invent in fiction, and it is not clear to everyone, even when see-ing the roaring fountain in the face of the cliff, exactly *what* Thunder Spring is. Fellow guide T. A. told me incredulously about one woman who never did grasp it.

"How does this water get here, T. A.?" she had asked.

"Well, there's an aquifer in the Redwall limestone that's imper-meable and collects groundwater moving into it from the Kaibab Plateau. The outlet for the aquifer is right there—Thunder Spring."

"Where does all that water come from?" she pressed.

Not thinking that her question was serious, T. A. answered, "Every 2,000 years a spaceship comes here and fills it up."

"No, really, who fills it up?"

Finally realizing that the gap in understanding was too great, T. A. told her what she wanted to hear, "The Park Service."

"I thought so," she said smugly.

Michael Ghiglieri also contributed "The Green Room" to Part One and "Jackass Canyon" to Part Four. This story was excerpted from his book, Canyon.

✳

Below us, the red rocks drop away at our feet. Surprise Valley spreads before us, a great bowl, green and yellow, vaguely mauve in the morning
light. Surprise Valley is a colossal slump block, a collapse feature situated at
an extraordinary concatenation of faults and subterranean springs. It is geologic shock. Along its east flank are Thunder and Tapeats springs; along
its west, Deer Creek Springs. As much as 40 percent of the discharge of the
Kaibab Plateau is funneled through that geologic plumbing.

—Stephen J. Pyne, *Fire on the Rim: A Firefighter's*
Season at the Grand Canyon

STEWART UDALL

* * *

Wild and Free

The Bass Trail tests old and young alike.

HIDING FROM THE SEARING SUN UNDER A PIÑON TREE 2,000 FEET above the Colorado River, I rebuke myself for being stupid. I should have known better than to try to hike out of the Grand Canyon on an abandoned mining trail in midsummer. And yet here I am—with my grandson Kyle Townsend in tow—wondering if my legs will get me to the South Rim by dark.

But I'm getting ahead of my story. Some months earlier, Grand Canyon Trust, an environmental organization, had asked me to host a week-long trip down the Colorado River for its members. Since I sit on the group's board, I happily accepted the invitation, but on the condition that I could bring Kyle. A last-minute change in plans, however, made it impossible for me to spend an entire week on the river. In hindsight, it would have been wiser to cancel. But, not wanting to disappoint Kyle, or the people from the Trust, I told them we would come for part of the trip.

And so, for three days before, our small party of adventurers had hiked down the Bright Angel Trail to Phantom Ranch where we met the rest of the group and embarked on the river. Kyle was the youngest participant, and I was the oldest. The head boatman put us in the bow of his oar-powered raft where he could keep a watchful eye on us as we bucked through Horn Creek, Granite, and Hermit rapids. It had been 24 years since I had been on the Colorado, and this was Kyle's introduction to river running, but both of us reveled in the white water. The next day, we ran the big one—Crystal—before making camp on the beach below Bass Rapids. From here, our plan was to hike up to the South Rim via the Bass Trail.

Having had a taste of the canyon's fiery heat, I was apprehensive about what the morrow might bring, and that night, after Kyle went to bed, I had a chat with our boatman. He, too, was worried.

Walking into the Grand Canyon is one thing; walking out on one of the hottest days of summer is another. This would be a challenging climb for someone in their prime. Though wiry for his age, Kyle was just 9—and I was 71. Were we up to it? Once we left the river, there could be no turning back. The only thing that made our plan feasible was that the Trust had sent one of its interns down the trail to cache water at two spots. He and an outdoorswoman who had run the upper part of the river would accompany us back out. Having two sturdy guides and water in place would make a big difference, I reassured myself.

The next morning, we rose before dawn. After a hurried breakfast in the dark, our boatman rowed the hiking party across to the trailhead. By sunup, we were moving. The first mile, in the coolness before the sun breasted the rim, was easy. When we reached the top of the Inner Gorge, we could see the jade-green river and our campsite far below. Kyle shouted and waved to the small, sticklike figures on the sandbar. Then, after saying goodbye to the boatman who had accompanied us this far, the four of us turned our attention upward. The real work lay ahead.

A long-abandoned mining trail that leaves the rim 20 miles west of Grand Canyon Village, the Bass Trail is rarely hiked. Winding through a wild reach of the Canyon, the unsigned path ascends 4,400 vertical feet in 8 miles. My companions put Kyle out front and let him set the pace. They also gave him the responsibility of picking out the cairns that mark the trail where it has been obliterated by rains and rockfall.

We made good time for the first hour or two, but then, as the heat began to build, my pace slowed. Every few minutes, I found myself needing a breather. Between us, we were carrying two gallons of water. By 11 a.m., most of it was gone. When we reached the first water cache, we thankfully refilled our canteens and ate something in the shade of an overhang.

By now the temperature was approaching 110 degrees Fahrenheit. No birds sang. Even the lizards and small creatures of the desert had vanished, seeking refuge in their burrows. After lunch, fatigued by the morning's exertions, I lay down on a rock and fell asleep. My nap ended when Kyle poked me in the ribs and said, "We've got to get going, Poppy."

Thirty minutes later, switchbacking our way up the Redwall, we suddenly found ourselves boulder hopping— we had lost the trail! Immediately, I called a halt. We couldn't afford to waste energy or to risk someone spraining an ankle. Sending our two companions back to relocate the trail, Kyle and I sought shade under a piñon tree, where I silently second-guessed my role in this risky venture.

"Are we going to make it out?" Kyle's voice interrupted my thoughts.

"We've got to go," I said. "Have another drink. You've been setting a nice steady pace."

We sat there for a few minutes—grandfather and grandson—

---

*A*rchaeological evidence shows that prehistoric Cohonina Indians used this route, followed in more recent times by Havasupai Indians.

Canyon pioneer William Bass improved the Indian footpaths for horseback travel. Bass developed a tourist camp on the South Rim and a winter camp and mines on the north side of the Colorado River.

Initially, he guided sightseers across the river by boat and then by cable crossing (now dismantled) to reach his trail leading to the North Rim.

◆

—Scott Thybony, *Official Guide to Hiking the Grand Canyon*

gazing out at the buttes and castles that rose shimmering out of the chasm. Our friends' shouts broke the silence. They had found the trail a few hundred feet above. We scrambled up to rejoin them.

The afternoon was a sun-baked grind, an agonizing test of a young boy's spirit and an old man's pride. Above the Redwall was a flat stretch across the Darwin Plateau, and the last water cache. Then came the final 1,000-foot climb. Kyle, showing no sign of his fatigue, stayed in front. My energies, though, were flagging, and I had to call for frequent, panting stops. Slowly, we inched skyward along the dusty trail.

And then, ten hours after leaving the river, it was over. We were on the rim.

"We made it, Poppy!" Kyle said, a note of triumph in his weary voice. I was proud of his spirit and stamina, and the praise that his newfound friends gave him seemed to make the whole ordeal worthwhile. "This is a hike you'll remember all your life," I said.

As I slumped, exhausted, into our vehicle, I wondered whether on this day I had passed the outdoor torch that my uncle had put in my hands in the White Mountains 60 years before.

Stewart Udall got his first taste of the wilderness when he was ten years old from his uncle while fishing for the elusive Apache trout in the White Mountains of northeastern Arizona. He later devoted much of his life to protecting and managing the environment, serving in the 1960s as secretary of the interior. This story was excerpted from his book, Arizona: Wild and Free.

*

About four o'clock in the afternoon of August 3rd, the writer was standing at Precipice View point on the North Rim with about thirty-five visitors and pointing to certain features on the Painted Desert. His right hand was grasping an iron railing, and his left arm was extended in the direction of interest over the canyon. Without warning, there was heard at the ends of his fingers a sound resembling that of a swarm of bees. Quite surprised, he pulled his hand in and examined the ends of his fingers to ascertain the cause. Of course, seeing nothing wrong, he again extended his arm and resumed speaking. Again, the same sound was heard, and once more he lowered his arm. At the same time, he called attention of the visitors to the phenomenon. Naturally, they all thrust their arms out over the railing, and the writer noticed a marked decrease in the amount of buzzing at the end of his own hand....

The secret of this interesting experiment was that the extended arms were conducting electricity to the ground through the bodies of the individuals from a cloud, either overhead or nearby, which was heavily charged with static electricity. The seriousness of this experiment, unbeknown to anyone in the group at the time, was that had this cloud been sufficiently charged so that the potential had been great enough, it could have easily attracted a bolt of lightning from any one of the several rainstorms nearby....

—Harold H. Hawkins, Ranger Naturalist, quoted in *The Best of Grand Canyon: Nature Notes 1926–1935*

SEAN O'REILLY

✳ ✳ ✳

Riders to the Rim

*Get out of your car and take
the iron horse.*

AT FIRST GLANCE, THE LOCOMOTIVE AT THE WILLIAMS DEPOT SEEMS impossibly large, like a machine from a planet of giants. Then you realize that at one point in our recent history, we really used to build things like this, and you are filled with admiration at the ingenuity of early 21st century metalworkers. Locomotive Number 20 was built in 1910, and the Harriman coach car next to it, in 1923. The town of Williams, the Depot, and the trains of the Grand Canyon Railway are steeped in this century's history. Presidents Teddy Roosevelt and Dwight Eisenhower and many other famous passengers rode in its coach cars to the rim. Part of the pleasure of a ride on the train today is a savoring of some of the same sights that these passengers must have experienced.

Train service to the rim of the Grand Canyon began in 1901 as part of the old Atchinson Topeka and Santa Fe line but ended in 1968, a victim to the penchant Americans have for driving themselves to scenic destinations. For twenty years, there were no trains to the rim, and the Williams Depot suffered the ravages of age and vandalism. The town of Williams also declined, as it lost both the revenue and employment provided by the trains. But the town revived in 1989 when the depot, the trains, and the Fray Marcos

Hotel reopened for business under the stewardship of entrepreneurs Max and Thelma Biegert. Now you can enjoy a ride that equals or surpasses those of the railway's earlier days.

The journey begins with a visit to an outlaw bull session outside the depot. The acting is good, and the actors seemed to enjoy their roles as they involve various members of the audience in a good-natured swapping of insults. The kids are treated to a shoot-out after the ensuing "insults" become too much for one of the outlaws to bear. By the time the cowboys start to dust themselves off, you are loading up into the railway cars, eager to see for yourself how riding the rails used to be. Since I was traveling with a pregnant wife and three small boys, we decided to go first class. This seating is aboard the *Chief Keokuck*, an authentic luxury parlor car built in 1927 by Pullman. Here, guests may recline on sofas and be waited on by cheerful attendants. The best of all though is the classic open-air platform on the back. Here, Theodore Roosevelt conducted one of his whistle stop presidential campaigns. My four-year-old son and I sat hypnotized on this platform as we watched the desert and swayed with the movement of the train. A light dust and thistle silk seemed to be blowing in the air, periodically catching the sun and washing us with fragments that could have come from the old west.

> *T*he Grand Canyon Railway carries approximately 130,000 passengers each year to the South Rim of the Grand Canyon. This is estimated to alleviate the influx of automobiles into the park by 50,000 vehicles.
>
> ◆
>
> —SO'R, JO'R, and LH

My reverie was suddenly interrupted by the sound of galloping horses and gunshots. Outlaws were attempting to board the train and rob us of our valuables! Well, not really, but you got a good taste of what such an ambush might have been like, and the kids loved it. We were actually warned in advance that we would be accosted, and all of those passengers from Los Angeles were jokingly requested not to use their firearms. Service in the *Chief Keokuck* was excellent. Club class is spacious and has a well-stocked mahogany bar. Good seating is also available in coach class in a fully restored 1923 Harriman coach that has plenty of headroom and leg-room. Strolling musicians pass through all cars during the trip and add a wonderful warm touch to the service.

The two-and-a-half-hour ride from Williams to the rim seems to pass effortlessly as the train passes old ranches, a deserted town, and the winding, limestone Coconino Wash. As we approached the Grand Canyon, there was barely any hint of the grandeur that awaits the first-time visitor. All of a sudden, the terrain has a slightly different feel to it, and the train begins to roll to a stop, and you are there, barely 100 yards from the rim. Mule deer lounge on the tracks, and you suddenly feel rested and ready to enjoy big-time vistas. Maybe you swagger a bit as you see all the visitors who drove their puny automobiles to the rim or rode on mere buses.

No matter how many times you have been to the Canyon—or if it is your first time—the view is staggering. The Grand Canyon is one place that lives up to its billing. Perhaps Swedish actress Signe Hasse had the best first reaction to the rim. "In Sweden, our mountains go up!"

Sean O'Reilly is an editor-at-large for Travelers' Tales.

✳

Railroading's return to the South Rim is particularly appropriate because, like the other great western preserves, Grand Canyon National Park was born with railroading—in this case, the Santa Fe—serving as midwife. The Great Northern, Northern Pacific, Union Pacific, and Southern Pacific all played roles in the creation of national parks like Glacier, Yellowstone, and Yosemite. The railroads recognized full well the potential of scenic wonderlands to generate passenger traffic.

One of the tightest of the park-railroad alliances, the Grand Canyon-Santa Fe partnership involved a critical third partner: Fred Harvey, a name that remains prominent even today on the South Rim. Harvey "kept the West in food and wives," according to Will Rogers, referring to the prim but attractive "Harvey girls" who waitressed in the depot lunchrooms that Harvey opened beginning in the 1870s along the Santa Fe's routes.

Even before boarding the train, today's Grand Canyon Railway patrons are introduced to Harvey history at Williams, Arizona, the southern terminus of the Grand Canyon branch and former interchange with the Santa Fe's east-west main line.

—Karl Zimmermann, "All Aboard for the South Rim"

✳ ✳ ✳

Legends of the Lost

Gold!

DEFIANT TO HIS LAST BREATH, JOHN DOYLE LEE STOOD IN HIS coffin that gloomy March day in 1877 and faced the five upraised rifles of the firing squad with seeming contempt.

"I am not afraid to die. I do not believe everything that is being taught and practiced by Brigham Young, and I do not care who hears it!" biographer William Bishop quoted him as declaring. "I have been sacrificed in a cowardly, dastardly manner!"

Suddenly his strident voice was silenced as shots rang out over the haunted expanse of Mountain Meadows in southwest Utah. In a bizarre final act to the drama, Lee was executed on the exact spot where he had participated in a massacre of 121 California-bound emigrants twenty years before. Of the 75 Mormon zealots involved in that slaughter, only Lee had to pay for the atrocity with his life.

Lee had avoided capture during those twenty years by disappearing into the lonely vastness of the Grand Canyon, where he spent much of his time prospecting for silver and gold. Rumor had it that he'd struck it rich. There were those who had hoped that Lee, in his last moment, would reveal the location of his legendary gold mine.

His attorney, Wells Spicer, was eager to go searching the depths of the Grand Canyon for that treasure trove. So was Emma, perhaps

Lee's favorite wife. But Lee would not reveal his secret—not to Spicer, not to any of his nineteen wives, not to his closest friends—not to anyone.

Hundreds of treasure seekers, some armed with maps or clues and others bolstered only by legends and hope, have combed the labyrinth of canyons and creeks along the Colorado River chasms between Vulcans Throne on the west and Lees Ferry on the east. But the mystery of the Lost John D. Lee Gold Mine remains unsolved to this day.

Somewhere in the almost impenetrable maze of Grand Canyon ravines and cliffs may lie untold wealth, waiting for some lucky and persistent searcher to discover.

The legend took shape in 1857, shortly after the Mountain Meadows Massacre, when Lee fled from the law to hide for the rest of his life in the safety of the Canyon. For some two years, he was reportedly a captive of the Havasupai Indians, and while living in their village, he may have discovered gold or silver near Vulcans Throne.

In 1871, Brigham Young directed Lee to establish a ferry across the Colorado River at the mouth of Paria Creek to enable Mormon pioneer families to reach northern Arizona. With wife Emma, he lived at the remote crossing, which she called Lonely Dell, until his arrest during a furtive visit to Panguitch, Utah.

Lee had plenty of time on his hands during those years of hiding, and he spent untold days and months searching for precious metals. Rumors that Lee had struck it rich ricocheted around the remote settlements of southern Utah for a decade.

And then came the revelation of Robert Hilderbrand, who as a lad of fifteen had lived with the Lees, almost a son, at Lonely Dell. Hilderbrand told some of the searchers for the mine that he had gone with Lee on several occasions some twelve miles downriver from the ferry to a meadow near the mouth of Soap Creek. There, he said, Lee left him in camp for two or three days and returned with an amazing haul: many tin cans full of rough gold nuggets. This was not placer gold from the river, but pieces broken from overhangs of lava rock.

Many years later, Utah historian Charles Kelly quizzed

Hilderbrand about the mine, but he was told that Lee would never reveal the exact location of his find. Hilderbrand was not the only believer in a lost John D. Lee Mine. John Hance, a legendary Grand Canyon storyteller, swore that he saw Lee packing silver ore on more than one occasion well downstream from his ferry. Hance told a Flagstaff friend in 1919 that the mine was probably in "a stubby canyon, under one of those high points" near the confluence of the Little Colorado with the Colorado.

Confusing? Perhaps there were two Lee mines—or who knows how many others?

There is much more to the story.

Isaac Haight, who participated with Lee in the Mountain Meadows slaughter and took the alias "Brown," believed Lee had given Emma a map revealing the location of his treasure find. But if she had the map, she refused to give it to him.

Haight, who had known Lee well, was convinced that Lee had buried seven cans of gold nuggets, probably in a cave near where the Little

I was requested by John Doyle Lee, after he had been sentenced to be shot for the part he took in the Mountain Meadows Massacre, to publish an account of his life and confessions....

Over 120 men, women, and children were surrounded by Indians, and more cruel whites, and kept under constant fire, from hundreds of unerring rifles, for five days and nights.... When nearly exhausted from fatigue and thirst, they were approached by white men, with a flag of truce, and induced to surrender their arms, under the most solemn promises of protection. They were then murdered in cold blood.... All this was done by a band of fanatics, who had no cause of complaint against the emigrants, except that the authorities of the Mormon Church had decided that all the emigrants who were old enough to talk, should die—revenge for alleged insults to Brigham Young.

♦

—William W. Bishop, Attorney of John D. Lee (1877)

Colorado flows into the Colorado River. He and brothers Sam and Bill Bass made at least two search attempts but came back empty-handed.

One legend says that Emma drew a rough map of the route to the mine, based on her recollections of Lee's chance remarks, and gave it to Bill Bass. He followed it to the best of his ability, but he found nothing except rugged scenery.

After Lee died, Emma married a miner named Franklin French, and he soon contracted a case of gold fever. Relying on Emma's scanty knowledge, he made repeated forays into the area where Haight had searched. His efforts had one lasting result: construction of the French-Tanner Trail down into the Grand Canyon near the mouth of the Little Colorado.

But French, too, met with nothing but frustration.

Another tantalizing Lee mine tale made the pages of *Desert* magazine in July 1980. Author George Thompson reported a conversation with an old cowboy named Rowland Rider, who told him of his 1909 encounter with a grizzled prospector at House Rock Valley near the

---

Some of the early pioneers in Grand Canyon were certain that such a wonderful natural phenomenon as the Canyon must contain vast riches in valuable ores, so much prospecting for gold, copper, lead, and zinc was a natural result. The large number of prospect holes to be found at several localities along the Canyon walls is mute evidence of their activities. These men often traveled along the Tonto Platform, which was the only practical way to follow the course of the Colorado without resorting to the plateaus along the rims. Good showings of copper were discovered in the Redwall limestone near Grandview. Considerable prospecting was done at a locality near what is now known as the "Corkscrew" on Bright Angel Trail.

◆

—Hugh H. Waesche,
The Best of Grand Canyon: Nature Notes 1926–1935,
edited by Susan Lamb

North Rim.

Rider said the old man had several bags of gold, which he said came from digging "near where Soap Creek goes into the Colorado." Thompson is sure the treasure came from Lee's lost mine.

Charles Kelly, who spent many years researching the life of John D. Lee, believes that his mine—if it really exists—is more likely to be found near Vulcans Throne.

There are doubters, of course, and some credible ones, as well. Dr. Robert Euler, the distinguished Grand Canyon archaeologist and authority on Canyon mines, says he has no solid knowledge that Lee's mine ever existed. Neither has Larry Winter of Los Alamos, New Mexico, a respected student of Western lost-mine stories. George Billingsley of the U.S. Geological Survey in Flagstaff is unaware of gold being discovered in any large quantity by anyone in the Canyon.

But still…

Where all that smoke has billowed over the past century, there must be some fire; and you can bet hardy searchers will continue to try to solve the mystery of John Lee's fabled mine.

Take your choice: look to the west, near Vulcans Throne. Or near the confluence of the Colorado and Little Colorado. Or, if you believe Hilderbrand, somewhere up the painted cliffs above Soap Creek. Remember that the Canyon is a national park, where mining claims can no longer be staked—but the thrill of solving this enduring riddle would be reward enough.

Author Thompson has some helpful hints for Soap Creek searchers: it's a big place, "so don't expect to find Lee's lost ledge on a weekend trip." Search near the Canyon bottom, because that's where Hilderbrand camped and where the prospector told Rider he had found his gold. And don't join the army of poorly prepared prospectors whose skeletons have been found in nameless gulches in that wild area.

John Doyle Lee lives in Western history for his role in the Mountain Meadows Massacre and for establishing Lees Ferry. His lost gold mine is little known, but its discovery could make his name a household word once more.

Dean Smith has been writing about Arizona subjects for some forty years, and is the author of fifteen books, most of them on Arizona history and biography. He and his wife Jean live in Tempe in the winter and in the cool mountains of Prescott in the summer.

✳

The discovery and looting of Mexico by Cortes in 1520 ignited the greatest treasure hunt in the history of the world. One of those treasure hunters, a thirty-year-old patrician named Francisco Vásquez de Coronado, was selected by the viceroy to explore northward into the present-day American Southwest.

Coronado's southwestern *entrada*, searching for the fabled cities of gold, lasted from 1540 to 1542. In August of 1540, his men reached the Hopi villages, disappointed, but still hopeful that the golden cities would be found. The Hopis told them of a great river to the west that sounded promising, and Coronado promptly dispatched another detachment under Cárdenas to locate and explore the river. The official account of that exploration, written for Coronado, has never been discovered. However, two narratives written by members of the Coronado expeditions do contain a description of the discovery of the Grand Canyon, presumably obtained from either the original written report or verbal descriptions by soldiers who accompanied Cárdenas....

Reading the two accounts in translation, 400 years later, there is no suggestion that the thirteen Spanish discoverers beheld anything of beauty. They were searching not for aesthetic values, but for tangible riches. And they were eager to get across only to see if anything more promising lay on the other side. The explorers tried unsuccessfully for three days to find a way to the bottom. Suffering for lack of water, "even though they had the river before their eyes," the party gave up, returned to the Hopi villages, and rejoined the main expedition for another two years of fruitless wandering upon the plains of New Mexico, Texas, and Kansas.

—Edwin Corle, *Listen, Bright Angel*

✳ ✳ ✳

Fishing Eagles

Few see the Canyon this way.

THE BOW OF THE BOAT GRATES ASHORE AT NANKOWEAP BEACH AT Mile 52.1. [John Wesley] Powell named Nankoweap using a Paiute name of rather confused etymology but never mind: it's a euphonious name and a beautiful place. Behind the tamarisk- and arrowweed-stalked beach, the terrain steps upward to the old high-water line, which in turn rises into a talus slope footing a high cliff that catches the first morning sun and houses a pair of peregrine falcons.

I pitch my tent in the tamarisk thicket, annoyed at the minute, prickly twigs that stick to everything and, in general, at this pushy intruder that spring floods once cleaned off and, with spring spates gone, has now taken over the riverbanks. Introduced from the Middle East at the end of the 19th century as an ornamental shrub, tamarisk probably entered the Canyon sometime after 1925 but did not proliferate until the 1950s. With its long taproot and ability to lose astronomical amounts of tufted, airborne seeds, it has spread throughout western watercourses. An efficient, greedy colonizer, it can withstand inundation for up to six weeks or low water for several years. At Nankoweap, a well-used beach, only the continual trampling of campers maintains paths and niches for camp spots.

In the midst of my carping, Bryan Brown, head ornithologist of this project, reminds me not only that Lake Powell inundated thousands of acres of riparian habitat upstream, but that throughout the Southwest 90 to 95 percent of lowland riparian habitat has disappeared. The postdam Grand Canyon, with its tamarisk thickets, has become a major new refuge for birds, ironically created by a dam that destroyed much of their original habitat. Displaced riparian birds moved downstream in an "instant migration." Of the 300 bird species listed along the Colorado River, 41 breed here, and 90 percent of those nest in tamarisk. In the summertime, tamarisk houses huge populations of leafhoppers and all manner of minute gnats and tiny bees, which make a munificent insect buffet for breeding and migratory birds.

In the tamarisk sheltering my tent, an avian architect engineered a teacup-sized nest in the fork of a branch, about five feet off the ground. Fashioned of tamarisk bits and scraps of paper, with strips of plastic woven in, it was constructed by a frugal bird that believed in recycling.

---

*O*ur Department of Agriculture imported two or three three species of tamarisks from the eastern Mediterranean around 1900 to line diversion canals and irrigation works of the Southwest to check bank erosion. Even though native riparian vegetation had been stabilizing stream banks here for thousands of years, Agriculture had looked elsewhere. Probably the irrigators were in too big a hurry to use slow-growing native plants.

The tamarisk story soon became a familiar one: the exotic panacea turned monster. When the introduced tamarisks matured, they sucked so much water out of the canals—every hour as much water as the weight of their canopy—that they more than canceled their value as preventers of erosion. Forty years after Agriculture planted the tamarisks, the Bureau of Reclamation tried to yank them all out. Then it spent millions to poison them, and failed.

◆

—Michael P. Ghiglieri, *Canyon*

Each of us is responsible for one shift a day at the observation point, with one day off a week. The morning team leaves camp early enough to be on post by first light at 7:00 a.m. The second shift sits from noon until dark at 5:30 or 6:00 p.m. At least four people staff each watch, three are constant observers, one or more as recorder. The main spotting scope is always focused on the creek mouth where the greatest activity occurs. An observer, binoculars affixed to face, stays glued to the bird he or she picks up, delineating the bird's actions to the recorder, who writes it down and marks activity time by the second. The forms record each foraging eagle and the age group to which it belongs, its success at taking a trout or lack thereof. We do not record what eagles do best of all, which is stand around.

Anticipating the chill that lack of movement brings in this 25-degree weather, I layer on one of everything I own, ending with a down jacket, which now for obvious reasons will not zip closed. Like an overstuffed penguin, I waddle up to the observation point along a circuitous path that meanders through willows and arrowweed, then through mesquites that trace the bottom edge of a terrace at the old high-water line. Some trees burned in an accidental fire in the summer of 1967, and now younger sprouts proliferate from the old roots, although the grove is far from recovered.

As the path rises, mesquite trees give way to desert scrub. The path breaks out into the open and begins a sharp climb up an ancient debris flow that rises almost 200 feet above the river. The gravels in the lower part of the hill are detritus from far upstream, studded with rocks brought in by the river when its channel ran farther west. The gravels in the uppermost part of the hill are local and match those in the Nankoweap Basin to the west. Over time, the ridge has been considerably eroded by the Colorado River, which borders it on the east, and Nankoweap Creek, which borders it on the north. If the river once flowed atop this ridge, it would solve the mystery of a pile of driftwood found in Stanton's Cave 20 miles upstream at Mile 31.7, a cave that opens 150 feet above present river level.

From the top of the ridge, the path hangs a left and goes straight up, paved with slippery, loose limestone scree, fraught with unstable handholds, one of those slopes vastly easier to negotiate going up than mincing down. The observation post nestled under a miniscule overhang 300 feet above and half a mile from the mouth of Nankoweap Creek, opening to a magnificent view of the river upstream and downstream and facing a grand 1,000-foot wall immediately across the river. To expedite locating eagles, we memorize the wall formations against which the eagles fly: Kaibab, Toroweap, Coconino, Hermit, Supai, Redwall, Muav, Bright Angel. The impact of this wall vastly exceeds the sum of its parts, and for all the hours I spend here, I never tire of looking at it, this record wall where animals snorkled in the silt and cycad fronds trembled in the rain, seas ebbed and flowed, continents melded and rafted apart, dunes sifted in, ancient rivers blew out of their banks, strange fish swam, fossils formed, species developed and expired, moons rose, suns froze, and whatever else that could happen did.

As watch begins, the landscape lies so far beneath us it resembles a dish garden scribed with a tiny pewter stream, a carved jade river, gray-green velour terrain, miniature wire trees, tiny sponge bushes, hovered over by pink cotton candy clouds. The river runs low, "Sunday's water" (from the day when dam releases are minimal) reaching here on Tuesday. From the adults we saw on the way downriver, we can assume that bald eagles have moved into the Canyon but

In the early 1960s, the Bureau of Reclamation proposed damming the Grand Canyon, both immediately upstream and immediately downstream of Grand Canyon National Park. For five years, the Sierra Club battled the plan, pioneering the use of full-page newspaper ads to rally attention to environment causes and enlisting the efforts of thousands of grassroots volunteers. The campaign lost the Club its tax-exempt status, but saved the Canyon.

◆

—SO'R, JO'R, and LH

are still dispersed because trout are not yet spawning and the peak of eagle presence correlates with the peak of spawning. Although trout cluster in the shallows in the river at the mouth of the creek and about a sandbar downstream, and although the river is high enough that fish can enter, only a very few have done so. We end the day with no bald eagle sightings but several soaring golden eagles noted, more interested in small rodents on the rim than in the fish in the river.

As late afternoon sunlight slants into the gorge downstream, the view is elegant, classic Colorado River. The bays and walls of limestone wedge the river into zigzags of turquoise green that angle out of sight in the floating light, dappling the water with alternating malachite and lapis lazuli shadows. The cliffs glow smoky rose, gathering in the afternoon shadows.

On early morning watch, when it becomes light enough to see, the river slowly recedes. Sunlight seeps down the Redwall, turning it deep salmon, then a blatant red orange. Upstream the Kaibab has a peculiar luminosity as sunlight glazes it pink. Five Canada geese skid onto the river with five splashes. Across the river, willows and arrowweed band the edge in gray green and rust, replicating the colors of the Muav and the Redwall, all doubled in a river that looks like warp-dyed silk.

Suddenly someone gasps, "Will you look at that!" Five pair of binoculars slide across the Redwall as we count: 6…8…9! 10! The eagles roost upstream, nobody knows where, but probably at a communal roost in a protected site where the concentration of birds in close quarters preserves body heat. But last night they roosted in niches in the Redwall across the river, basalt statues in marble niches.

Below, a raven materializes, struts about, pecking in desultory fashion carrion left from yesterday. Another glides in and lands on a mesquite branch. A third, then a fourth and fifth, arrives, and then suddenly there are over a dozen. Generally, early-morning action follows a daily pattern: after the ravens land, the eagles arrive and wait some distance away before coming in themselves, and may

well watch the ravens for any sign of disturbance. So far, no eagles
have been observed preceding the ravens. The first eagle usually
alights just before seven, followed by a few more. Some sneak in,
some materialize out of a solid rock wall, others swoop in with a
panache of a Parisian model on the runway. When one arrives, others generally follow. Typically, after they arrive, nothing happens for
up to an hour or more, a period scientists interpret as "staging time."

But this morning, because it is windy, the eagles stay high after
they lift off the Redwall, and fourteen bald eagles float across the
sky in lazy helices, catching the early thermals, adjusting their pri-
maries individually, like the spoiler on a jet plane's wing, increasing
their stability and ability to maneuver, reducing turbulence. Their
alternate soaring and gliding takes about a twentieth of energy that
flapping does, which they generally do only on take off or to insert
themselves into a thermal.

The wind lessens, and the eagles zoom in like kamikazes. This
morning, they begin moderately high, wings spread, spiraling
downward. Once over the creek, they drop. They don't stoop to
gain velocity like falcons, they don't close their wings so that they
are bullet-shaped like swallows, they don't glide like pelicans. They
choose a spot, angle in, and plummet. Like a stone. The medieval
chronicler who depicted them as "coming down like a thunderbolt"
had not watched Nankoweap eagles.

One eagle stalks to the creek edge. Over 75 percent of their foraging takes place within the first 40 feet of the creek mouth, so any
trout entering or leaving runs a gauntlet. The eagle waddles into the
creek, nails a fish, and hops to shore with its catch in its talons—
whomp, whomp, whomp—battering the poor fish with every hop.
A focused, fierce eater, it strips the fish with its beak. One fish
weighing a pound or a pound and a half is adequate for a bald
eagle's daily diet, since eagles need consume only 6 to 11 percent of
their body weight each day. The eagles take more trout than they
can consume, but in the end all the leftover fish are consumed by
somebody, most commonly golden eagles and ravens. During high
forage times, birds take anywhere from 50 to 75 trout a day. With
up to 1,000 trout in the stream some days, the food supply is

essentially unlimited. Rather than by food availability, the eagle population here is determined by social tolerance, human disturbance, and other habitat limitations. Eagles present on these days of high trout concentration total twenty or more, paralleling the concentration of trout. And as always in close attendance, like lugubrious, sharp-eyed, 19th-century undertakers, are the ravens.

Another young eagle stands in the river at the mouth of the creek when a trout wiggles past. The eagle takes two steps toward it, pounces on it, and has it on shore but at a minute when it is pirated by another subadult. Pirating another eagle's catch is simply a way of life with eagles, and there is less display of animosity than one might expect (at this time of year, eagles are not territorial). Evidently there's a quick assessment of the other eagle's size, the most important factor in releasing pray or defending it. Pirating is opportunistic, and eagles do it only when it takes less energy than getting food other ways, which may explain why more pirating usually occurs when a very large fish is involved. Here, where there is ample food and hunger is not a factor, pirating takes on a rather perfunctory, ho-hum aspect and would confirm Benjamin Franklin's suspicion that eagles are of bad moral character.

Usually five to ten seconds elapse before a fish is pirated. One fish, taken by a young eagle, is pirated first by another immature one, second by a subadult, and third by yet another youngster. Generally, immature eagles will pirate from an eagle of any age, whereas adults predominantly pirate from other adults. Adult males often challenge each other but seldom challenge females, thus female pirating attempts have the highest success rate. Pirating occurs with ravens as well. Two ravens can work an eagle like a confidence man and his shill. A pair of ravens land beside a feeding eagle, one bobs and weaves at the eagle's head while the other tweaks its tail. When the eagle drops its fish to confront its tormentor in the rear, the front raven pirates the fish. Honest: Teresa saw it.

At 10:20, an adult golden eagle sails into the mouth of the creek. It trots four feet along the bank, pounces on a fish in the water, hops to shore with it, mantles over it, and devours it on the spot. Its whole aspect is dark, a Dracula-like specter, wings raised like a great, dark cloak. Goldens dominate bald eagles, who immediately abandon their fish without challenging the goldens. Even the ravens do not hassle them. When this golden flies off without finishing its kill, the ravens swarm in like jackals.

Two adult bald eagles stand downstream where pockets of trout blacken the water. After what seems an eternity of standing on one foot and then the other in what looks like eagle body language of reluctance and indecision, one eagle finally walks into the water and impales a fish. Curious about the amount of time an eagle stands around, we later clock an eagle that remained for an hour before making a forage, and this is the rule, not the exception: eagles can spend a lot of their time, sometimes over 90 percent, just standing around.

Finally, as the day wanes, only one immature eagle remains. It grabs a foot-long fish and takes it up on the bank but abandons it to the ravens. The bird may be full, but it keeps on catching fish anyway. In most bald eagle populations, the ratio of young to adult is 1:1. Here the ratio is consistently 2:1 or higher, and it goes up even further when the adults migrate out first. Adult bald eagles range widely in winter, remaining in one place as long as the food supply lasts, but young move around more and also need more food sources than adults because they forage less efficiently. At Nankoweap, immature eagles, not yet skillful hunters, have a very high success rate, perhaps up to 95 percent, and the number of young eagles here surpasses that for the river as a whole. They remain here because foraging is so easy, and their proficiency enables them to build up more fat and strength to help in migration. Already dressed for success, a new adult pounces on a fish and drags it up on shore immediately, a trick younger birds usually do not practice, often losing their fish as a result.

Since midmorning, a minimum of four to five eagles have been in view all the time, but within the hour, all exit, and there comes a sudden quiet. Only three ravens remain. An inventory of the common perching sites shows none on the Bright Angel Ridge below;

across the river, none; in the mesquite trees, none; on the big rocks at the entrance to the river, none. Only one eagle soars. A day's-end comes at noon.

Ann Haymond Zwinger is known not only for her books of natural history—Beyond the Aspen Grove, Land Above the Trees, A Desert Country Near the Sea, A Conscious Stillness, Wind in the Rock, The Mysterious Lands, *among others*—*but for the evocative illustrations of plants, animals, and landscape that grace her work. Her essays have appeared in many anthologies and in* Audubon, Orion, *and other magazines. Zwinger lectures widely and teaches "The Natural History Essay" at Colorado College, and lives in Colorado Springs. This story was excerpted from her book* Downcanyon: A Naturalist Explores the Colorado River Through the Grand Canyon.

❋

The impacts of Lake Mead on the riverine ecology of the Grand Canyon are almost inconsequential when compared to the changes brought about by the 710-foot-high Glen Canyon Dam. Officially operational in 1963 and located 17 miles upstream from the park boundary, Glen Canyon Dam has completely altered the Colorado River within the park. The dam has changed the physical and biological characteristics of the river while simultaneously enhancing river recreation activities.

Today, the demand for hydroelectric power controls the river's flow. When distant cities need more power, more water is released from the penstocks of Glen Canyon Dam. Because the water is released from 200 feet below the lake's surface (the hypolimnion), it is perpetually cold and virtually sediment-free. River temperatures in the Grand Canyon now range from 45° to 55°F (7° to 13°C) where they once approached 80°F (27°C). The sediment entering Lake Mead has been reduced to less than fifteen percent of the total predam sediment volume. The water's flow rarely exceeds 28,000 cubic feet per second (cfs) now and averages a mere 10,000 cfs.

The difference in sediment concentration and water temperature has had a profound impact on the aquatic ecosystem. The clear, cold water now released from the dam has changed the river's productivity from low to high. Solar radiation previously reflected from the surface of muddy water now penetrates to the bottom of the river, allowing abundant production of algae and associated periphyton. This new productivity is the basis for a food chain that supports a trout fishery recognized as one of the best in existence.

—Steven W. Carothers, *The Grand Canyon: Intimate Views,*
edited by Robert C. Euler and Frank Tikalsky

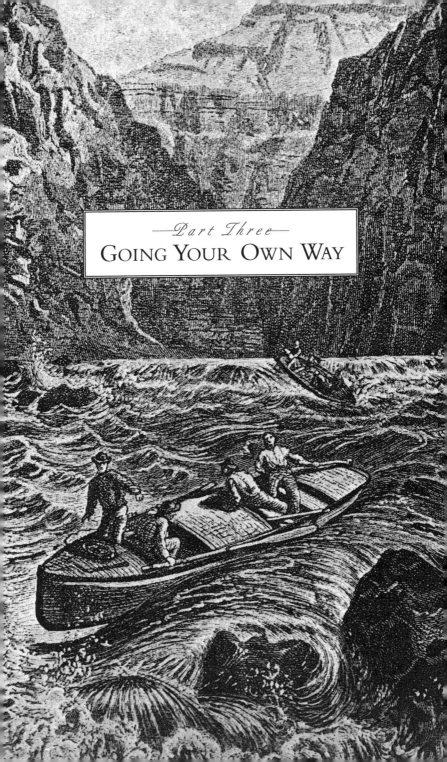

Part Three

GOING YOUR OWN WAY

SCOTT THYBONY

✳ ✳ ✳

Shamans' Gallery

Treasure is in the eyes of
the beholder.

LITTLE IS KNOWN ABOUT THE FIRST HUNTERS TO VENTURE INTO the Grand Canyon 3,000 to 4,000 years ago. They climbed into caves and left ritual offerings—willow twigs bent into shapes resembling bighorn sheep, sometimes with spearlike sticks piercing their sides.

Another clue to the ceremonial lives of these early Indians turned up a few years ago. A cowboy and former trapper named Gordon Smith stumbled across a cliff wall, in a remote corner of the Grand Canyon, covered with images painted at least 3,000 years ago. A few weeks before this most recent hike, I asked Smith to take me to a place called Shamans' Gallery.

Driving across sagebrush flats, we headed toward the brink of the western Canyon. Smith put on a pair of dark glasses as I angled the truck into the sun. The 32-year-old mule packer from Beaver, Utah, wore a trophy rodeo buckle on a tooled-leather belt and a blue silk scarf around his neck. A baseball cap from the Renegade Lounge covered all but a tuft of red hair.

The western Canyon has a different feel to it. The lines are simpler—a band of outer cliffs falls 1,500 feet to a prominent bench called the Esplanade, several miles wide in places. Then it drops again into a sheer inner gorge thousands of feet deep.

We grabbed our packs and began walking. The trail followed a good descent route to the Esplanade. Gordon mentioned he'd led a string of mules down here several times. "It can be a real lonely place when you're by yourself," he said with a rounded Utah drawl. "But I need to be on my own to find things. Most people don't know where to look. I know this country. To find things, you have to think like an Indian."

Finding a break in the lip of the Esplanade, we reached a ledge running halfway along a cliff of red sandstone. It dropped 50 feet to a dry wash bordered by a few clumps of scrub oak. We followed the shelf as the cliff flared above.

Painted figures spread for 60 feet across the rough back wall. Mythical beings stretched up the rock face, long and narrow. Ghost figures as tall as a man crowded together with geometric-shaped and antlered animals.

One image held my attention longer than the others: a painted face with a black band across the eyes, topped with a feather and balanced on the back of a green animal with red claws. Farther along, two green suns floated above a spectral figure, outlined in the color of dried red blood. Red and yellow designs overlapped those in whites, blacks, and greens. Superimposed images added depth— visionary figures appeared to emerge from deep within the rock, rising to the surface for a moment before sinking back.

The first time Smith came here, he almost missed them. "It was getting dark," he said, "and I was right under the spooky figures before I seen anything. It scared me. I thought I was seeing things."

He paused a moment as the deep quiet of the place returned. "I don't know what they mean. But I'll tell you what, I wouldn't be caught camping here alone."

The prehistoric site was unknown to park service archaeologists until Smith reported it. He then guided rock-art specialist Polly Schaafsma to the panel. She reported that archaic hunter-gatherers had used the ritual site to communicate with the supernatural.

The mule packer and I sat on the ledge and dug out our food. I offered him part of a sandwich, but he preferred his cowboy grub— beef stew, cold out of the can. Resting beneath the pictographs,

Gordon told me about another finding of his—a place whose location he'd kept secret.

Seven years ago, he said, he was exploring the country north of the Canyon on his mule. He had stopped to smoke a cigarette and felt air blowing from between some rocks. Clearing them away, he found a cave entrance and crawled inside with a flashlight in hand. The passageway opened into a chamber. He swung the dim beam of his light around the room and stopped. Laid out before him were a couple of bodies. Scared, he left without exploring the rest of the cave. "It's spooky in there all by yourself," he said. "You wonder if one of the bodies is going to start moving."

Resealing the entrance, he left the area and didn't return for five years, he told me. When he did go back, he searched the entire cave and found more than two dozen bodies, each covered with a blanket. Masks inlaid with precious stones leaned on the wall with a number of wooden canisters—one filled with feathers, another with leather scrolls. And, naturally, treasure.

As the cowboy told his story, he wove into it tales of lost tribes and the legend of Montezuma's hidden treasure. Smith said he planned to show the world someday but was in no rush. "I don't care if anybody believes me," he said.

It is written that the Spanish cavalier and explorer, in quest of the seven cities of gold, pushed the prow of his boat so far into the waters of this fearful chasm of colors that on looking up at midday he could see the stars; and it is written that overcome with religious awe, fearing perhaps that he was daring to approach the gates of Paradise before his time, he raised the cross, bared his head, gave this color world its name, and drew back and away, to come again no more. But still the tradition was that at least one of the cities of gold lay with and under the protection of these fearful walls of flaming red.

◆

—Joaquin Miller, *The Grand Canyon of Arizona* (1909)

"I know it's true. I've sat on it for seven years. I can sit on it the rest of my life if I have to."

Climbing up from the river in the dark, I followed the trail up the Inner Gorge, heading for the Tonto Plateau. At night, the Canyon exerts a presence as powerful as it does during the day—its raw beauty darkened but intact. As I picked my way up the trail, I wondered about those who spend their lives searching for hidden treasure when it lies all about them, wide open, even at night.

Too tired to keep going, I found a place to stretch out. The night grew colder as I watched Orion step over the rim, advancing slowly across the dark field. The air held tight.

I must have drifted asleep. When I awoke, winds were gusting across the Tonto, shaking the stiff branches of the blackbrush next to me. Orion had moved high above the horizon. Nearby, a trail scar cut across the dark talus slope, past rock forms reshaped by starlight. Too cold to sleep and drawn by the beauty of the night canyon, I got up and began walking again.

Scott Thybony also contributed "Beneath the Rim" to Part One.

⁜

Ramparts Cave was used extensively by the now-extinct Shasta ground sloth, and the floor is deep with deposits of sloth dung mummified over millennia in the dry desert air. The site has been known to archaeologists for decades; an exploratory trench divides the deposits, and a metal gate guards the cave entrance, located about five hundred feet above the river just before the Canyon ends at Grand Wash Cliffs. But someone has broken in and, deliberately or accidentally, has started a fire. The dung glows to life, and smoke from the cave is spotted by river trippers.

The South Rim fire crew instantly claims jurisdiction on the grounds that they control the park helicopter, that initial attack and resupply will require extensive helo use. We are powerless to protest. Stiegelmeyer, now foreman of the South Rim crew, gloats at his power over his former North Rim buddies.

When the initial crewmen arrive at Ramparts, they land on a ledge and walk into the smoking entrance, then abruptly turn around and walk out. So dense is the smoke that they can see absolutely nothing. The stench of smoldering sloth shit is excruciating. While scientists and administrators at park headquarters debate what to do, the South Rimmers decide to treat the cave fire as they would a house fire, and they return with structural fire equipment. They don breathing apparatus and turnout coats, set up a ventilating fan, even erect a portable tank and, using a helo bucket, fill it with water from the Colorado while a portable pump charges their lines. They enter the cave, spray wildly, and retreat again. Unlike in a structural fire, conditions in the cave make ventilation impossible. The heat turns the water instantly to steam, and huge chunks of the cave walls and roof threaten to spall off; the roof will have to be shored up before anyone can safely enter the cave again. And so it goes. Each solution only creates another problem.

—Stephen J. Pyne, *Fire on the Rim: A Firefighter's Season at the Grand Canyon*

* * *

The Journey's End

Or is it the beginning?

I'VE NEVER HAD A DESIRE TO DINE WITH ROYALTY. I'VE NEVER visited a locker room to shake hands with a professional athlete, and I've never asked a movie star for an autograph. But when I heard the story of Rona Levein's escape from the 20th-century tiger trap of money and power, I knew I needed to meet her.

It's not easy to meet Rona. She lives in a vast and lonely part of Arizona sometimes called "the American Tibet." More commonly known as the Arizona Strip, it's the 9,000-square-mile northwest corner of the state cut off from the rest of Arizona by the Colorado River and the mile-deep gorge of the Grand Canyon.

The Arizona Strip is larger than the state of Massachusetts, yet its total population is on the short side of 4,500, and most of these people live in the communities of Fredonia and Colorado City. Otherwise, fewer than 700 permanent residents are to be found in this vast expanse of beautiful but unsettled country.

The only Arizona entry into the strip is over a sturdy 60-year-old bridge that hangs 500 feet above the Colorado River at Marble Canyon. Rona lives at a place called Vermilion Cliffs, a tiny way station, appropriately named because it sits in the shadow of the 3,000-foot Vermilion Cliffs.

The little settlement consists of a small motel, a restaurant, and a few houses down the road at a place called Badger Creek. That's where Rona lives. Once she had a prestigious address in Manhattan and a plush office in a glass skyscraper. She was a corporate officer for one of the world's largest advertising agencies and worked among the trendsetters of the fashion and cosmetics industries.

*R*ona is now happily retired and still living at Badger Creek.

♦

—SO'R, JO'R, and LH

Today, she delivers mail on a postal route that has taken her, by her own estimate, more than a quarter-million miles through the sparsely populated land she now calls home. On some days, she carries no more than a few dozen pieces of mail. She says that never, ever, does it cross her mind to go back to her old way of life.

I had an assignment to write an article on the Toroweap Overlook, one of the most remote points on the North Rim of the Grand Canyon. Toroweap, accessible only through the Arizona Strip, is 154 lonely miles from U.S. Route 89 at Bitter Springs of the Navajo Indian Reservation. The final 63 miles are over a dirt road that undulates and twists through plateau country totally uninhibited except for a ranger station at Tuweep near the North Rim of the Canyon.

I decided to ask Rona if she would accompany me on this trip into the heart of her adopted homeland. I had been informed she had hiked, alone (four days), through the remote and precipitous canyon of the Paria River. She had rafted numerous times down the rapids of the Colorado and through the Grand Canyon. She was a logical companion who could supply unique views on the land and its history.

But my real reason for wanting to take Rona along was to see if she would share her formula for breaking free from the siren songs of materialism and prestige. What was the impetus that permitted her to turn her back on the jet-set life? What propelled her into the semiwilderness on a quest for peace and harmony?

On a pleasant August day under a sky of purest blue, we set out on the journey to Toroweap from Rona's home at Badger Creek. She suggested we travel in her 1970 Volkswagen van. "It knows the country," she tells me.

So, we pile in, Rona (in the driver's seat); myself; my college-age son Bart; and photographer HelenLau Running. Also along is Pal-o-mine, a part-collie/part-coyote sheepdog that Rona acquired on the Indian reservation. And finally, Pal-o-mine's pal, a peculiar-looking, mixed-breed pup with one blue eye and one brown.

It's a tight squeeze because Rona's vehicle is loaded—on an ever-ready basis—with items needed for treks through a lonely land: shovels, ground cloths, cans of motor oil, bug repellent, ice chests, and a small tent.

We start west on U.S. 89A, driving below the weather-carved escarpments of the Vermilion Cliffs; then across House Rock Valley where one of the West's largest buffalo ranches is located, up to the 8,000-foot crown of the forested Kaibab Plateau; then down the other side on State 389 with the red rock country of southern Utah far in the distance.

Somewhere on the downside of the Kaibab Plateau, I tell Rona I worked for a number of years with ad agencies, and I had lived in several big cities as well. "I've known a multitude of people who said they wanted to drop out of the rat race. But very few do."

Rona is a diminutive woman with light-brown hair and a wide smile. Somewhere in her early middle years. She turns on the smile, "You escaped," she says.

"Partially and slowly," I reply, "but you made a quantum leap from one end of the spectrum to the other, almost instantaneously. Will you tell me about it?" She nods, still smiling.

"In college," she says, "I began experiencing a strong desire for recognition. I wanted to do things that would mark me as a woman of accomplishment. I was graduated from Barnard.

"After graduation, I took the ocean liner *La Liberté* to Europe for a six-month postgraduate holiday. When I came back, I put on a blue suit, white gloves, and went out looking for success."

In the small farming and lumbering community of Fredonia, we stop for lunch and find a Mexican restaurant serving good tacos and tamales.

"I started as a secretary," Rona tells me. "Then I got a chance to write a documentary movie. That led to a job at NBC as a community writer, and from there, I moved to the position of assistant creative director in the advertising department of a cosmetics firm. I job-hopped to an ad agency and doubled my salary. At the age of 35, I became a vice president at Foote, Cone and Belding."

After lunch, we top off the gas tank and move on. About 12 miles ahead is Pipe Spring National Monument, one of the last outposts of civilization on this route. To the south and west are thousands of square miles that harbor no signs of man, except for a few crumbling shacks and generally unreliable dirt roads. Not much water, either. There is not a single permanently running stream or lake in this entire 9,000 square miles.

The road to Toroweap, a left turn nine miles west of Fredonia, doesn't look too bad. "Well, most of the time it's okay," Rona tells me. "But, after a good rain, it turns into a quagmire."

Ahead, I can see the road, snaking its way through strands of sagebrush all the way to the horizon. Far distant and off to the right are the dim blue silhouettes of Mount Trumbull, Mount Logan, Mount Emma, all more than 7,000 feet in height.

Bart is in a rear seat listening to a tape. Pal-o-mine sleeps on his lap. Photographer HelenLau is dozing, too. The dog with the funny eyes is lost in the pile of bedrolls. "So, now you are a vice president," I say, resuming our conversation.

"My salary keeps going up, my interest level down," she says. "And I'm starting to think: Is this all there is? Something's missing."

I turn and look behind us. All I see is distance and our dust trail. Distance ahead. We haven't passed a single car. "Let me guess. It's about time for a geographic cure," I opine.

"Right," she replies. "Six months in Greece and Portugal. When I came back, I went to work for Charles Revson at Revlon. But somewhere along the way, I realized that recognition was no longer meaningful, and I felt a need to search for something else."

A pickup truck passes, going in the other direction, the first and only vehicle we will see on the road to Toroweap.

"Isn't it strange…the things that can totally change our lives," Rona muses. "One day, I picked up a brochure from the Museum of Natural History advertising a geological field trip on rafts through the Grand Canyon. I went. I saw. And I was totally captured by the serenity I found in the silence, the peace in the great visible distances."

Now, we are entering Toroweap Valley (sometimes called Tuweep Valley), one of the many tributaries of the massive lava flows that, eons ago, spilled out of the nearby volcanic peaks and flowed to the Grand Canyon. There are more than 60 volcanic cones in the region. Geologists tell us that giant lava spills once created a dam across the Colorado River that was more than 500 feet high. One of the earlier lava streams flowed more than 84 miles downstream. But the force of the mighty river eventually broke through the dam more than a million years ago.

"I made two more raft trips through the Canyon," Rona continues. "Then in October 1978, I left New York to try living in the strip country. I had been earning a very nice income, but I hadn't saved much. I had enough to last about four months. I moved into a tiny room at Lees Ferry Lodge near the Vermilion Cliffs. The small café had a jukebox and a pool table: a place where river-raft crews gathered to socialize. When money ran out, I worked as a maid at Marble Canyon Lodge down the road."

She finally landed the job delivering mail. Later, she bought an old house with a hole in the wall where a pickup truck had backed into it. She restored the house, started an orchard and vegetable garden, terraced the land, and planted shade trees and a profusion of flowers. Her front porch looks out on the immense, upthrusting mass of the Vermilion Cliffs. "Sometimes," she says, "I climb up into the cliffs and shout Shakespeare into the wind."

We stop along the road from time to time. HelenLau takes pictures. The dogs chase jackrabbits through the sagebrush. It is late afternoon by the time we reach the ranger station where we inquire about a campsite. There aren't many at Toroweap, and they are primitive. The ranger tells us that one, off-road and remote, is close by. He gives us directions.

As we approach the rim over a road that finally becomes only a pair of ruts, I can see Vulcans Throne off to the right. It's an old and impressive volcanic cone that erupted and formed at the Canyon's edge more than 100,000 years ago.

Dusk is falling, and heavy clouds are rolling in over the Uinkaret Plateau to the north. We forgo a look into the Canyon and navigate between gnarled juniper trees and over a surface of red sandstone. The road has entirely disappeared.

A picnic table under a jutting overhang of rock tells us we have arrived. We build a fire, prepare food. Droplets of rain are falling, but the overhang blocks most of them. We sit by the fire and talk.

While Rona has made the strip her permanent home, I find that she ranges far and wide in pursuit of her "close-to-Nature" lifestyle. A few years back, she traveled to Nepal, hiked alone to Hillary's old base camp at the foot of Everest. She has kayaked down the Green River, a tributary of the Colorado, and, in two weeks, she will leave for a pack trip through the Canadian Rockies.

"Why Nepal?" I ask.

"The Grand Canyon and the Himalayas were the yin and yang, the antithesis of one another. Deep down in the Canyon are the oldest exposed rocks on Earth. After being there, it seems natural to travel toward the highest point on Earth."

Nightfall and cloud cover create a world of near-total blackness beyond the little island of our fire. I ask Rona, "What has the move done to you, for you?"

She slowly stirs the fire with a stick. "I think we become one with the landscape we live in. I would suggest that people look around. Take a good look at your landscape. Out here, I have good landscape. The more I blend with it, the happier I get."

Transient drops continue to fall. Rona decides to sleep on a pallet in the van. Bart assembles a one-man tent under a pine tree. I find a large flat rock five feet above the ground and toss down my sleeping bag. Experience tells me that sleeping on a flat boulder beats the bumps of rocky ground. HelenLau pulls the picnic table back under the overhang and arranges her bedroll on the tabletop.

Hours later, I suddenly come awake; I'm on my back looking skyward. The clouds are breaking up. Those remaining march across the face of a brilliant moon. A coyote yips from the cliffs to the north and receives a mournful answer from the woods to the east.

Breakfast is a slapdash affair. Bart makes himself a peanut butter-and-jelly sandwich. Mine is a granola bar and a cup of juice. With the first rays of early morning sun, we hop into the van and bump our way to Toroweap Overlook.

The dropoff point is about 50 yards away. A dozen steps from the edge, my "trepidation meter" clicks on and keeps going up. Six feet from the rim, I'm getting strong psychological beeps. My steps get shorter, a flock of butterflies takes flight internally. Two feet from the edge my knees lock. That's as close as I intend to go. Some might call it a fear of heights. I call it an automatic application of common sense. Who needs a 3,000-foot free fall on a beautiful, sunlit morning? Not me.

Here, at Toroweap, the

We came upon the aspen-ringed meadow after six miles of hiking and immediately declared there was no question about it: this was the scenic centerpiece, the undisputed gem of the Ken Patrick Trail.

A couple of miles later, we blithely jilted the wildflowers in favor of what was positively the zenith of the route: a view into the mesmerizing depths of the Grand Canyon from 8,803-foot Point Imperial, the highest spot on either rim of the Canyon.

That is the way it goes on the Ken Patrick Trail, a ten-mile linear wonderland on the Grand Canyon's North Rim. Virtually every segment of the trail, from tall forests to elegant meadows to heart-thrilling Canyon overlooks, would be the top attraction to many other routes.

◆

—Douglas Kreutz,
Arizona Highways

Grand Canyon narrows to a width of less than a mile and offers the longest straight-down drop along its 277-mile course. Off to my right looms Vulcans Throne and an incredible path of black lava stretching from ground level all the way down to the Colorado.

I stretch my neck. The green and twisting ribbon of the river is down there. In its middle is a great black monolith, a huge plug of basalt called Vulcans Anvil. Downstream is a maelstrom of froth: Lava Falls, considered one of the world's fastest and most terrifying navigable rapids.

We walk about…chat…point…take pictures. After a while, I walk alone to the east a distance, find a large rock at rim's edge, sit down. I try to free my mind of everything, let my eyes take me down into the erosion-blasted depths past the ragged cliffs and tiers of tumbled rock, deep into a yawning gorge essentially devoid of vegetation.

I sit quietly. Strangely, perhaps, the word "hell" floats down the corridors of my mind. I'm getting a feeling, but it is not of the cartoon hell of frolicking little devils with pitchforks. I am thinking of the hell of complete isolation. Overwhelming loneliness.

I imagine being placed in the awesome depths down there, alone for all eternity, cut off from communication with God and all living creatures. A shudder runs up my spine. Then I shift to another channel of perception. I see the brilliant shafts of sunlight streaming down, a slice of blue sky, drifting fluffs of cumulus, two tiny dots that are rafts in the river below, a hawk soaring on an updraft. Heaven.

Maybe that's as good a way as any to describe the Grand Canyon from Toroweap Point. In one long glance…from heaven to hell and back again. The ultimate in contrasts.

Hardy early explorers John Wesley Powell and Clarence Dutton described the Grand Canyon in lengthy and meticulous detail. I have always gotten lost in their narratives, and I have always felt that there is too much in the Grand Canyon for complete human description. The more you tell, the further away the essence of it seems to float. I like the few words that author Frank Waters wrote about it:

"[It is] the sum total of all the aspects of nature combined in one integrated whole. It is at once the smile and frown upon the face of nature. In its heart is the savage, uncontrollable fury of all the inanimate Universe, and at the same time the immeasurable serenity that succeeds it. It is Creation."

We linger into the afternoon. Just looking, soaking it up. A car with three college students on a tour of the Southwest arrives. Later a pickup truck with an elderly couple pulls in. There is a register at the site. I glance through it. Ours seems about an average day at Toroweap: two, three, maybe four vehicles. Not a very busy part of the Canyon, not when you consider the more than four million visitors who view it from the South Rim's more accessible sites each year.

I walk with Rona up to higher ground, another vantage point. I ask the question. "What is the secret? What propelled you into this life?"

"I don't know. It's not anything I did. It was what happened to me. It was the effect of the river and the canyon walls on my mind. The visual and spiritual power. I was flattened by the immensity of the walls, the power of the river, the vividness of the colors. I think it may have created an absence of my ego."

For a person who doesn't know, her statement seems profound.

William Hafford passed away in 1992.

★

For me this river had become more than a river. It was both the ultimate freedom and a prison. Was my wondering about the flow merely one more symptom of my increasing self-questioning on whether it made sense any more for me to keep coming back here?

I steered the van off a 470-foot cliff onto the narrow bridge. The rattle of the van and the hum of its tires echoed off the steel railings. Far below us, the Colorado flowed by serenely, a translucent green snake crawling blindly to Mexico. Most of the water down there would not complete that journey. Instead, it would end up saturating some salt-loaded field of alfalfa. At any rate, the flow here seemed to be in the midteens; Crystal would be a cinch.

From the shotgun seat, Fabry, just arrived from Sonora to work his first trip of the year, stared down at the river as if at a vision of the Virgin and said, "There she is."

What was the magnetism? We returned every spring like migratory animals. Neither of us could stay away. I glanced at him, still absorbed in gazing down past the steel rails into Marble Canyon at the West's most famous river. For both of us the magnetism was not just rivers. We had run dozens. I had rowed or paddled wild rivers on every major continent on this planet. The magnet was the Colorado, and not just the Colorado—the Colorado here, in Grand Canyon. This place had become holy. It had nothing to do with the Grand Canyon being one of the Seven Natural Wonders of the World and a World Heritage Site. This was sacred ground for far more personal reasons.

A bulky Winnebago motor home lumbered onto the narrow bridge—it was only eighteen feet wide—from the north and crept toward us at about ten miles per hour. Both riders in front craned their necks to scan the depths below us. I imagined their conversation: "What do you suppose it's like down there, Martha?"

I knew.

—Michael P. Ghiglieri, *Canyon*

G. B. and the Rangers

*Doesn't everyone love the men
and women in khaki?*

NATIONAL PARK RANGERS AND NATIONAL FOREST RANGERS ARE my heroes. I discovered them many years ago. They were friendly, peaceful, well-educated individuals who loved the earth and all its inhabitants. Every creature was treasured by rangers, as was every plant, rock, and bit of soil.

Once in the wee hours of night, I roused my three children from their sleep, and told them "Adolf" (the car) was packed. Then I asked if they would like to get dressed and go to the Grand Canyon. I did not realize at the time, this would be the first of a succession of such camping trips from Canada to explore the American Southwest, its national parks, forests, and monuments.

On these trips, we were escorted by rangers on trail walks, delighted by rangers at the nightly fireside talks, and watched over by rangers as we slept in the campgrounds.

We often traveled during the school year, so I assigned several hours a day of study time to the children. Those hours were spent with the rangers either in the museums or at the visitor centers. They took notes while the rangers related colorful details of the natural and geological history and of the people who dwelt there.

When the day's studies were complete, Lee would head down

the canyon trails, and the girls would clad themselves in bell anklets and chicken feather headdresses to watch the Indian dancers perform in front of the Hopi House, by the rim of the Grand Canyon. After each performance, the rangers would expound on what they had just viewed.

The rangers were our heroes, and for Nana, the baby of the family, they were more than that. She loved the rangers. My little tomboy, with her long, blond curls tousled by the wind, would escape her brother and sister to chase, stop, and smile up at every ranger who passed her way.

When my children were grown, I met and married G. B. Madison, a wild old Okie boy who was superintendent of the production division of Western States Stone Co., in Ash Fork, Arizona, the "Flagstone Capital of the USA" I presumed G. B. would see rangers as I saw them. But I was in for a rude awakening.

While Nana and her young daughter Morgan were visiting us from Canada, G. B. decided to take us up to the Grand Canyon for a day's outing. When we reached the park entrance, Nana spotted a ranger inside the gatehouse and excitedly pointed him out to Morgan.

G. B. failed to discern the admiration in Nana's voice, and as soon as we paid the park fee and received our receipt, map, and park newspaper, he began to mumble, "I hate them danged, pooshy, Forest Service, government, bloodsuckin' leeches so bad Charle, dammit!"

Nana, Morgan, and I turned as one to stare incredulously at him, while the ranger in his gatehouse politely pretended not to hear.

"G. B., are you talking about the park rangers? We love park rangers!" My voice was high and quivering in disbelief. I could not believe what I had just heard, and in front of Nana, Morgan, and the ranger too!

G. B seemed not to hear my question or my opinion and carried on with, "Parks, Forests an' Mines, it's all the same. Them ignorant, self-assertive, bossy government devils stop me cuttin' new roads into quarries, an' I have to stand around an' listen to their Goll-danged demands an' threats an' then wait fer my master to leave—

so's I can finish cuttin' roads into my very own quarries! An' if a rock doodler leaves his cabin empty fer a little bit, they have it burned down faster'n a man can scrape gnats off a dead frog!" And off he drove.

As we passed the cutoff for the East Rim Drive, G. B. pointed out curbstones which "he" supplied to the park, then he drove right past the Mather Point and Yavapai Point lookouts, because he was "fixin'" to show us something.

G. B. stopped at the Visitor Center—not to show us the exhibits, books, and Grand Canyon videos, not to get pamphlets or go to the bathroom—he wanted us to examine, in detail, the flagstone forecourt, the stone for which was also supplied by G. B. and the stone company.

Nana wanted to take Morgan down into the Grand Canyon, so we strolled along the rim to the Bright Angel Trail, where they began their short descent. G. B. and I sat in the shade of a piñon pine to wait for them, and I gazed out across the Canyon. Its jagged opening into the ages was veiled in the soft lavender, blue, and dusty pink hues of the noontime light, and I wondered if Canada geese momentarily interrupted their migration flights to frolic and soar in air currents boiling there.

"Y'all have to go down," G. B. blurted out to a pair of doddering old tourists who were looking over the edge, "Even jes' a li'l ways. Y'all need to feel the true wonder of it, an' y'all can't do that up on top."

After a rest and lunch, G. B. sent Nana and Morgan into the Hopi House to shop.

"Y'all graze 'round in thar an' get y'all somethin', Morgan too. An' take y'all's time," he added.

We sat down on a bench, and after a few minutes G. B. grumbled, "How long can they stay in thar? What're they doin'? Dammit Charle...go get 'em. I got a lot to show 'em yet today, an' the day's near over!"

Nana and Morgan had left the Hopi House, and were in front of it, looking at the old dance platform. Nana was talking and gesticulating to Morgan, and I murmured to G. B., "She must be telling

Morgan about the Indian dancers she saw there when she was little."

Tears welled up in his eyes as he thought for a moment, then said, "Y'all leave 'em be Charle, but don't let 'em disappear on ye."

G. B. finished giving us his tour of the park and headed for home. We had just turned south onto Route 64 from the East Rim Drive, when G. B. abruptly stopped the car in the middle of the road and told us to get out. Either the car was going to blow up, or he had spotted a "snattlerake," but instead he led us to the curbstones.

"Girls, while they was a-workin' on the curbstones, I came up here one day with a load a' rock, so's I could check on their progress, an' I saw they was doin' it all wrong. It wasn't enough to tell 'em how to do it, I had to SHOW the dang fools how to do it."

As he spoke, vehicles began to stop. Tourists left their cars, campers, vans, and motor homes to gather around the man in khaki-colored clothes and a broad-brimmed cowboy hat, thinking he was connected to the Park Service. Instead of hearing a talk on the flora and fauna bordering the roadway, they received a lesson in curb-stone construction.

G. B. spoke with such color and authority on the subject that he kept his audience captivated until he finished his spiel, at which time he took a few moments to pose with a Japanese gentleman while the gentleman's wife took their picture. Then G. B. simply walked back to the car—with us in quick retreat, and drove away, leaving the crowd to deal with the park ranger approaching in his pickup truck with the flashing yellow light.

Charlotte Madison is an author and artist who currently resides on the "big island" off the coast of British Columbia. She has roamed the American Southwest, playing hermit, painting and writing, since the Petrified Forest was green and thriving. Her passion for the desert compels her to return to it annually. Nana Cook is a self-confessed Southwest fanatic who lives with her husband Gary in a log house on the "wet coast" of Vancouver Island. Since childhood, she has explored the Southwest, loving the land and its inhabitants. When not reading about, writing about, or painting the Southwest, she and Gary are riding through it on their Harleys.

※

Rangering becomes more than a job; it is a state of mind. The ranger mind is designed to function in crises, real or imagined. It delights in juggling many thoughts and decisions but within a context whose purpose is predetermined and whose context demands only a choice of techniques, not of philosophies. It is a mentality of triage; it works rapidly but shallowly; it detests contemplation and shuns moral or philosophical ambiguity. On the surface, it appears to be an odd state of mind for future park administrators to cultivate, but it explains the almost total absence of any kind of contemplative study within the agency. No park ranger has ever written an important statement of national parks values or purposes. Instead, the ranger reacts to crises, and if existing crises are not enough, new ones must be invented. The best bet is crime.

The emphasis on law enforcement is staggering.... Where the Fourth of July used to be associated with rumors of the monsoon, it now rings with rumblings about bikers. Motorcycle gangs are descending on the North Rim. The rangers organize us for riot control drills. The fire crew, outfitted with batons, will form a wedge, while rangers behind us wield shotguns and handcuffs. The strategy is for us to hide in the trees by the entrance station and, if trouble develops, to pour out of the woods, assume formation, and attack the bikers....

But no confrontation occurs. The bikers—the Dirty Dozen—agree to set up camp along the main haul road on the national forest. When they enter the park, they do so under escort. Quickly between them and the rangers a symbiosis develops. The bikers revel in their armed escort; the attention is intoxicating. The rangers thrill no less to their status as public protectors. To prevent a real crisis from intervening, the rangers and the bikers hold preliminary conferences to work out protocol. Before the bikers leave, they invite the rangers to a beer bust. They promise to return the next year. Gonzo orders t-shirts to be made with the inscription "Bikers, 35, Rangers, 5. Rangers Win."

—Stephen J. Pyne, *Fire on the Rim: A Firefighter's
Season at the Grand Canyon*

PAUL RICHFIELD

✳ ✳ ✳

The Turbulent Times

There are some things which shouldn't fly.

CLIMBING UP TO 7,500 FEET, THE AIRPLANE'S NOSE BOBS SLOWLY
from left to right and back again as the light chop intensifies on the
lee side of the ridge. I reflexively apply pressure to both rudder
pedals in order to "stiffen the tail" and thus keep the nose straight.
Without warning, a small yellow dot appears directly in front of my
right cornea. What the heck? I take off my sunglasses and swipe the
lens across my pants leg. Replacing my glasses, I find that the yellow
dot is still there. Could it be on the inside of the lens? No, that's not
possible…but looking closely, I establish that the particle has
impacted the inside center of my right sunglass lens from the right
rear and below at approximately at 45- to 50-degree angle. Please,
God, no. I twist my head to the right and lock eyes with a flaxen-
haired toddler, Gustaf, who having "flung his gauntlet" stares at me
malevolently, a creamy, yellow, bilelike substance covering his face,
the floor, and, of course, my back.

It is said that the Eskimos have a hundred words to describe
snow. Figuring prominently in the course of their day-to-day lives,
the white stuff is a common topic for conversation—snow's temperature and consistency, its many shades, its textures and variations.
So it is with Grand Canyon tour pilots and human vomit; the list of

157

descriptive terms is as varied and colorful as the contents of the barf bags themselves. Anyone can tell you what appears to be in the Sic-Sac, but it takes an experienced tour pilot to tell you with certainty not only which food group the stuff started out as, but from which buffet line it originated.

Just when you drop your guard is when the passengers are most likely to cross that fine line between excitement and trepidation, usually as they realize that the window is not a television screen and their lives truly are in the hands of that maniac in the left seat. Even the beautiful girl you strategically placed in the copilot's seat can turn on you, flirting one minute and throwing up loudly the next. Intimate, but not what I had in mind. I assume nothing, having seen jumbo jet captains fill bag after bag. Alaska bush pilots beg to go back, and fighter pilots mumble with fear, their hands furtively searching for an ejection handle that exists only in their minds.

Speaking of fear, a passenger who becomes catatonic (eyes closed) is said to "vapor lock," or "go off-line." Customers whose heads appear to be locked directly forward, eyes and mouth open wide, skin pale and sweating, are "utterly fascinated," or "too scared to puke." Tourist who make it the whole way without throwing up or passing out, yet collapse in a heap next to the aircraft on the tarmac, are "technical knockouts," or "TKOs," even if they're just faking it in order to gain sympathy or attention from a friend, loved ones, or me. Those who race to the fence and collapse, or hold back just long enough to vomit into trash cans, urinals, water fountains, or each other, are "limp-offs." Customers who pretend to require oxygen, or are well enough to demand medical evacuation by ambulance or helicopter, are said to have "gone camping," or are "renting a car." Customers who are genuinely in need of medical attention are extremely rare.

Often the scenic-tour pilot is a victim of complex family politics within a passenger group. I recall a family from the Middle East, which consisted of the obviously Western-educated father, the traditionally garbed mother and daughter, and the very traditionally garbed grandmother/matriarch whom we'll call Ma-ma. Ma-ma was big, requiring two seat-belt extensions, and she was loud. The moment my wheels left the pavement, Ma-ma let out a scream, the kind of plaintive, Koranic wailing usually reserved for executions, massacres, and natural disasters in the Third World. Ever the diplomat, I asked the nice lady if there was a problem, and if not, then I would consider it a personal favor if she would please knock it off. Having made her point, she resigned herself to groaning from time to time lest we overlook her displeasure. Just because her son-in-law was head of the household and wanted to take his family on an air tour didn't mean that she had to like it. Stranger still, the rest of the family happily ignored her, as if her performance were standard operating procedure for family outings. They were content to take photographs and listen to my narrative. Everyone had a great time, even Ma-ma, who gave me a dollar and patted me on the head after the flight.

People understand that this business of flying people through the Grand Canyon is almost always a pleasant experience. When it's nice and smooth out, I'm a hero—expert pilot, tour guide, soothsayer, comedian, and guardian of our greatest natural wonder, all things to all people and a great role model for children, a future airline captain. But when it's bumpy, lo and behold, in the passengers' eyes I metamorphose into a more sinister figure—dissipated, disheveled, a tough-talking, hard-drinking loser of the skies, condemned to fly these journeys through hell no doubt due to delayed combat stress disorder and repeated smuggling convictions. Heck, honey, I'll bet the little monster doesn't even have a pilot's license. Then we touch down, one of my characteristic smooth landings, and I'm the hero again. To date, I've carried more than 15,000 people from 150 countries over the Grand Canyon, 9 at a time.

Paul Richfield wrote this story for Flying *magazine.*

❊

We are now ready to start on our way down the Great Unknown. Our boats, tied to a common stake, are chafing each other, as they are tossed by the fretful river. They ride high and buoyant, for their loads are lighter than we could desire. We have but a month s rations remaining. The flour has been resifted through the mosquito-net sieve; the spoiled bacon has been dried, and the worst of it boiled; the few pounds of dried apples have been spread in the sun, and reshrunken to their normal bulk; the sugar has all melted, and gone on its way down the river; but we have a large sack of coffee. The lighting of the boats has this advantage: they will ride the waves better, and we shall have but little to carry when we make a portage.

We are three quarters of a mile in the depths of the earth, and the great river shrinks into insignificance, as it dashes its angry waves against the walls and cliffs, that rise to the world above; they are but puny ripples, and we but pigmies, running up and down the sands, or lost among the boulders.

We have an unknown distance yet to run; an unknown river yet to explore. What falls there are, we know not; what rocks beset the channel, we know not; what walls rise over the river, we know not. Ah, well! We may conjecture many things. The men talk as cheerfully as ever; jests are bandied about freely this morning; but to me the cheer is somber and the jests are ghastly.

—Major John Wesley Powell

Women in the Canyon

They did more than they got credit for.

"HEY, YOU HAGS, ARE THE BOATS UNLOADED YET?"

Lorna and I turned to see another boatman grinning up at us. "Sure," we said, laughing. "Here, catch these!" and within seconds he was dodging flying gear bags.

The nickname "hags" sounds grating to most people, but the women who row for one river company use it with affection. To us, it symbolizes the feel of our oars pulling through water, the sweet comfort and awesome beauty of 5,000-foot cliffs, the roar of rapids, and the laughter of our passengers. To us, being a hag means being a woman river guide on commercial trips through the Grand Canyon.

It can also mean working long hours. No matter which company a boatwoman works for, she doesn't punch out at five o'clock each day during the 225-mile trips that last eight to eighteen days. Sometimes we row against seemingly endless upstream winds. Our skin is dried out by too much sun, and our brains are fried by hundred-degree heat. We face other assaults on our bodies, the latest being some incurable form of foot rot. But for the six-month river season, these minor irritations are more than offset by watching that massive pile of rock, the Grand Canyon, work its particular magic on folks.

And then there's the river…

∗

Before Georgie White rowed her first boat through the Grand Canyon, boats running the Colorado may have had women's names, but never women pilots. Back in 1869, John Wesley Powell commanded the wooden *Emma Dean* on his exploration of the Grand Canyon. Twenty years later, Robert Brewster Stanton's expedition rode downriver on the *Sweet Marie* and the *Bonnie Jean*, as the crew surveyed the Canyon for a railway route west.

Previous to Powell's expedition, history records two other Grand Canyon river journeys—one planned, one unplanned. Hopi legends tell of a young man who, riding in a hollowed-out log and using a magic wand to maneuver, floated through the Canyon and on out to the sea. In September of 1887, prospector James White allegedly rode through the Canyon on a makeshift log raft, hastily put together to escape attacking Indians on the upper Colorado. Controversy still rages as to whether White actually made the journey.

No one denies Powell the credit for being the first white man to lead a planned expedition through the Grand Canyon. His wooden boats put on the water up in Green River, Wyoming. When they encountered rapids, the oarsmen, their backs facing downstream, rowed like crazy while the stern man shouted commands and ruddered. (In 1897, trapper Nathaniel Galloway developed the rowing technique prevalent in rapids today—only one oarsman rowing and facing downstream. But when it is time to make a powerful cut across the water, modern oarsmen and -women still turn their backs downstream and row like crazy.) Like many expeditions that were to follow, Powell's men lined or portaged the worst rapids. *Lining* meant trying to control the boats by rope from shore; *portaging* meant unloading supplies and carrying the heavy boats around the rapid. Both techniques involved back-breaking labor. Powell's trip met with misfortune, hunger, and desertion, but three months after his party started, it emerged from the depths of the Canyon.

During the next 60 years, more adventurers ran the rapids of the Colorado, hoping to make their fortunes from recording or retelling their adventures. That was the intent of Glen and Bessie Hyde, who spent their honeymoon in 1928 floating through the Grand

Canyon, or almost all the way through. After they failed to arrive at their planned destination, a search party found their empty, flat-bottomed wooden scow bobbing near shore, with its bowline wedged between two rocks, just 39 miles short of the end of the Canyon. What happened to the honeymooners has remained a mystery to this day. Unclear, too, is how often Bessie handled the sweep oars attached to the bow and stern of their 25-foot scow. In any case, what with unplanned swims, repairs, and lining rapids, the trip must have been a physical ordeal for them both.

The first women to float through the entire Grand Canyon were Elzada Clover and Lois Jotter, passengers on pioneer river runner Norm Nevills's first Grand Canyon commercial trip in 1938. Elzada, a botany professor, had met Nevills in Mexican Hat, Utah, when she was collecting specimens. Nevills, who had already run two tourist trips downriver through Glen Canyon to Lees Ferry, asked Elzada if she would be interested in planning an expedition through the Grand Canyon to study botany. The next year, Nevills's three wooden boats headed toward Lees Ferry, but apparently there were personality conflicts along the way. When they arrived at the Ferry, their trip began to disintegrate. Some historians believe that the trip continued only because of Elzada's determination to find replacements for the deserting boatmen.

When Buzz Holmstrom, an adventurer who had just traversed the canyon solo the year before, heard of Nevills's intended trip carrying women passengers, he remarked, "Women have their place in

---

*R*iver runners can be divided into three general groups: "privates," the people who outfit and operate their own trip; "commercial boaters," professional guides who conduct river tours for a fee; and "people," the folk who hire guides to take them down the river.

♦

—Kim Crumbo, "The Canyon by River," *The Grand Canyon: Intimate Views,* edited by Robert C. Euler and Frank Tikalsky

this world, but they do not belong in the canyons of the Colorado."

Well, he was a little mistaken. A few women have been in the Grand Canyon almost 20 years, and in November of 1990, more than 200 people gathered at a river outfitter's warehouse to celebrate Georgie's 80th birthday and 40th year on the river. In the spring after her next birthday, Georgie would be gone, passing on to her next adventure. But that night, her blue eyes shone like a teenage girl's as she danced at her birthday bash. One boatwoman said, "To be eighty years old in the Grand Canyon...you wouldn't think of your grandma running a boat in the Grand Canyon. Georgie doesn't care. That's her life. That's her happiness. As long as she's alive, she intends to partake in it—and there's a lot of people who love her for it."

Georgie said, "I was born under a lucky star." But, actually, in 1911, she was born into a poor, essentially fatherless, family in Chicago. Perhaps Georgie's mother was her lucky star. "My mother said, 'You can't get any lower because you're on the bottom, [but] you've got good health and spirit, so go for it!'" And Georgie did. After marrying at 16 and giving birth to a daughter, Georgie and her husband set off for California on bicycles to find their fortune, "which was not a stunt; we didn't have any money." She loved Los Angeles and soon sent for the rest of her family. During the war years, she trained to ferry military planes within the States. In 1944, her daughter was killed in a bicycling accident, a tragedy Georgie may never have gotten over. But she did find renewal on the river.

Encouraged by friends, she attended a Sierra Club lecture by Harry Aleson, which led to the two of them swimming the Colorado. (Georgie was no stranger to cold water, she had grown up swimming in frigid Lake Michigan.) She and Harry hiked into the lower Grand Canyon with meager supplies and life jackets and jumped into the river. They tried to stay together by holding each other's wrists as they swam, or more literally, as they were tossed, spun, and submerged for four days by the muddy river, which was speeding along at 48,000 cubic feet per second (cfs). Georgie fell in love—with the Colorado. She and Harry came back into the lower canyon the next year, this time bringing a small, flimsy raft but nearly dying of thirst while hiking in. In the following years, she ran many southwestern canyons, including Escalante, Cataract, Lodore, and Glen Canyon. Using the small military surplus rafts available after World War II, Georgie spent her vacations (from her Los Angeles real estate business) running share-the-expense vacations for friends and acquaintances. In 1952, she rowed through the entire Grand Canyon, with the exception of a few portages where she was helped by two boatmen who were now running Nevills's river company. Georgie had found her home and spent the rest of her life sharing it with others.

When she was running the high and wild Colorado back in 1954, she was frustrated with how frequently her small rafts flipped. Georgie had no fear of swimming and loved the big water. "I like rapids—always did and always will." But figuring that the idea of swimming rapids would not attract many passengers, she lashed three 14-foot rowing rafts together. These "triple rigs" were nicknamed *G-rigs* (for Georgie) and handled with sweep oars. Not only did this design make the boats more stable, it greatly increased the passenger-carrying capacity. Further, Georgie could save time by using a motor during the flat stretches. Using big boats and motors attracted more passengers, and began discussions about river-trip aesthetics that continue to this day.

In 1955, Georgie put together her giant G-rigs—three 37-foot, inflatable, military-surplus bridge pontoons tied together, creating a 27-foot-wide motorboat. Other early adventurers and outfitters had used various boat types: wooden boats and various-sized inflatable rafts propelled by either oars or motors. Georgie's new rig design, with some modifications, would be used by the majority of Canyon river companies. Georgie said, "They'd call me crazy woman when I'd come into Temple Bar [a takeout on Lake Mead]. I'd just have to laugh, have a beer, and go on because it didn't bother me any." Georgie could afford to "pay no attention," she was her own boss, doing what she loved—an inspiration to all women who saw her on water.

Fewer than 200 people had floated through the Canyon when

Georgie started running her G-rigs. Running rivers was considered a reckless thing to do, and only a few daring individuals attempted the roaring rapids of the Colorado. But soon, more and more people were discovering river running, the Grand Canyon, and perhaps a wilder side of themselves. In the 1960s, Americans were becoming aware of the wildland vacations available to them. Tourists signed on with outfitters like Georgie, who ran trips themselves or hired boatmen to assist with the essentials of running a river trip. Their job was to successfully navigate a boat from put-in to take-out, cook meals, talk about the ecology and history of the place, lead hikes, handle emergencies, and—most important—show people a good time.

Today, some river companies still are operated by or carry the names of some of these early outfitters: Hatch, Sanderson, and Ron Smith, to name a few. What began as a hobby eventually became a business. And for many river guides, what began as a summer job eventually became a career—albeit a seasonal career, May through September, with no retirement or health benefits.

In 1964, 15 miles above the beginning of the Grand Canyon, the gates of Glen Canyon Dam closed, shutting off the natural, muddy flow of the Colorado River. Spring floods of 120,000 cfs would be seen no more. The dam caused major ecological changes along the river, most visibly tamarisk growth, lack of driftwood, beach erosion, and clear water. The water flowing out from the deep artificial lake behind the dam was clear and cold, about fifty degrees. The dam helped catalyze a business boom because river runners could count on a fairly consistent flow between 3,000 to 29,000 cfs. The water would drop out from under boats in the autumn or rise suddenly from unusual rain or spring runoff. (However, as we will see, there would be some unplanned events.)

Between 1965 and 1971, the number of people going down the river grew from 547 per year to 10,385. By 1972, almost 16,500 people had floated through the Canyon. The Grand Canyon National Park Service realized that, unless limits were set, overcrowding would destroy the pristine river corridor and the river experience. In 1973, the Park Service essentially froze the number of people allowed down the river, holding to the 1972 use level: 92 percent of the allotment was for commercial trips and the remaining 8 percent for noncommercial or private use. (Years later, due to public and business pressure, the private trip percentage and the total number of trips would increase.) The existing outfitters were given first preference for national park commercial concessionaire status. After 1973, anyone who wanted to float through the Canyon had to apply either for a private permit (and probably wait years for a turn) or pay one of the licensed outfitters, or river companies, for a trip. If someone wanted to carry paying passengers, he or she had to work for one of the outfitters—not always an easy task if that someone happened to be a woman.

The women after Georgie were in a different world. By the early 1970s, the pioneer days of river exploration and creating river companies in the Grand Canyon were past. Georgie—a remarkable character with many adventures behind her—was in her early 40s when she rowed the Canyon for the first time. The women who followed were in their 20s. The early '70s were also a time of transition, where women as well as men were changing their ideas of what constituted women's work.

There weren't nearly as many women as men asking to work as adventure guides; but a few who *were* asking heard some interesting responses. "You're a pretty girl, but we won't hire girls," said the manager of one river company to an eager applicant. That was in 1981—30 years after Georgie started running her boats and almost 4 years after other Canyon boatwomen had begun leading river trips. The hiring of women guides continued to evolve unevenly, because each of the 20 river companies were like different countries with different traditions, crews, and leaders. Some of them, depending on their backgrounds and deeply ingrained ways of thinking, were more receptive than others to the idea of women running boats down the Colorado....

All the early Canyon boatwomen, through a combination of luck and desire, were able to set the groundwork for more women to work in the Canyon. "If we'd screwed up, history would have to be rewritten," said one boatwoman. "If we hadn't been able to handle the boats, do you think they would have put another one of us on? It would have been a long time. So we did it! And it was fun!"

It was, indeed, the best of times.

Louise Teal is a writer who has been published in Arizona Highways, Backpacker, *and* Bicycling *magazines. This story was excerpted from* Breaking into the Current: Boatwomen of the Grand Canyon.

★

One effect of this river that I never would have guessed is that of psycho-analysis—it reveals the depth, or lack of it, of a relationship. Couples arrive at Lees Ferry either with a thriving relationship or one held together by the weak glue of habit, or finances, or status, or insecurity, or you name it. The river will weld the people who are bonded in a healthy relationship even tighter—happy and dreaming together and newly aware of how blessed they are to have one another. In contrast, it will dissolve weak relationships like a lump of sugar.

Why? Because the Grand Canyon challenges people. Day after day, it freezes them, scorches them, wears them out, torments them with thirst and hunger, drenches them repeatedly, hurries them up and then slows them to a dead stop, scares the living daylights out of them and then soothes and consoles them like some gigantic guru. It forces people to trek in blistering heat, climb on rock hot enough to refry beans and on exposed routes above falls that if they fell would mangle them like doomed bison driven off a cliff by Paleo-Indians. The canyon sucks the moisture out people fast enough to make a prune farmer turn green with envy. Then it showers them in a cold rain that will not stop. It strips away all sophistry. It makes people feel as insignificant in the shame of things as a gnat and, worse, pointedly shouts that their life spans here on Earth are just as fleeting.

People here fall out of love—and into love. The canyon is the elemental catalyst of primeval passions, good and bad. It nurtures what is strong and destroys what is weak, especially in marriages. We see it all the time.

—Michael P. Ghiglieri, *Canyon*

W. PAUL JONES

Trinitarian Thoughts

Take a look. Everything is connected.

HIKING FROM THE SOUTH RIM OF THE GRAND CANYON TO THE
Colorado River floor is, physically, no major challenge. The most
dangerous part is not slipping after an incontinent mule team passes.
Many hike it, although those who do the fourteen-mile-round-trip
Kaibab Trail in one day may be a more select group. And among
these, fewer still attempt the marathon as a spiritual pilgrimage.

My longing to do so began several years earlier when, in a
Navajo healing ceremony, I encountered the "Sipapu." This small
hole in the hogan's floor is a ceremonial focus for the power of the
mysterious womb hole from which all spirits are birthed. The real
"divine center" is known only to the gods, but many believe it to
be the Grand Canyon. Into that huge hole I hiked, the one from
which all of us may have come—dust to dust, life to life—on a pilgrimage from sunrise to sunset.

The first half mile was a welcomed contrast to the resortlike
atmosphere of the rim. My eyes, at first, were those of the artist. My
imagination fashioned a necklace from the maze of switchbacks,
stringing together the mellow colors of carefree buttes and pinnacles and palisades. In time, I became more contemplative, emptied
of thought, merging and floating with the birds, now at eye level.

169

Other persons must have been so affected, for the map identified a point immediately in front as Buddha Peak, the one to the right as Vishnu Temple. Some time after the third hour, the pilgrimage became decidedly physical and, simultaneously, more spiritual. Thirst was my first clue that I did not belong here. Toads, lizards, a coiled rattlesnake—they all seemed at home—even a vulture overhead, circling with growing interest my slowing steps. A sign put the matter graphically: "Danger! Those without a gallon of water each, turn back now!" Life was as thin as a canteen strap.

With heavy panting, I seemed to be entering the electronic museum display on the rim. It had a beeper that went off every second for three minutes. The total beeps marked the advent of the Canyon within the whole span of time. As I hiked, one fact became increasingly heavy: only with the last beep did the human species appear. In fact, human history is so minuscule that this last beep included not only "us" but all the extinct mammoth animals of prehistory.

To understand what was happening to me, one must understand that I am a theologian, philosophical by training, biblical by choice. History has long been my foundation for theological exploration. But with human figures still visible on the rim, I had quickly walked far beyond the symbolic equivalent of recorded history. And yet, stretching far below me, winding for miles down into the Canyon, strata after strata, stretched endless symbolic layers of a nonhuman time. Billions of years without us. Each of my downward steps was like going back in time a hundred years, as each mile-sign translated beeps into alienation.

It was close to 10 a.m. when I was swept by a childlike thought: Where was God all this time? Intellectually, this was no new question. But the artistic eye with which I began, displaced by eyes more contemplative, were now very physical eyes, cutting straight through the romanticism of my theological metaphors. I had to get down and back out by sunset. With night temperatures well below freezing, and my water half gone, conclusions were simple. Lost in this symbolic immensity of time, I as a conscious being was a freak. We simply do not belong.

I picked up a pebble at my feet. The time it reflected, compared with the time in which self-conscious life has been on earth, staggers the mind. In a universe twenty billion years old, the first dated year in history is 4241 B.C. How utterly insignificant to this bleak wholeness is the fact of self-conscious mind. Standing deep within the Canyon, feeling like a humorless afterthought of a mindless whole, my operating assumption as a theologian became a strange non sequitur. How can one any longer take this recent phenomenon of self-consciousness as *the* image for understanding the meaning of whole? From that point on the trail, I knew myself to be a misfit, for I alone was self-conscious. Impossible to shake was a portrait of the newest kid on the cosmic block, arrogantly insisting that behind everything was one of his kind.

Violating all techniques of suspenseful storytelling, let me just say straight out that I made it down and back in one day. But the price was costly. Merton claimed that in the desert the wrestling with God is until one receives a new name. In the Canyon that day, I knew that my wrestling would be until God, too, was renamed. The irreversibility of this awareness became clear the next day. I drove to Mount Palomar. The conclusion became indelible. Whether I looked into the earth or away from it, the effect was the same. Through that telescope one can see a billion light years away, which is staggering when one remembers that a light year itself is six trillion miles. And while our solar system is seven billion miles in diameter, from outer space it is simply one star in a gigantic galaxy—which itself appears as only a minor smudge with at least 100 million observable galaxies much like our own.

What the Grand Canyon does for time, Palomar does for space. With the arrival of consciousness late on a freaklike speck in an inconceivable vastness, how can one any longer propose self-consciousness as the defining analogy for comprehending the totality? As Freud observed, "I personally have a vast respect for mind, but has nature? Mind is only a little bit of nature, the rest of which seems to be able to get along very well without it."

Existence is the search for *the* analogy by which to be ordered. A generation ago, Dorothy Emmet concluded that the future of metaphysics (and thus theology) depended upon the emergence of a new analogy capable of igniting the imagination. She recognized, apparently, what is becoming clearer now, that we have crossed a threshold in which deity as self-conscious being can no longer be entertained as anteceding the cosmos. Whatever validity Christianity may claim, it must be in the full face of our cosmic loneliness and the absurd abyss of prior aloneness for any professed deity.

The Canyon, however, focused a second childlike question. If we persist in projecting a self-conscious God as creator-designer of the whole, the question of God's *doing* becomes even more devastating than God's *absence*. It was noon when I reached the bottom. Beside the surging Colorado River, I ate a sandwich, watching the pink and orange swirl of clouds stir the Canyon into a cauldron of peach froth, when a motion far closer refocused my eyes. I had been watching the sky through a spider web and in the center was a healthy-sized spider, riding the breeze patiently, oblivious to the peach display. A fly struck the web. With three venomous assaults on the terrorized insect, the spider began sucking it apart, savoring lunch with contentment. How can I stomach a God who designed such an arrangement, especially when, sooner or later, each of us will experience the

---

Once more the strange, infinite silence enfolded the Canyon. The far-off golden walls glistened in the sun; farther down, the purple clefts smoked.

The many-hued peaks and mesas, aloof from each other, rose out of the depths. It was a grand and gloomy scene of ruin where every glistening descent of rock was but a page of the earth's history.

It brought to my mind a faint appreciation of what time really meant; it spoke of an age of former men; it showed me the lonesome crags of eagles, and the cliff lairs of lions; and it taught mutely, eloquently, a lesson of life—that men are still savages, still driven by a spirit to roam, to hunt, and to slay.

♦

—Zane Grey, "An Appreciation of Grand Canyon"

whole from the vantage point of the fly? The spider may think such an arrangement to be fine, but only until a bird sees its lunch being a spider in the middle of that web. In collecting firewood the previous day, I saw, under a log, what as a child we called "roly-polies." I wondered if they hurt anything. At the Canyon bottom, I knew the absurdity of such a question. There is nothing alive that is not bad news for something. The only image of God that could any longer be viable would be one that permitted me to stare bald-faced at both fly and spider.

Ernest Becker's Pulitzer Prize–winning book, *The Denial of Death*, is deadly to any God who would dare peer out from behind the death and decay woven irradicably into the fabric of "creation." Staring unblinkingly into the repulsive extravagance in time and blood that has brought evolution to where we are, Becker asks, "What are we to make of a creation in which the routine activity is for organisms to be tearing others apart…everyone reaching out to incorporate others who are edible to him?" God cannot be guiltless, whether as the informing "wisdom" of nature's bloody plan or, conceived more distantly, as the force functioning intrusively as "acts of God," specializing in earthquakes and plagues, either willed or permitted. Every attempt at theodicy founders, for any self-conscious deity must be brought to confession by the portrait of a "nightmare spectacular taking place on a planet soaked for hundreds of millions of years in the blood of all its creatures," turning the planet "into a vast pit of fertilizer." A fully conscious creator forces the enigma that confounds every theodicy: the inconceivability of affirming a loving will as having designed a creation in which it is the routine activity of every organism to devour something else for its livelihood. Either we have for this "terror of creation" a sadomasochistic Designer or an Impotent Watcher or else we must forfeit primal self-consciousness as our informing image. Teresa of Avila was enough of a mystic to put it charitably, "I do not wonder, God, that you have so few friends from the way you treat them."…

The Grand Canyon is indeed a cauldron of death, symbol of creation's bloody chalice. Its restless sides teem with life, propelled by an insatiable drive to endure, indeed, to prevail. Wind, river, clutching root-fingers of trees, lean varmints in crouched determination—all are sister-brothers in the surging restlessness. We can feel this straining deeply within ourselves. Life is thrashing about, expanding, reaching out, in uncertain directions for seemingly unknown reasons. But here one can sense strangely that consciousness is not alien, but a breakthrough—within and for the whole. Ironically, while such emergence brings the alienating burden of knowing what nothing else in creation seems yet to know, it opens the religious threshold: greeting self-consciousness as the emergence of the whole.

W. Paul Jones has taught at Yale, and Princeton, St. Paul School of Theology and has published widely both in journals and books. He alternates life in the inner city with being a Trappist monk. He has five daughters which is quite interesting for a Roman Catholic Priest. The last mountain he and his daughters climbed was Chair Mountain near Marble, Colorado two years ago.

★

John Hance loved the Grand Canyon. Its mysticism touched him, and once that happened, he was destined to live on the rim and in the bottom for the remainder of his life. It was a shrine, and he had come to it; it was a sanctuary, and he devoted himself to it; it was his pet, and he liked to have it perform for strangers while he told tall tales about it. Hance was a religious man. One of his friends once said, "Oh, he believed in God—I guess. But he believed mostly in the Canyon and John Hance." If he had been told that the Canyon had appealed to his latent sense of teleological inquiry he would have been nonplused and would have countered with some remark intended to astound his visitor and put him on the defensive.

His excuse for living on the South Rim was a mine. It was an asbestos mine deep down in the bottom where the second geological era had fused and pressed its elementary constitutents some billion years ago until it had created this heat-resistant mineral. Asbestos mines are not common. Hance thought that he had a good thing, and he had. But like most other mineralogical efforts to make the Grand Canyon pay dividends, it failed because the cost of getting the product out of the Canyon was prohibitive. Hance came, in time, to understand that his mine was impractical. But he never quite gave it up. It remained his excuse for living at the South Rim, although the real reason was his love for the Canyon itself.

—Edwin Corle, *Listen, Bright Angel*

EDWARD ABBEY

* * *

Havasu

Many years ago, the famous activist
almost didn't make it out of
the Grand Canyon.

ONE SUMMER I STARTED OFF TO VISIT FOR THE FIRST TIME THE CITY of Los Angeles. I was riding with some friends from the University of New Mexico. On the way, we stopped off briefly to roll an old tire into the Grand Canyon. While watching the tire bounce over tall pine trees, tear hell out of a mule train, and disappear with a final grand leap into the Inner Gorge, I overheard the park ranger standing nearby say a few words about a place called Havasu, or Havasupai. A branch, it seemed, of the Grand Canyon.

What I heard made me think that I should see Havasu immediately, before something went wrong somewhere. My friends said they would wait. So, I went down into Havasu—14 miles by trail—and looked things over. When I returned five weeks later, I discovered that the others had gone on to Los Angeles without me.

That was fifteen years ago. And I still have not seen the fabulous city on the Pacific shore. Perhaps I never will. There's something in the prospect southwest from Barstow which makes one hesitate. Although recently, driving my own truck, I did succeed in penetrating as close as San Bernardino. But was hurled back by what appeared to be clouds of mustard gas rolling in from the west on a very broad front. Thus failed again. It may be, however, that Los Angeles will come to me. Will come to all of us, as it must (they say) to all men.

But Havasu, once down in there, it's hard to get out. The trail led across a stream wide, blue, and deep, like the pure upper reaches of the River Jordan. Without a bridge. Dripping wet and making muddy tracks, I entered the village of the Havasupai Indians where unshod ponies ambled down the only street and the children laughed, not maliciously, at the sight of the wet white man. I stayed the first night in the lodge the people keep for tourists, a rambling, old bungalow with high ceilings, a screened veranda, and large, comfortable rooms. When the sun went down, the village went dark except for kerosene lamps here and there, a few open fires, and a number of lightning bugs or fireflies which drifted aimlessly up and down Main Street, looking for trouble.

The next morning, I bought a slab of bacon and six cans of beans at the village post office, rented a large comfortable horse, and proceeded farther down the Canyon past miniature cornfields, green pastures, swimming pools, and waterfalls to the ruins of an old mining camp five miles below the village. There I lived, mostly alone except for the ghosts, for the next 35 days.

There was nothing wrong with the Indians. The Supai are a charming, cheerful, completely relaxed, and easygoing bunch, all one hundred or so of them. But I had no desire to live *among* them unless clearly invited to do so, and I wasn't. Even if invited, I might not have accepted. I'm not sure that I care for the idea of strangers examining my daily habits and folkways, studying my language, inspecting my costume, questioning me about my religion, classifying my artifacts, investigating my sexual rites, and evaluating my chances for cultural survival.

So, I lived alone.

The first thing I did was take off my pants. Naturally. Next, I unloaded the horse, smacked her on the rump, and sent her back to the village. I carried my food and gear into the best-preserved of the old cabins and spread my bedroll on a rusty steel cot. After that came a swim in the pool beneath a great waterfall nearby, 120 feet high, which rolled in mist and thundered over caverns and canopies of solidified travertine.

In the evening of that first day below the falls, I lay down to sleep in the cabin. A dark night. The door of the cabin, unlatched, creaked slowly open, although there was no perceptible movement of the air. One firefly flickered in and circled my bacon, suspended from the roofbeam on a length of bailing wire. Slowly, without visible physical aid, the door groaned shut. And opened again. A bat came through one window and went out another, followed by a second firefly (the first scooped up by the bat) and a host of mosquitoes, which did not leave. I had no netting, of course, and the air was much too humid and hot for sleeping inside a bag.

I got up and wandered around outside for a while, slapping at mosquitoes, and thinking. From a distance came the softened roar of the waterfall, that "white noise" as soothing as hypnosis. I rolled up my sleeping bag and in the filtered light of the stars followed the trail that wound through thickets of cactus and up around ledges to the terrace above the mining camp. The mosquitoes stayed close but in lessening numbers, it seemed, as I climbed over humps of travertine toward the head of the waterfall. Near the brink of it, 6 feet from the drop-off and the plunge, I found a sandy cove just big enough for my bed. The racing creek as it soared free over the edge created a continuous turbulence in the air sufficient to keep away all flying insects. I slept well that night and the next day carried the cot to the place and made it my permanent bedroom for the rest of July and all of August.

What did I do during those five weeks in Eden? Nothing. I did nothing. Or nearly nothing. I caught a few rainbow trout, which grew big if not numerous in Havasu Creek. About once a week, I put on my pants and walked up to the Indian village to buy bacon, canned beans, and Argentine beef in the little store. That was all the Indians had in stock. To vary my diet, I ordered more exotic foods by telephone from the supermarket in Grand Canyon Village, and these were shipped to me by the U.S. Mail, delivered twice a week on muleback down the 14-mile trail from Topocoba Hilltop. A little later in the season, I was able to buy sweet corn, figs, and peaches from the Supai. At one time for a period of three days, my bowels seemed in danger of falling out, but I recovered. The Indians never came down to my part of the Canyon except when guiding occasional tourists to the falls or hunting a stray horse. In late August came the Great Havasupai Sacred Peach Festival and four-day Marathon Friendship Dance, to which I was invited and in which I did participate. There I met Reed Watahomagie, a good man, the Chief Sinyala, and a fellow named Spoonhead who took me for five dollars in a horse race. Someone had fed my mount a half-bushel of green figs just before the race and didn't inform me.

The Friendship Dance, which continued day and night to the rhythm of drums made of old inner tube stretched over #10 tomato cans while ancient medicine men chanted in the background, was perhaps marred but definitely not interrupted when a drunken free-for-all exploded between Spoonhead and friends and a group of visiting Hualapai Indians down from the rim. But this, I was told, happened every year. It was a traditional part of the ceremony, sanctified by custom. As Spoonhead told me afterward, grinning around broken teeth, it's not every day you get a chance to wallop a Hualapai. Or skin a paleface, I reminded him. (Yes, the Supai are an excellent tribe, healthy, joyous, and clever. Not only

To the west of the Havasupai for 108 miles, the walls and the South Rim of the Grand Canyon lie within the domain of the Hualapai Indians. Half the width of the Colorado River, too, say the Hualapai. No part of the river, says the park. Here also, as in Navajo country, the boundary remains in dispute. The Hualapai indisputably own a ragged crescent of a million acres, plateau and canyon land, and there's a lot going on out there.

Hualapai boatmen run river trips. Other river runners ramp on and ramp off at Diamond Creek by permission of the Hualapai, who own the only road that runs down to the Colorado in the entire 277-mile stretch of the Grand Canyon.

♦

—Seymour L. Fishbein, *Grand Canyon Country: Its Majesty and Its Lore* clever, but shrewd. Not only shrewd but wise: e.g., the Bureau of Indian Affairs and the Bureau of Public Roads, like most government agencies, always meddling, always fretting, and itching and sweating for something to do, last year made a joint offer to blast a million-dollar road down into Havasu Canyon at no cost whatsoever to the tribe, thus opening their homeland to the riches of motorized tourism. The people of Supai or at least a majority of them voted to reject the proposal.) And the peach wine flowed freely, like the water of the river of life. When the ball was over, I went home to my bunk on the verge of the waterfall and rested for two days.

On my feet again, I explored the abandoned silver mines in the canyon walls, found a few sticks of dynamite but no caps or fuses. Disappointing; but there was nothing in that area anyway that required blowing up. I climbed through the caves that led down to the foot of Mooney Falls, 200 feet high. What did I do? There was nothing that had to be done. I listened to the voices, the many voices, vague, distant, but astonishingly human, the Havasu Creek. I heard the doors creak open, the doors creak shut, the old forgotten cabins where no one with tangible substance or the property of reflecting light ever entered, ever returned. I went native and dreamed away days on the shore of the pool under the waterfall, wandered naked as Adam under the cottonwoods, inspecting my cactus gardens. The days became wild, strange, ambiguous—a sinister element pervaded the flow of time. I lived narcotic hours in which like the Taoist Chuang-tse I worried about butterflies and who was dreaming what. There was a serpent, a red racer, living in the rocks of the spring where I filled my canteens; he was always there, slipping among the stones or pausing to mesmerize me with his suggestive tongue and cloudly haunted primeval eyes. Damn his eyes. We got to know each other rather too well, I think. I agonized over the girls I had known and over those I hoped were yet to come. I slipped by degrees into lunacy, me and the moon, and lost to a certain extent the power to distinguish between what was and what was not myself: looking at my hand, I would see a leaf trembling on a branch. A *green* leaf. I thought of Debussy, of Keats

and Blake and Andrew Marvell. I remembered Tom O'Bedlam.
And all of those lost and never remembered. Who would return?
To be lost again? I went for walks. I went for walks, and on one of
these, the last, I took in Havasu, regained everything that seemed to
be ebbing away.

Most of my wandering in the desert I've done alone. Not so
much from choice as from necessity—I generally prefer to go into
places where no one else wants to go. I find that in contemplating
the natural world my pleasure is greater if there are not too many
others contemplating it with me, at the same time. However, there
are special hazards in traveling alone. Your chances of dying, in case
of sickness or accident, are much improved, simply because there
is no one around to go for help.

Exploring a side canyon off Havasu Canyon one day, I was
unable to resist the temptation to climb up out of it onto what cor-
responds in the region to the Tonto Bench. Late in the afternoon,
I realized that I would not have enough time to get back to my
camp before dark, unless I could find a much shorter route than
the one by which I had come. I looked for a shortcut.

Nearby was another little side canyon which appeared to lead
down into Havasu Canyon. It was a steep, shadowy, extremely narrow defile with the usual meandering course and overhanging
walls; from where I stood, near its head, I could not tell if the route
was feasible all the way down to the floor of the main canyon. I had
no rope with me—only my walking stick. But I was hungry and
thirsty, as always. I started down.

For a while, everything went well. The floor of the little canyon
began as a bed of dry sand, scattered with rocks. Farther down, a few
boulders were wedged between the walls; I climbed over and under
them. Then the canyon took on the slickrock character—smooth,
sheer, slippery sandstone carved by erosion into a series of scoops
and potholes which got bigger as I descended. In some of these
basins there was a little water left over from the last flood, warm
and fetid water under an oily-looking scum, condensed by pro-
longed evaporation to a sort of broth, rich in dead and dying

organisms. My canteen was empty and I was very thirsty, but I felt that I could wait.

I came to a lip on the canyon floor which overhung by 12 feet the largest so far of these stagnant pools. On each side rose the canyon walls, roughly perpendicular. There was no way to continue except by dropping into the pool. I hesitated. Beyond this point, there could hardly be any returning, yet the main canyon was still not visible below. Obviously the only sensible thing to do was to turn back. I edged over the lip of stone and dropped feet first into the water.

Deeper than I expected. The warm, thick fluid came up and closed over my head as my feet touched the muck at the bottom. I had to swim to the farther side. And here, I found myself on the verge of another drop-off, with one more huge bowl of green soup below.

This drop-off was about the same height as the one before, but not overhanging. It resembled a children's playground slide, concave and S-curved, only steeper, wider, with a vertical pitch in the middle. It did not lead directly into the water but ended in a series of steplike ledges above the pool. Beyond the pool lay another edge, another drop-off into an unknown depth. Again I paused, and for a much longer time. But I no longer had the option of turning around and going back. I eased myself into the chute and let go of everything—except my faithful stick.

I hit rock-bottom hard, but without any physical injury. I swam the stinking pond dog-paddle style, pushing the heavy scum away from my face, and crawled out on the far side to see what my fate was going to be.

Fatal. Death by starvation, slow and tedious. For I was looking straight down an overhanging cliff to a rubble pile of broken rocks eighty feet below.

After the first wave of utter panic had passed, I began to try to think. First of all, I was not going to die immediately, unless another flash flood came down the gorge; there was the pond of stagnant water on hand to save me from thirst, and a man can live, they say, for thirty days or more without food. My sun-bleached bones, dramatically sprawled at the bottom of the chasm, would provide the diversion of the picturesque for future wanderers — if any man ever came this way again.

My second thought was to scream for help, although, I knew very well there could be no other human being within miles. I even tried it, but the sound of that anxious shout, cut short in the dead air within the canyon walls, was so inhuman, so detached as it seemed for myself, that it terrified me, and I didn't attempt it again.

I thought of tearing my clothes into strips and plaiting a rope. But what was I wearing? — boots, socks, a pair of old and ragged blue jeans, a flimsy t-shirt, an ancient and rotten sombrero of straw. Not a chance of weaving such a wardrobe into a rope 80 feet long, or even 20 feet long.

How about a signal fire? There was nothing to burn but my clothes; not a tree, not a shrub, not even a weed grew in this stony cul-de-sac. Even if I burned my clothing, the chances of the smoke being seen by some Hualapai Indian high on the South Rim were very small; and if he did see the smoke, what then? He'd shrug his shoulders, sigh, and take another pull from his Tokay bottle. Furthermore, without clothes, the sun would soon bake me to death.

When I first hiked from Mile 157 at the bottom of the Grand Canyon upstream along the aquamarine creek flowing and tumbling between the thousand-foot walls of pink Muav, Temple Butte, and Redwall limestones of Havasu Canyon, I was stunned by its beauty. My brain seemed reluctant to file the images I was seeing as genuine. "Are you hallucinating?" it seemed to accuse. Each bend of the wide, U-shaped canyon revealed a new roaring waterfall spilling blue-green water over curving red terraces of rimstone dams flanked by lush wild grapes and flickering velvet ash. No place on earth could be this beautiful and be real.

◆

—Michael P. Ghiglieri, *Canyon*

There was only one thing I could do. I had a tiny notebook in my hip pocket and a stub of a pencil. When these dried out, I could at least record my final thoughts. I would have plenty of time to write not only my epitaph but my own elegy.

But not yet.

There were a few loose stones scattered about the edge of the pool. Taking the biggest first, I swam with it back to the foot of the slickrock chute and placed it there. One by one I brought the others and made a shaky little pile and about two feet high leaning against the chute. Hopeless, of course, but there was nothing else to do. I stood on top of the pile and stretched outward, straining my arms to their utmost limit and groped with fingers and fingernails for a hold on something firm. There was nothing. I crept back down. I began to cry. It was easy. All alone, I didn't have to be brave.

Through the tears, I noticed my old walking stick lying nearby. I took it and stood it on the most solid stone in the pile, behind the two topmost stones. I took off my boots, tied them together and hung them around my neck, on my back. I got up on the little pile again and lifted one leg and set my big toe on the top of the stick. This could never work. Slowly and painfully, leaning as much of my weight as I could against the sandstone slide, I applied more and more pressure on the stick, pushing my body upward until I was again stretched out full length above. Again I felt for a fingerhold. There was none. The chute was smooth as polished marble.

No, not quite that smooth. This was sandstone, soft and porous, not marble, and between it and my wet body and wet clothing a certain friction was created. In addition, the stick had enabled me to reach a higher section of the S-curved chute, where the angle was more favorable. I discovered that I could move upward, inch by inch, through adhesion and with the help of the leveling tendency of the curve. I gave an extra little push with my big toe—the stones collapsed below, the stick clattered down—and crawled rather like a snail or slug, oozing slime, up over the rounded summit of the slide.

The next obstacle, the overhanging spout 12 feet above a deep plunge pool, looked impossible. It was impossible, but with the blind faith of despair I slogged into the water and swam underneath the drop-off and floundered around for a while, scrabbling at the slippery rock until my nerves and tiring muscles convinced my numbed brain that *this was not the way.* I swam back to solid ground and lay down to rest and die in comfort.

Far above, I could see the sky, an irregular strip of blue between the dark, hard-edged canyon walls that seemed to lean toward each other as they towered above me. Across that narrow opening, a small white cloud was passing, so lovely and precious and delicate and forever inaccessible that it broke the heart and made me weep like a woman, like a child. In all my life, I had never seen anything so beautiful.

The walls that rose on either side of the drop-off were literally perpendicular. Eroded by weathering, however, and not by corrosion and rushing floodwater, they had a rough surface, chipped, broken, cracked. Where the walls joined the face of the overhang they formed almost a square corner, with a number of minute crevices and inch-wide shelves on either side. It might, after all, be possible. What did I have to lose?

When I had regained some measure of nerve and steadiness I got up off my back and tried the wall beside the pond, clinging to the rock with bare toes and fingertips and inching my way crabwise toward the corner. The water-soaked, heavy boots dangling from my neck, swinging back and forth with my every movement, threw me off balance, and I fell into the pool. I swam out to the bank, unslung the boots, and threw them up over the drop-off, out of sight. They'd be there if I ever needed them again. Once more, I attached myself to the wall, tenderly, sensitively, like a limpet, and very slowly, very cautiously, worked my way into the corner. Here, I was able to climb upward, a few centimeters at a time, by bracing myself against the opposite sides and finding sufficient niches for fingers and toes. As I neared the top and the overhang became noticeable, I prepared for a slip, planning to push myself away from the rock so as to fall into the center of the pool where the water was deepest. But it wasn't necessary. Somehow, with a skill and tenacity I could never have found in myself under ordinary circumstances, I managed to creep straight up that gloomy cliff and over the brink of the drop-off and into the flower of safety. My boots were floating under the surface of the little puddle above. As I poured the stinking water out of them and pulled them on and laced them up, I discovered myself bawling again for the third time in three hours, the hot delicious tears of victory. And up above the clouds replied—thunder.

I emerged from the treacherous little canyon at sundown, with an enormous fire in the western sky and lightning overhead. Through sweet twilight and the sudden dazzling flare of lightning, I hiked back along the Tonto Bench, bellowing the "Ode to Joy." Long before I reached the place where I could descend safely to the main canyon and my camp, however, darkness set in, the clouds opened their bays, and the rain poured down. I took shelter under a ledge in a shallow cave about 3 feet high—hardly room to sit up in. Others had been here before: the dusty floor of the little hole was littered with droppings of birds, rats, jackrabbits, and coyotes. There were also a few long gray pieces of scat with a curious twist at one tip—cougar? I didn't care. I had some matches with me, sealed in paraffin (the prudent explorer); I scraped together the handiest twigs and animal droppings and built a little fire and waited for the rain to stop.

It didn't stop. The rain came down for hours in alternate waves of storm and drizzle, and I very soon had burnt up all the fuel within reach. No matter. I stretched out in the coyote den, pillowed my head on my arm and suffered through the long, long night, wet, cold, aching, hungry, wretched, dreaming claustrophobic nightmares. It was one of the happiest nights of my life.

Edward Abbey the legendary author of The Monkey Wrench Gang *and many other critically acclaimed books, was born in Home, Pennsylvania, in 1927, and died at his home in Oracle, Arizona, in 1989.* Desert Solitaire, *from which this story was excerpted, established the author as one of the country's foremost defenders of the natural environment.*

✳

Havasupai worry that their water supply, the blue-green springwater flowing down Havasu Creek, will become polluted with radioactive uranium and will no longer support normal life. They also worry that Red Butte, the region they hold most sacred—it is as significant to them as the Sipapu along the little Colorado is to the Hopi—will be damaged beyond the powers of the universe to heal.

Why? For many of the details of this issue, I owe a debt to Flagstaff environmental journalist Dan Dagget and to Kathleen Stanton. The source of the radioactivity problem is geological: there are thousands of breccia pipes scattered on the Colorado Plateau on both sides of the Grand Canyon. Breccia pipes here are caused by the collapse of overlying strata— say of Supai, Hermit, and the others all the way up to the Kaibab and beyond for an additional vertical mile of Mesozoic formations that have now vanished due to erosion—into giant solution caverns that have formed beneath them in the Redwall aquifer. These breccia pipes tend to store collapsing rock, funnel groundwater, and concentrate many minerals that are far more dispersed in the surrounding bedrock—minerals that were present in those now-vanished upper strata.

—Michael P. Ghiglieri, *Canyon*

Transition

*A solo journey on foot leads
to inner discovery.*

As I STOOD WATCHING THE PLANE CONTRACT TO A SPECK AND finally dissolve in the black distance, I think I already knew that my journey had moved on. It was no picnic yet, let alone a pilgrimage. But I had taken the critical steps. I had crossed the amphitheater. And by taking my airdrop at the alternate site I had proved beyond all reasonable doubt that I could meet the Canyon's physical challenge.

It was not until evening, though, just after sunset, that I really grasped what the airdrop had meant. I was stretched out on top of my sleeping bag and doing nothing but gazing up into the pale blue sky when, far overhead, a jet airliner glinted briefly in the rays of the already-hidden sun. But the plane was flying so high that its whisper did not really damage the silence. And its remote presence did not even touch the solitude.

And all at once, I realized that the airdrop had not touched my solitude either. Had not penetrated my cocoon of peace and simplicity. For there had been no feeling of personal contact. Even on the Cessna's final run, I had, curiously, seen no figures in the plane's cabin. And I realized now that I had not really connected the plane and its roar with actual happenings in the outside world. I had seen it as a mere convenience. As an impersonal instrument fulfilling my personal needs. And now, looking up at the remote speck that was the airliner, I saw, in the sudden and overwhelming way you do when the obvious at last forces itself on your awareness, that the important thing was my cocoon of peace and solitude. The fact that a cocoon existed. I had, I saw, finally escaped from the paradox of simple living. The trivia were still there, and would be until the end of my journey. But I had overcome them. Had broken free at last from the din and deadline of the outside world.

I promptly held a celebration: I prefaced dinner with the week's menu-spicing delicacy, a can of smoked sliced lobster, and afterward I tempered the pemmican and dehydrated potatoes with claret. At the meal's end, for a semidelightful five minutes, I was half-canyon over.

Yet, the turning point that I had sensed did not immediately materialize. I even managed to spend the next three days pressed tighter than ever to the sweaty world of effort.

All through those three days, I reconnoitered, hard, in Fossil Canyon. No one, it seemed, had ever found a way down this narrow cleavage in the rock, almost 2,000 feet deep. But I knew that if I succeeded, I would be able to travel beside the Colorado and avoid the appallingly long and apparently waterless extension of the Esplanade that still separated me from the cache I had hidden just below the rim near Bass Camp.

(As far as I knew, this terrace was without any natural water source; but halfway along, just below the rim at Apache Point, I had put out my only other cache, and it included four gallons of water.)

The idea of pioneering a route down Fossil Canyon had attracted me at least as much as the practical advantages, and for three days, based on my airdrop camp, I walked and scrambled and climbed and inched my way down and along and then back and along and then across and up and along an endless succession of terraces and ledges and cliffs. Twice I followed tapering cliff-face cracks until I was out in places I should never have been. And there was one talus slope I hope some day to forget. On the third evening, I came back to camp exhausted. My left hand was a throbbing pin cushion: in a

sudden moment of fear, on a sloping rock ledge strewn with rub-
ble, I had grabbed blindly for a handhold and found a prickly pear.
And for the third straight day, I had failed to find a break in the
Redwall cliff that is Fossil Canyon's major barrier.

It was as I lay in my mummy bag waiting for dinner to cook that
I realized that by concentrating on the reconnaissance I had lost
sight of why I had come down into the Canyon. Once the idea had
occurred to me, the stupidity of the mistake became quite clear.
And I decided that I would rest for two days beside the large rain
pocket at the head of Fossil Bay—the rain pocket that had been the
proper alternate drop site—and then strike out along the terrace
toward Bass Camp.

The decision was the real turning point.

I do not mean that I discovered at once the things I had come
to find. But from then on, I moved steadily toward them. Moved
closer to rock and sky, to light and shadow, to space and silence.
Began to feel their rhythms.

Of course, the change did not appear clear-cut. If you had
asked me almost any time during the week how the journey was
progressing, I would have answered, I think, with reports on water
supply and condition of feet and quantity of food left and distance
remaining to the next cache. These were still the things I measured
progress by. Most of the time, anyway.

On this important and insistent level, the week was a period of
steady and straightforward physical progress. I rested as planned for
almost two full days beside the deep rain pocket at the head of Fossil
Bay, then struck south. The terrace that led to Bass Camp was four
times as long as the one I had barely managed to complete on that
first Butchart test day to Sinyala Canyon, and even with my halfway
cache at Apache Point, it looked as if it would be the toughest leg
so far. But now I was ten days better tuned, and the operation went
off exactly according to plan.

I left the head of Fossil Bay in the cool of evening, as I usually
do when a long day lies ahead. I carried three gallons of water and
camped barely two hours out. By six o'clock next evening I had
crossed the precipitous head of Forster Canyon—a barrier that wild

burros cannot pass, and which marks the eastern limit of the bighorn country; just as the amphitheater under Great Thumb Mesa marks its western limit. At nightfall, I camped close under Apache Point, on the first map-marked trail since Supai. This Apache Trail, though betraying no hint of human use, turned out to be a busy burro turnpike (the burros are the National Park's unpaid trail maintenance crew), and I made good time along it. By noon the next day, I had reached and found unharmed the five gallon can of supplies and the four gallons of bottled water that formed my cache at Apache Point. (I arrived with only sixty-five cc of water left, but the situation was much less critical than it sounds: before climbing the steep, thousand-foot talus slope below the cache I had lightened my load by drinking most of the quite adequate supply left in my canteens.) In the cool of that evening, I carried three gallons of water back down to the terrace and camped. Next day, I broke the back of the long, zigzag, burro-trail swing around Aztec Amphitheater. And by ten o'clock on the fourth morning after leaving Fossil Bay, I was standing on Bass Trail with half a gallon left in my canteens and luxuriating in the comfortable knowledge that the Bass Camp cache lay only a thousand vertical feet above. The week's physical progress was as simple and straightforward as that. The deeper progress of these days was even more satisfying—but neither so simple nor so straightforward. It came erratically and hesitantly, so that later I remembered the week less as a steady stream of events than as a montage of moments.

They often came, these moments, quite unexpectedly.

About ten o'clock on the morning after I had abandoned the Fossil Canyon reconnaissance, I was breaking my airdrop camp in leisurely fashion for the move to the head of Fossil Bay when I noticed a small, green-speckled lizard move speculatively out from a crack in the red rock. Jerkily, with many interrogatory genuflections, it investigated my toothbrush. Then it strolled across my outspread washcloth, mounted the stone that was holding it down, closed its eyes, and basked. I went quietly about my business. Quarter of an hour, and the lizard opened its eyes. A minute passed before it moved; but when it did, it no longer strolled. It flicked forward; halted; inspected the world; riveted its attention on a shrub; rocketed toward it; leaped. The leap carried it a full five inches off the ground. At least, I received the impression of a five-inch jump. But all I really saw was a blur—and then a re-landed lizard smacking its lips and looking very pleased with itself and obviously more than ready for another fly if one should be so ill-advised as to settle within jumping range.

Now, every sunlit desert morning has a magic moment. It may come at five o'clock, at seven, or at eleven, depending on the weather and the season. But it comes. If you are in the right mood at the right time, you are suddenly aware that the desert's countless cogs have meshed. That the world has crystallized into vivid focus. And you respond. You hold your breath or fall into a reverie or spring to your feet, according to the day and the mood.

The leaping lizard heralded

---

*I*t is remarkable how soon the world fades into complete oblivion, and this rock-bound solitude is the only existence which seems real.

I once spent ten days on the plateau. At the end of the week, I had forgotten the names of my most intimate friends, and on the ninth day, I spent several minutes trying to recall my own name. I was so insignificant a part of those terrific silences, to have a name hardly seemed worthwhile.

One could forget a great sorrow here in a month.

◆

—Winifred Hawkridge Dixon, "Westward Hoboes," excerpted from *Grand Canyon Deeps* by Benjamin J. Kimber

---

such a moment. I do not mean that anything very dramatic happened. A waspish-banded fly took a hovering look at my nylon rope, then snapped away into invisibility. A butterfly landed on one of my red socks. A hummingbird buzzed the sock and the butterfly flickered, vanished. The hummingbird cased the orange parachute, rejected it, up-tailed away to nearby bush, and perched there with constant nervous quivering of its violet-banded neck.

That was all, I suppose. That, and a sharpening of the sunlight, a thickening of wind-borne scents, or perhaps, a deeper vibration somewhere down in the silence. But I know that all at once, standing there on the red rock terrace, still watching the lizard, I was knife-edged alive.

It did not last, of course. They cannot last, these climax moments. In five minutes or ten or thirty, the heat begins. Gently at first, it clamps down on the desert, stifling the day's vitality. And you sink back from your peak of awareness. In a little while, that sunlit morning on the red rock terrace, I sank slowly and sadly back; but afterward, all through the two days I rested beside the big rain pocket at the head of Fossil Bay, I remained aware of simple things that trivia had been smothering. I stood in silence beneath the curving harmony of three huge sandstone boulders. I wondered what lived down a tiny vertical shaft in hot red sand. I even found myself really listening—to a piercing, intermittent blast so like a referee's whistle that it kept stopping me in my tracks; and to a soft, contemplative warble that repeated, endlessly: "Years and years and years and years and years…."

When I saw another bighorn sheep—clear and sharp this time, in sunlight, and quite close—I realized that I had come to understand something about the lives of these graceful and dignified creatures. I am not talking now about hard zoological facts. Nor even about such practical information as that these nimble-footed individualists are mediocre trailmakers. (Their most heavily used highway never amounted to much more than a suggestion that a couple of little bighorns might have passed that way in Indian file about the time of Custer's last stand.) I am thinking of less tangible matters.

During my reconnaissance of Fossil Canyon, cloven tracks in rain-smoothed sand pockets had shown me that bighorns travel by preference along the brinks of precipices. I had discovered too that they choose their hideouts, or at least their habitual lying-down places, far out along perilously inaccessible rock ledges. Most of the heavily patrolled precipices and all the hideouts commanded magnificent, sweeping panoramas of the kind that no man can look at unmoved. After a day or two, it occurred to me that bighorns' choice might be no coincidence; and the more I thought about it, the more difficult I found it to avoid the idea that these dignified animals appreciate scenic beauty.

During the two days' rest at the head of Fossil Bay, I even found myself looking differently at inanimate objects. Brooding over the map, I found that instead of worrying only about the way ahead, I was reading history. The map—a work of art as well as an astonishingly accurate cartographic document—eased me, step by step, into the past.

The survey which produced the map was begun in 1902 by one François Matthes and was finally completed in 1923. I could grasp this date firmly: I was born in 1922. Stanton Point carried me back around the turn of the century: in 1889 and 1890, Robert Brewster Stanton was first a member and then the leader of two survey parties that investigated a part of the Colorado on behalf of an optimistic railroad company, and lost three men by drowning within six days; not altogether surprisingly, he failed to convince anyone that they should build a railroad through the Canyon. I map-dreamed on, and Bass Trail and Hance Trail took me back another decade: in the late 1880s and early 1890s, two miners named William Bass and John Hance, quite independently and in different parts of the Canyon, began to turn from mining to dude wrangling and so begat the local tourist industry. Other place names recalled key figures in the Canyon's white-man history: Powell Plateau honors the one-armed Major John Wesley Powell who in 1869 led the river party that forced the first passage of the Canyon and who later became director of the United States Geological Survey; and Ives Point commemorates the efforts of Lieutenant Joseph Christmas Ives, who in 1857 led the first government exploration of the area. And Cárdenas Butte was obviously named for García López de Cárdenas, one of Coronado's captains, who led the party that "discovered" the Canyon in October 1540.

Other names on the map probed back more deeply, though less obviously, into time. A man who gave buttes and pinnacles such names as Vishnu Temple and Krishna Shrine and Tower of Ra and Wotans Throne had clearly been moved to feelings beyond the here and now. But religion is not the only mystery that can move a man. Near the head of Bass Trail lay Darwin Plateau. From its northern rim ran Huxley and Spencer terraces. And between them, sure enough, nestled Evolution Amphitheater. As I brooded over the map, there beside the rain pocket at the head of Fossil Bay, it seemed to me that these last names were the ones that carried the heaviest load of meaning.

Sometimes now I found myself thinking, quite specifically, about the longer time spans.

From the earliest planning days, I had expected that as I walked I would ponder a great deal about the rock. After all, the Canyon is above everything else a geological phenomenon. But it had not happened this way. The rock had always been there, but by and large, my eyes had seen only its surface. Had seen only route and obstacle, shape and shadow, or at the most, magnificent sculpture. Back on the Esplanade, even a striking example of a toadstool rock had seemed little more than an oddity, a chance photogenic freak. I had seen, in other words, only static things, not imprints of a flowing process.

For stimulation along the way, I had put in my pack a small paperback book on geology, but in the first two weeks there had been no time to do more than glance at it. But now, resting beside the big rain pocket at the head of Fossil Bay, I began to read.

Perhaps the book was one reason why, as I bathed one morning in the water from the rain pocket, standing in warm and soothing sunshine, I noticed that I had a shell-patterned bathroom wall. The big white boulder had broken away quite recently, I saw, from the cliffs above. Less than a million years ago, certainly. Probably no more than a few hundred thousand years ago. Perhaps it had even fallen since that yesterday in which García López de Cárdenas and his party stood awestruck on the rim. And as I stood wet and naked in the sunshine, looking down at the shells that were now fossils (they looked exactly like our modern cockleshells), I found myself understanding, vividly and effortlessly, that they had once been the homes of sentient, breathing creatures that had lived out their lives on a dark and ancient ocean floor and in the end had died there. Slowly, year after year, their empty shells had been buried by the minute specks that are always settling to the floor of any ocean (specks that are themselves often the shells of tiny creatures that have also lived and felt and died). For a moment, I could visualize this drama quite clearly, even though what had once been the slowly building ocean floor was now 400 feet of solid limestone high above my head, gleaming white in the desert sunlight. I could feel the actuality so clearly that the wetness of that ancient ocean was almost as real to me as the wetness of the water on my body. I could not comprehend in any meaningful way when all this had happened, for I knew that those shells in my bathroom wall had lived and died 200 million years before I came to wash beside them: and 200 million years, I had to admit, still lay beyond my grasp. But after the moment

> This incredible pageantry of sunlight and chasm, I thought, is our nearest approach to fourth-dimensional scenery. The three dimensions are on such a scale that some of the fourth has been added. You do not see, hung before you, the seven million years that went to making of these walls and their twisted strata, but you feel that some elements of Time have been conjured into these immensities of Space....
>
> ◆
>
> —J. B. Priestley, "Midnight on the Desert," excerpted from *Grand Canyon Deeps* by Benjamin J. Kimber

of understanding had passed, as it soon did, I knew with certainty that in its own good time the Canyon would show me the kind of geology I had hoped to find.

The evening I struck south from Fossil Bay, the look and challenge of the terrace that stretched out ahead, on and on, inevitably screwed my mind back to the present. Two hours out, as night fell, I camped—because it happened at that moment to become too dark to go on—beside a dead juniper tree. "Damn!" my notebook complained. "Back to the press, press, press. Back to Butcharting."

But by nine o'clock the next morning, I had covered half the straight-line distance between Fossil and Apache, and the pressure began to ease. Then, as I swung around an outcrop and for the first time that morning came to the very lip of the terrace, I stopped in my tracks.

Since leaving Supai, I had glimpsed the Colorado only briefly, a short segment at a time, framed deep in the V of a side canyon. It had remained remote, cut off from my terrace world. But now there opened up at my feet a huge and unexpected space. On the floor of this space, 3,000 feet below, flowed the river. It flowed directly toward me, uninterrupted, down the long and arrowlike corridor of a tremendous gorge.

The whole colossal scene was filled and studded and almost ignited by the witchery of desert sunlight, and the gorge no longer looked at all a terrible place. Compared with the gloomy chasm in which I had made my reconnaissance, it seemed broad and open and inviting. Now the Colorado no longer swirled brown and sullen; its bright blue surface shone and sparkled. And although the river lay far below me, I found that it no longer existed in a totally different world.

Yet, because of the size and the beauty and the brilliance of this magnificent unexpected view, I felt in that first moment on the lip of the terrace something of the shock that had overwhelmed me when I first stood, a year earlier, on the rim of the Canyon. It even seemed that, once again, I was meeting the silence—the silence I thought I had grown accustomed to—as something solid, face to face. And just for a moment, I felt once more the same understanding and acceptance of the vast, inevitable sweep of geological time.

The understanding did not last, of course. I was too firmly embedded that morning in the hours and the minutes (though I stayed for almost an hour, gazing at and then photographing that stupendous corridor, which the map calls Conquistador Aisle). But when I walked on eastward again—hurrying a little now, to make up for lost time—I remembered that moment of shock when I first saw the corridor open up in front of me. And I knew that, like the shell pattern in my bathroom wall, the moment had been a promise.

There is something of a gap, then, in my montage of moments. For the next two days, in unbroken sunshine and growing heat, it was all yard and mile, minute and hour; zig and then zag again along terrace and talus, terrace and talus, terrace and talus; a scrambling, sweaty climb to Apache Point; the long swing around Aztec Amphitheater. But the cool of each evening was an intermission.

The first of these nights I camped—again because that was where I happened to run out of daylight—beside a big juniper tree. As I went to sleep, black branches curved up and over against the stars. The next night, I once more camped beside a juniper tree. This time, I camped there because it grew on the brink of a precipice that promised magnificent moonlight vistas. I lit no fire, so that nothing would block me off from the night. And before I went to sleep, I sat and watched the promised vistas materialize, gloriously, and felt the hours of sweat and effort sink back and away.

The third night, I stumbled on one of those strokes of luck that you seem almost able to count on when things are going well.

I had not actually run short of water, but by dusk, I was conscious that I would have to drink a little sparingly until I reached my Bass Camp cache, sometime the next day. Then, as the burro trail I was following skirted a smooth shelf of rock, I saw out of the corner of my eye what seemed in the failing light to be a glint of dampness. I stopped, took two paces backward. Nothing more. I drew a finger across the dampness. For a moment there was a causeway of dry rock. Then moisture had welled over again, slowly but without hesitation, and erased it.

I held my breath and listened. A rhythmic rippling of silence, barely perceptible. I climbed down a few feet of layered rock below the dampness and found, sure enough, a little overhang; and when I put a cooking pot beneath it, the metallic and monotonous drip, drip, drip of the single drops of water made beautiful and moving music.

I camped ten feet from the seep, beside a white-flowering bush that overhung a precipice. From my bedside, the bush framed with Japanese delicacy an immense blue-black pit that was filled not so much with shapes as with suggestions of shapes—gargantuan shapes that would have been deeply disturbing if I had not known by heart now exactly what they meant.

That night, again, I lit no fire. And as I was waiting for dinner to cook—cut off from the silence, inside the roaring world of my little stove—I watched the evening sky grow dark. Slowly the darkness deepened. But the blue-black pit below me remained blue-black. Began, even, to cease back from the brink of blackness. For as the last daylight sank away, the moon took over, casting shadows at new angles, constructing new shapes, warding off the blackness with a new and cool and exquisitely delicate blue.

When I took dinner off the stove, I found myself looking at the fire ring, shining red-hot out of the darkness. Found myself, unexpectedly, appreciating that it too was a thing of beauty and value. And when I turned off the stove, I heard all around me, as always happens, the sudden and surprising silence.

While I ate dinner, with the silent blue-black pit opening up below me, I found myself savoring the sense of newness and expectancy that now came with every step of my journey—the always-moving-forward that now filled each day of my life. Soon, I began to contemplate the clock that measured this daily progress; and all at once I was feeling, as if I had never understood it before, the swing and circle of the sun. Sunrise and sunset; sunrise and sunset; sunrise again; and then sunset. It happened everywhere, of course, all over the Earth. But now I could detect in the beat of that rhythm an element I had never felt before. Now, I could feel the inevitability of it. An inevitability that was impersonal and terrifying and yet, in the end, comforting. And as I sat looking out over the huge and mysterious blue-black space, it occurred to me that the pioneers who crossed the American prairies in their covered wagons must have felt, many days out from sight of mountains, the power of this ceaseless rhythm. For them, the understanding would have been generated by the monotony of the plains. For me it had something to do with the colossal sameness of the Canyon; but that was a sameness not of monotony but of endless repeated yet endlessly varied pattern. A prodigal repetition of terrace mounting on terrace mounting on terrace, of canyon after canyon after canyon after canyon. All of them, one succeeding the other, almost unknown to man, just existing, existing, existing. There seemed at first no hope of a beginning, no hint of an end. But I knew now, more certainly and more easily, that the regularity and the existence were not really timeless. I knew they were echoing reminders of a time, not so very long ago, before the coming of the noisy animal, when the earth was a quiet place.

When I had finished my dinner, I lay still and listened to the silence. To the silence and to the music of the water splashing metronomically down into my cooking pot. Before I fell asleep — warm and comfortable inside my mummy bag, passively at ease now inside the silence and darkness — I knew that at last I stood on the threshold of the huge natural museum that is Grand Canyon.

You cannot, of course, enter such a museum without preparation. It is not a mere place of knowledge. It is not really a place at all, only a state of understanding. As I lay in the darkness, staring up at the stars and hearing how the silence was magnified by the drip, drip, drip of water, I knew that after all my days of effort and silence and solitude, I was almost ready at last to move inside the museum.

But a journey is always, before anything else, a physical thing.

By ten o'clock next morning, I had begun to climb up Bass Trail toward my cache. In his note with the airdrop, Ranger Jim Bailey had said that he might be able to check whether I had found the cache. But I knew that he would hardly come down into the Canyon to look for me: it would be like combing Africa for Livingstone, and no natives to question. I climbed up the steep trail, watching the red terrace unfold below, watching it grow less red with distance and more and more orange. I turned onto the last twisting stretch of trail before my cache. And then all at once, there was an animal, coming down toward me. A broad, green animal. A large animal, walking upright.

My voice sounded strange. It was the first time I had heard it in two weeks.

"Mr. Stanley, I presume," it said.

"Well, I'll be damned!" said Jim Bailey.

Colin Fletcher was born in Wales and educated in England. He lived in Kenya, Zimbabwe, and Canada before moving to California in 1956. Soon afterward, he spent a summer walking from Mexico to Oregon across California's deserts and mountains. Later, he became the first man known to have walked the length of Grand Canyon National Park within the canyon's rim. Each of these feats generated a book: The Thousand-Mile Summer *and* The Man Who Walked Through Time, *from which this story was excerpted. He continues to explore and write books:* The Complete Walker *(revised four times),* The Secret Worlds of Colin Fletcher, *and* River: One Man's Journey Down the Colorado, Source to Sea.

*

At Point Sublime—midway in the Canyon—you can see everything.

Every other viewpoint is inevitably compared with the perspective at Point Sublime, and every other viewpoint is found wanting. Each has its special signature, and many are better than Sublime for this effect or that. But Sublime has everything, and it has it all the time. It is the universal Canyon overlook. So effective is it at orchestrating Canyon scenery that it almost loses its own identity, and that may be its unique attribute. At Sublime, the Kaibab becomes vanishingly small. The rim is reduced to an infinitesimal presence, like a mathematical point. You see the Canyon as though suspended over the brink. The sweep of the Canyon matches the sweep of the sky. At sunrise, it appears as a great lake of shadows that breaks up into shafts of sunlight and glowing rock. At noon, it is clear and still and sunburned with Canyon colors. At sunset, it presents two panoramas from a common vantage point, one with the sunset and the other against it, as shadows sweep like ether around butte and gorge, and the sun and moon move in a minuet of light and space. At Point Sublime, there is only the Canyon, and a Beyond—an enormous tableland that stretches to mountains that appear blue and purple along empty horizons beneath an endless sky.

> —Stephen J. Pyne, *Fire on the Rim: A Firefighter's Season at the Grand Canyon*

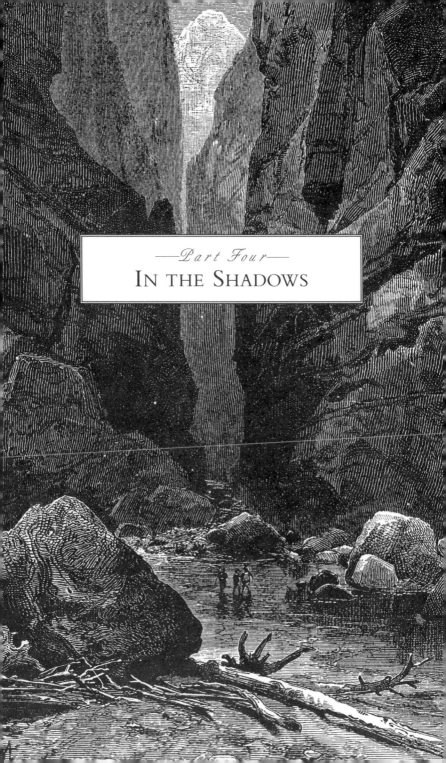

—*Part Four*—
IN THE SHADOWS

⁕

Flash Flood

*On the Colorado River, everything
can change in an instant.*

It seemed just like any other day at Havasu, except the air
was cool and it was early August. I was on an oar trip with
Wilderness, and we pulled three snouts, two canyons, and a Maravia
into the mouth of Havasu and tied up. Down at the lower pull-in
were two Wilderness motor rigs and two Western motor rigs. A
private trip pulled in and tied up two boats deep in the mouth and
used our boats as a bridge. Nine kayaks and a canoe were able to
squeeze by all the boats and skinny through the six-foot slot to
paddle to their own private dry dock near the first waterfall 100
yards upstream.

We got all the passengers off the boats and assembled them on
shore to get their premade lunches for the all-day Beaver hike we
had planned. Some of the boatmen looked up Havasu Canyon and
saw a few scattered clouds, but only enough to remind you that a
flash flood is a possibility. Okie was in charge and made a hard call
due to less than perfect weather. The Beaver hike was changed to
a one hour up to the first pools and back, and then early to camp
to play volleyball. Tony Anderson had made a similar call and
already had his people coming back from a quick visit to the pools.
Western had pulled in early and had people well on their way to

Beaver. This typical, pleasantly sunny day was about to change dramatically.

After a brief visit with the Wilderness boys at the lower pull-in, myself and a few other Wilderness boatmen returned to the boats in the mouth to grab some food, water, and shade, along with some of the nonhiking passengers. I lay down on my ice chest and stared up at the clouds that were moving very quickly but provided decent patches of shade to my boat in the sun.

Just then, a distant roar started to turn my ears up like a deer noticing a strange sound. The roar got louder and soon revealed its identity as distant thunder. I looked over at a passenger who was watching my peculiar paranoia, and I lay back down. Just moments later, another low-frequency roar began, except this time it was up Havasu Canyon and was slowly getting louder—and rhythmic. It was a helicopter 100 feet off of the Havasu Canyon floor coming down the canyon. For two seconds, I wondered what the hell the chopper was doing, and then I saw a hand making a wave-like motion much like splashing water in a pool. I screamed over the choppers roar along with four other boatmen. "FLASH FLOOD! EVERYBODY OUT!!! OUT, OUT, EVERYBODY OUT!! NOW!!"

It was mass confusion. Some people thought that we meant get on the boats to leave. Parents ran around looking for their children. One parent came up to me as I was screaming at his son, who was deep in the mouth of the pull-in spot, trying to get the vest that was blown into the water from the chopper. He finally heard the panic in our voices and left the life jacket in the water and ran across the boats.

With everybody off the boats, everything seemed strangely calm. What do we do?, I thought as I looked at the eight perfectly calm boats sitting in the mouth. Is this a two-minute warning or a twenty-minute warning? Should we cut the boats loose? Is this a debris flow or just a mild flood? If we have even three minutes, we can get some of these boats out of here. It felt like what I imagined to be a bomb on its way to destroy the boats.

Since two of the boats were almost completely out of the mouth of the canyon, it seemed to make sense to try and move one at a time out of the main path of the imminent water. It didn't make sense at the time to cut the boats loose because we didn't know what was coming—since it was high water, maybe the lake that was there in the mouth would slow down a small flood. Standing on those boats and untying them felt like having a shoelace caught on a train track, with a train coming full speed. We were deeply aware of anything that might indicate the water being near, and none of us would commit to going into the mouth where there was no immediate escape route up the sheer 25-foot walls. We managed to untie one of the boats and positioned it in the current of the main river—about 30 feet downstream from what is considered to be the mouth. We went back to get the second boat, and then we heard the horrible sounds—absolutely terrifying. The sounds were not of the water, but of people way upstream screaming in terror and warning those downstream. Okie and I were in the mouth and stopped what we were doing. We sat there frozen for about ten seconds listening to the yelling and screaming getting closer.

And then, there it was. It seemed to be coming down the canyon at automobile speeds. I had always envisioned a flash at Havasu to be a wall of muddy water crashing through the canyon with reckless abandon, but this moving water was smooth and beautifully blue. It came like a wave on the ocean, 5- to 6-feet tall, perfectly smooth, with about a 45 degree angle to it. As the wave moved into the narrowest part near the boats, the water instantly stood up and filled the 6-foot-wide slot completely to the top of the cliffs with about an 80-degree, if not perfectly vertical, 10-foot wall of blue water. Within seconds Okie and I were on the safe ledge we had chosen as the escape route, and we watched the carnage happen.

All the ropes seemed to snap at once like popcorn well into the popping stage. One of the boats that was tied to a "bomber" tie off, resisted the current for about three seconds, flipped onto another raft, and slid back into the water upside down snapping a D-ring off. Oars were swinging everywhere as eight boats pulled out at the same time on the new muddy water pushing them. Trees and kayaks stuck up out of the water like daggers between rafts from all the congestion. One log about 30 feet long was somehow lifted into a vertical position from all the debris and constriction, and glanced off one of the boats when it crashed back down again.

There was a hellacious vortex of water where the Havasu water met the Colorado, that violently shook and turned the boats as they exited the mouth. The rafts floated out in the current and underneath the chopper hovering over the Colorado. The flow seemed to be about 90 percent water and about 10 percent wood, and we began to wonder what to do if we saw any people or bodies. An occasional life jacket, or piece of clothing would surface and then submerge again—causing an instinctual urge to jump into the river to help. All we could do was watch for people and watch our boats go downstream.

The chopper pilot, Michael Moore, had saved the day. His warning was all that was needed to get everyone to high ground. Apparently, he saw the flood coming way upstream and broke some rules of radio contact and flight zones, and went on the warning mission. You could easily argue that he saved a dozen lives that day.

Everyone was running around wondering what to do. Pat Phillips thought it wise to jump onto one of the Western boats that had already snapped one of two *Queen Mary* bowlines because of the newly introduced current from Havasu. The upstream pontoon was about 70 percent underwater, and the water actually ripped away one of the kitchen boxes tied on the side of the raft. The Western boat was a smart place to be to watch for people, since everything that came out of the mouth either crashed into or went underneath those boats. Okie, the lead on the Wilderness trip, started calling everyone together to count heads and see what the next step was. The one snout that was moved out of the mouth was still there in the current, but was stressing the rope to its limit. There was a feeling that the trip was definitely over—that there was no way we could recover a trip from this situation. Several minutes had passed at this point, and it seemed apparent that the chopper had done its job—there were no bodies that day.

It seemed pointless to just sit there and watch the remaining snout break away and go downstream, so Pat and I carefully boarded the boat. The line was so tight it was unapproachable. Brett Starks cut the line at the tie off point with just a touch of a dull Gerber Shorty knife. Pat and I were catapulted like an accelerating sports car into the current and bounced off the Western boats we couldn't avoid. We had a few ideas of how we might pull some of the boats to shore, but we were hoping that T. A. and his motorboats didn't go too far for lunch, since the oar boats were several minutes ahead of us.

At the mouth, the chaos had just begun. One of the passengers on the private trip was in the water near the first pools when the flood hit and was rammed in the ribs by a log. Unable to pull herself out of the current, she screamed for help. Patrick (Mowgli—the ex-Marine) was there and helped her to higher ground. A quick assessment revealed not much more than some possible broken ribs, and an embarrassed need for Mowgli's shirt.

Near the first crossing spot, one of the passengers, struck with fear, interpreted "get to high ground" as "scale the cliffs." Climbing in panic, the softspoken band teacher soon realized he had climbed too far and froze 60 feet up on the cliff on a narrow ledge. Matt Penrod, an experienced climber, began an hour and a half rescue with a harness and some climbing equipment he acquired from the Park Service that had recently landed to assess the situation at the river—things were mild compared to the 600 people stranded upstream near the Havasu village, and the Park Service could only help so much. Matt scaled the 5.8−5.9 cliff to the stranded climber and was able to assist in a 30-foot down climb to a spot where a harness could be used to lower the passenger.

Upstream near Beaver Falls, a dozen or so passengers began a series of harrowing chopper flights through the canyon to get back to the boats. One of the Western boatmen made an impossible trek along the talus to get back to the boats for help and information.

Down on the Colorado River, T. A., Christen, Aaron, and Katie came to the rescue of the boats. They had the difficult task of pushing the boats to shore, while driving in a bog of driftwood and debris. Pat and I met up with T. A. just as he had pulled all the boats ashore. We righted the flipped raft and began making triple rigs with the boats for a speedy trip down to Tuckup. At this point, we were asked by the Park Service over the radio if we could continue the trip. Amazingly, we accounted for every boat, including kayaks, and gave the Park Service the thumbs up for our ability to continue. Two Western boats, who were unable to pull in because of the flash, met up with T. A. and took on the responsibility of transporting the equipment for the private trip. The brigade of oar boats tied to motorboats quickly drove down to Tuckup and met up with Jason and Mike on the Wilderness support boat, who had also been rescuing kayaks and equipment. Every boat downstream had kayaks filled with driftwood on board.

With all boats at Tuckup, T. A. and the Western boats went downstream to continue their trips. And there we sat—setting up a kitchen, a chopper pad, and listening to the aircraft radio—eighteen boats, four crew members and 45 people upstream.

Hours passed, and at Havasu the stream slowly began to diminish. Some spots became crossable with the assistance of life jackets, some strong shoulders, and lines strung across the river. The whole process of getting everyone back to the boats was horrendously slow, and people began to approach their limits. To make matters worse, a severe thunderstorm was rolling in and nightfall was approaching. All the Park Service could do was to make a final drop of food supplies and life jackets, and take off into a dark and stormy night. With 90 people rain gear-less and shivering, the crew members made the call to get to Tuckup via the two Western rigs. The boats were heavy and slow and extremely wet from splashing. To make matters worse, walls of rain began dumping on the rafts. The lightning was flashing like a bad discotheque, dozens of waterfalls crashed off every cliff, and the last mile was driven in complete darkness.

At Tuckup, the chaos began again. Ninety people pulled into camp in a horrendous rainstorm, all looking for their bags and equipment strung about like a chaotic yard sale. No one could find anything in all the chaos. The halogen flood lamp and the generator saved the day. With light on the scene and the smell of hot food cooking, people were able to get situated. Some shivering children were quickly taken to the shelter of an overhang and bundled up in dry sleeping bags. With the camp situated, food in our bellies, bodies warmed, and fears behind, ninety people went to bed that night with a memory of a lifetime.

In looking back on that day, I think the most impressive aspect of how everything came together was the reactions of the people involved. Every passenger and crew member rose to meet the occasion. There was no time for judgment or ego. Some people became leaders, some people became invaluable followers. Virtually every decision was logical, and the first priority was always safety. The Park Service was there and gave exactly what help was needed. The chopper pilot made the move that he knew he had to make—rules or no rules, he couldn't have lived with himself had someone died that day.

From a humanistic perspective, I think the most impressive thing that happened that day was that people found that they had limits beyond what they knew about themselves. I think when people are pushed beyond their known limits, a strengthening of spirit occurs and there is a rekindling of what our real values are in life—being alive with loved ones—having a healthy body.

On behalf of everyone involved with that incident, I would like to thank the chopper pilot, Michael Moore, for his brilliant job of warning everyone in Havasu Canyon. I'm sure that there are dozens of incidents deserving of praise and recognition, and I apologize for not being able to include these in this story. My personal view is that the crew members of Western and Wilderness orchestrated a brilliant recovery from that day and that the situation could not have been handled in a better way. The Park Service, as always, fit perfectly into the recovery, and a special thanks should go to all who were there.

Tom Janecek (T. J.) has been a commercial river guide in the Grand Canyon since1986. He resides in Flagstaff, Arizona with his wife Kelly, and his Yellow Labrador Retriever "Crystal" (named after the rapid).

✳

For nearly a century, the Havasupai Reservation had been squeezed into a section of Havasu Canyon, a wedge of 518 acres. The tribe struggled for years to enlarge it. Then in 1975, when the national park was extended to nearly twice its size to include Grand Canyon and Marble Canyon national monuments, the Havasupai won an expansion of 185,000 acres. The increase seems enormous, 350 times bigger than the canyon wedge, but there may be less there than meets the eye. By law, the land must be kept forever wild, restricted mainly to traditional use, essentially grazing. In effect, the Havasupai, numbering more than 600 members, today own the plateau grazing lands they had been using all along with permits from the former owner, the national park.

—Seymour L. Fishbein, *Grand Canyon Country:*
Its Majesty and Its Lore

GAIL GOLDBERGER

Under Lava

This is one place you do
not want to be.

THE DAY HAD BEEN LONG AND HOT, WITH THE SANTA ANA WIND blowing hard from the south, the direction into which we are heading. For most of the afternoon, we had turned our boats around and backstroked downwind. It was easier than pushing ourselves forward, which is how we oared much of the river.

A mile before the rapid, a tall chunk of lava juts out of the middle of the river, like an evil finger warning us away. It is called Vulcans Forge, or Winyataloopa by the Hualapai. We pass and are silenced.

The thundering roar of water sounds the approach to any rapid. Before you reach the point where the current starts to pull you in, it is advisable to pull over to the side and scout the rapid. The flow of rapids changes depending on the volume of water released at the dam, and the deposits of rock and mud that came down from side creeks in storms. By scouting a rapid, you can see how the river runs at any moment and chart your course.

As we tie our boats off to the right, upstream of Lava, other groups are gathered on both sides of the river, scouting and waiting to go. Our crew climbs to a black, rocky rise to watch boats and study the river. We look ahead, evaluating the flow of the rapid, the holes, and the waves. We stare down the whole gnarly run of it.

A few motorized rubber rafts go first and have a buckaroo kind of ride, with people whooping and hollering, some holding on for dear life, some falling into the boat, others leaning over the sides and back with raised beer cans and champagne glasses. Then the group ahead of us prepares to go. They are in George Litton's wide canoes called dories, the only wooden boat company on the river. All the other companies use rubber rafts: either long ones with motors that seat ten to twenty people or shorter ones powered by humans with oars or paddles, like ours. Smaller rafts and wooden dories alike carry only three to four passengers.

We watch as all six dories go through Lava Falls, an extremely long stretch of river that drops 26 feet in 100 yards. The last dory to go enters the rapid just a little too far to the right and careens toward rock litter at the bottom of the rapid. The strongly moving current collides the dory into a steep rock. The dory rides up the side of the rock, spilling people and gear into the river. The dory continues to bob in place, pinned against the rock by the press of the water.

The passengers and gear are caught by other boats. The dory itself remains stuck between the rushing water and the rock, and a call comes upriver for help. All our crew except Mary Lou run down the canyon to try to liberate the boat from the rock. Using rope, and different angles, they try to work the boat up and off the rock. They struggle for at least an hour, and they fail. The force of the steeply dropping rapid is just too great.

As the crew attempts to dislodge the dory, the passengers and trainees from our seven-boat excursion remain behind. Seeing a boat turn over like that puts us deeper into our fear, which has been building not for one day but for ten!

Ken, the other trainee, left the group to walk up a rise over to the right of the beginning of the rapid. When I go to look for him, I find him scrunched under a scrubby tree staring at the rapid to our left and the boat downriver.

"Thinking about going down there to help?" I ask.

"No," Ken says, "I'm too nervous to help."

Together we contemplate the rapid. The most difficult thing about Lava is the point of entry. If you enter too far right of center like the dory did, the river draws you inexorably into rocks at the bottom-right of the rapid. Entry to the left of center is simply not possible, as an enormous wave stretches from the middle of the rapid clear across to the left-hand side of the bank forming a hole, or trough—the wildest trough of water turning back on itself I have ever seen! Like a waterfall, dropping 10 to 12 feet with an equally high wave curling back into it, it stretches left, 30 feet across the river.

Just to the right of the trough is a narrow slot, or bridge, a straightway of sorts, and the safest entry of the rapid. Our boat company, Oars, Inc., has been using the bridge to run Lava successfully for years.

Ken and I stare at the hole, leering at us like a sinister mouth.

"See that trough?" Ken asks, as though I could miss it. "If I saw my boat go in there, I'd jump out to the right to avoid it. I don't think you can get out of that hole."

*T*he way a dory handles is like night and day compared to a raft. Oh, a dory's just so responsive—it breaks the water so beautifully, it pivots so fast, it glides. I mean, you can track in the water and not lose momentum in the wind. But mostly, it's the way a dory feels over waves—instead of just sploshing through them, a dory slices through waves. It feels everything, so it's responding to every up and down. They are just such a joy to row.

There is a downside to the dories. Because of their narrow six-foot beam, they do flip easier than a raft. And if they hit a rock, they tend to crunch. Dory boatmen sometimes scout rapids through binoculars to see the precise shape of waves and to look for chine diggers, rocks just below the surface.

♦

—Louise Teal, *Breaking into the Current: Boatwomen of the Grand Canyon*

Oh great, I think to myself. It's always dangerous to spill into a standing wave, or "curler" as they are called. The force of water turning back on itself can keep you spinning in a circular motion, not putting you down deep enough to swim out beneath the wave, and too powerful to keep you from punching through the wave.

If you get stuck in a "curler" and keep recycling, it is the only time you are advised, as a last-ditch effort, to get rid of your life jacket. Buoyancy works against you, in a case like this, keeping you aloft in the wave. Cutting loose from your jacket is a very risky move, however, as the rest of the rapid awaits you. I think about this as I watch the falls curl.

We slowly head back to our boats, feet pressing into the black gravel trail. It is 6 p.m., over 100 degrees, and even our strong, amazingly capable crew must be tired.

Tired myself of waiting, I busy myself back at the boats, rearranging gear, packing loose items away. I tighten my life jacket and rummage through a rubber sack for Coke, to greet the returning crew. Five minutes later, I put the cans away. They'll be too warm if I leave them out any longer. Everything in the boat looks secure. I chat with the other women.

Our crew straggles back. Matter-of-factly, the first group of three boats prepares to leave. The trainee boat pulls out with this group. Earlier that day, I succumbed to fear and decided to change boats. I wanted to ride through Lava with a certified guide—I wanted to ride through with Tom—I felt secure with him. Mary Lou was rowing the trainee raft, and I remembered our backwards run through Upset Rapid. Mary Lou was flustered when I asked to change boats and said she wished I would come with her as she could use the extra weight. By the time she pushed off to run Lava with Kim and Ken on either side of her, she seemed confident, unconcerned.

The long wait has made me anxious, and I feel depleted, but I especially want to see how the trainee boat fares. I run downriver, back up the blackened rise kicking sand, and watch. Neusom goes first, rides precisely over the "bridge," and then is in it! The edge of the trough catches the underside of his left oar, popping it out of its oarlock. In a millisecond, he shoots up and pounds it back into place, meanwhile navigating and steering with his right oar. He remains standing and pulls hard on both oars, and his raft jettisons through the deepest holes and highest waves on the entire river. The holes and waves are very close together and must be pulled through rapidly and strongly. He makes it and we all cheer wildly.

Mary Lou goes next. My heart is pounding. She is oaring the raft in which I have traveled most of the river. She places well also, though a little to the left. She pulls quickly on the right oar and rides smoothly over the bridge. Boatwomen are often great technical navigators. They have to make up for less muscle with more agility and accuracy. They need to steer the boat to the right place and react quickly if they don't. They can't rely on being able to "power" themselves out of trouble with strong upper bodies.

"Pull, Mary Lou," I scream, "pull!" She almost glides through, has a beautiful run. So much for lack of confidence in my own sex and a fellow trainee.

Bruce follows next, but by now I race back. The second group of boatmen are preparing to go. As Tom readies our boat, I see that his head and shoulders are hanging down. He looks tired. Three passengers and I arrange ourselves across the front. I sit all the way to the right. By taking myself out of the trainee boat, I

*U*nique in so many ways, the Canyon has its own 10-point rating system for the rapids. "Generally," said boatman Jeff Schloss, "Canyon ratings are about twice what they would be on the national 6-point scale." In contrast to small white-water streams that require constant maneuvering, Jeff said, "the Colorado is a big, pushy river, with the entrances to the rapids very important, and there's not much maneuvering once you get in."

◆

—Seymour L. Fishbein, *Grand Canyon Country: Its Majesty and Its Lore* add extra weight to Tom's boat. No one complains. I'll never know if it mattered. Tom stuffs loose gear away.

Earlier that afternoon, under the slim shade of a tree, Tom confided to me that he hated running big rapids late in the day, after oaring hard for so many hours in the heat. Canyon temperatures in August reach 100 during the day. Winds blow up from the south at 30–35 mph.

"I'm already worn thin," he said. "And I don't like looking at the rapid with the sun at horizon level either."

We are the second of our group of three boats to pull away from shore, and Sam, the trip leader, yells back, "Tom, make sure those folks have their life jackets on good and tight."

Tom leans forward and checks us one by one, pulling back straps to see if they're tight enough. Our boat swings around and moves into the smooth, wide tongue of water that is the approach to the rapid. Tom begins spouting instructions about what to do in case we flip. "Feet out, take deep breaths when you surface, backpaddle, get away from the boat." I've never heard him sound so serious before, so on guard.

We move ahead very slowly into the broad, quiet water. And then, I hear rushing sounds. I look over my shoulder at Tom, whose eyes strain fixedly ahead. They look wild, open extrawide to take everything in. I feel the fear in him, and in me. I'm holding the ropes of the raft tighter than I've ever held anything in my life.

Tom yells, "There's our first mark!" We sail over a trail of little bubbles and a smooth edge of water and then…we're sliding down a chute at about a 70 degree angle.

We are face to face with a massive wall of water curling back at us. Are we in the trough? I wonder. In a fraction of a second, I realize there is no way we are going to punch through this wave like we have punched through other standing waves. It is higher than our boat is long, and way too wide. Our angle is too steep, we entered the rapid too far to the left. We are in the trough!

In a moment that stretches before me like an hour, the boat flips, ever so slowly, over my shoulder, left to right. Swearing to myself, Oh, shit!, I kick away from the boat hard, with a presence of mind that surprises me. My leg grazes something, the boat probably, and I am free, away from the boat.

I tumble over and over in the water. I have swum rapids before, and I usually feel in control. But not here, not now. I come up for air and am immediately dashed underwater again, tossed this way and that. I am unaware of forward, backward, right side up or upside down. I think about thrusting my legs forward like I'm supposed to, but can't.

I emerge a second time and get ready to gulp a breath of fresh air. I open my eyes and am horrified by a 15-foot standing wave curling over my head. Oh God, I think. Brace yourself! I don't remember getting a breath. I am too stunned by the sight of the wave coming down on me. I am shot straight down like a cannonball in reverse. I am fortunate that this is a deep river and a deep rapid. I hit no rocks, encounter no obstacles, though later I learned that the rapid is strewn with huge boulders. I am shoved way down and straight down. It is all black around me, and still.

Well, this could be it. I might die in this rapid. I have no idea how far down I've been pushed. I'm in the bottom of the worst navigable rapid in North America, and I may drown. The feeling sinks in, and I give in to it at some level. I relax. I am not breathing, nor am I struggling for air.

I am calm, and able for the first time to straighten out my body. I put my feet in front of me and feel that I'm on my back, being carried swiftly forward. Mercifully, I have hit a straightaway in the rapid for I'm no longer being tossed this way and that. I imagine myself coursing downriver, like I'm flying. I open my eyes and spread my arms out wide. I feel very free. And then the blackness of water becomes brown. I keep moving through lighter and lighter shades of brown, and I get excited thinking that this is good. This means I'm getting nearer the surface. I'm suddenly aware of tremendous pressure on my chest. It feels as though two enormous clamps have mysteriously found me and are pulling me up. It is the power of the swiftly moving water meeting the buoyancy of my life vest. I continue to feel powerfully lifted up and, then, out of the water. Oh, my sweet life jacket!

I pop out of the water, slicing through the surface at 20 miles per hour. I see ahead of me a line of choppy standing waves and am grateful. Although each crest and trough are 6–8 feet high, I've swum rapids like these before, feet out in front of me, and I know I can do it. I'm moving fast now, dropping down into the bottom and up and over the crest of the wave. No one is in front of me, and no one can hear me, but every time I slide down and rise over a wave I bellow, "I'm alive, I'm alive, and I'm swimming Lava Falls!"

Tom is behind me now, shouting the name of one of our passengers, "Dale, Dale!" I twist around and yell back. I think he is calling my name. I see him and Mona hanging from the sides of our now upside-down raft. Off to our right and a little in front of us is Chris, bobbing pale green and not looking good. He has had the flu since yesterday. His father is in the raft right behind us and has to watch our boat spill his son in the river.

Dale is nowhere to be seen, so Tom continues to call out her name. It turns out that she went to the right of the rapid, unlike the rest of us who went left, and got picked up by another boat company.

I am in front of Tom, Mona, Chris, and our boat. I can now see downstream. The four rafts in front of ours are off the river to the left, gone to a natural spring to fill our water containers. A call must have gone out when we flipped, for I see people running and boats hurled into the water to try to get to us before we get swept into Little Lava Falls, another big rapid, right below Lava! The current is strong here; I see oars churning and bodies pitching and flailing as they hurry out to catch us.

The rapid carries me right up to the raft. Someone grabs me under my arms and yanks me in. I'm soaked, chilled, and crazed with an odd mixture of fear, gratitude, and exultation. I yell, "Swimming at the Y will never be the same!" (Thank God!)

I never did become a river guide. It was too scary for me, in the end, and too physical. But I learned to read water and steer boats, and later, canoes, all over the Midwest. That was more my speed. I learned a lot about myself and trusting my instincts. Rivers helped me build strength and independence, which I was seeking.

And rivers started me writing. My first poem was born on the banks of the Rogue River in Oregon, the evening of my last trip with the rafting company. Rivers shook my senses awake, and inspired me to begin laying down words.

Lava Falls is no longer the worst rapid on the river. Crystal has that distinction. It changed from a rapid rated #8 to a rapid rated #10 during the flood years, 1983–1984, when the dam released 92,000 cfs to keep Lake Powell from overflowing. The already challenging rapid rearranged itself, becoming longer and adding lateral waves at the head of the rapid to the legendary "Crystal Hole." It can't be gotten through neatly, and there is no bridge to safe passage. They say that prayers, luck, and low water help.

A year later, on my second rafting trip through the Grand Canyon, I huddled around a campfire with river guides from a different rafting company and retold the tale of my first training trip. I can still hear their voices in chorus, "Oh, no, not the Colorado. It's a terrible river to train on. It's too big."

Indeed.

Gail Goldberger, a native of Chicago, works at jobs where writing is her major responsibility. Her swimming is mostly confined to a very unturbulent YMCA pool in Evanston, Illinois.

✳

The Hualapai name for the Colorado River is *Hautata*, which means Backbone of Mother Earth.

—Sylvia Qwerta, Hualapai tribal member

MICHAEL P. GHIGLIERI

✳ ✳ ✳

Jackass Canyon

Sunset waits for no one.

THE CAMP HERE ON THE JACKASS CANYON SIDE OF BADGER CREEK Rapid was a long beach stretching upstream to border the rapid. Scattered in the sand were huge slabs of tan sandstone that had peeled off the cliff thousands of years ago and now looked like the raw material for a do-it-yourself Stonehenge. As I pulled in, clouds of hot sand lifted off the beach and flew back toward Wyoming like horizontal rain, only to be deflected back toward the river by a 700-foot cliff. At its base, in more fallen slabs of Coconino sandstone sand-blasted to silky smoothness, were some beautiful fossil footprints of predinosaurian reptiles.

I stared off the cliff. I had learned a lesson here, but not about footprints. On second thought, footsteps had been important. It was in September. I had just returned to the river after two weeks off—so my "sun clock" for Badger was a month behind. Michael Boyle warned me that I did not have enough daylight to hike everybody out of Jackass Canyon to the plateau, walk them the extra mile to the cliff overlooking this camp, and get them all back down before dark. But because I loved this hike and had just done it successfully a month earlier, I wouldn't listen. Boyle had been right, though; I couldn't pull it off this late in the year.

I had ignored other signs as well. When I gathered everyone for the hike, our three stewardesses asked me to wait while they finished putting on their makeup. Yes, stewardesses—one English, one Irish, and one Greek—for Saudi Arabian Airlines. The kind that we hear about from other trips but never see. But these were the real thing. All were in their twenties, and each had a perfect body. I would soon find out how perfect. They did not need makeup. They were runners. Maybe they ran to escape lusting Arabs.

We also had a seventy-one-year-old German I was worried about, but again I was wrong. At least I was consistent. Herman hiked like Reinhold Messner.

Another sign I ignored also came early, among the garage-sized boulders strewn in the Hermit shale in the first third of the hike, where a couple who wouldn't watch those ahead of them never knew where to go next. They slowed us down, but still I was too stubborn to cut back on my plans.

When I finally got all of them up the rope at the 25-foot waterfall and then on to the assault through the U-shaped canyon in the Coconino, Toroweap, and Kaibab formations, I still thought I had it made.

I made a big mistake right after we zigzagged to the top of the Kaibab and escaped Marble Canyon. Sunlight still burned the Echo Cliffs crimson, but only an hour of light remained. I should have congratulated them and then done an immediate about-face. Instead, I tried to give them everything. I warned them that we were running out of light and *should* head back, but I said that if they hustled the mile out to the rim and back, they would get the view of their lives. Of course, they all went for the view.

But as they marveled at the fantastic view down to Badger Rapid and our camp, I looked back at the Echo Cliffs, and my stomach sank. Direct sunlight had vanished. I rounded up everybody and hurried them back.

We were missing four people. Skip Horner was my only other guide, and this was his first time up here. I asked him to keep everybody moving while I ran back. Mike Anderson, our trainee, said he had tried to get the stewardesses and a woman from New

York to leave, but they had shooed him away to take photographs.

When I got within 50 yards of the drop-off, the Greek with the classic body—who was wearing nothing but her shoes and a camera—motioned me to stop. The other three were naked and posing inches from that 700-foot drop. I regretted not having my own camera. Among other things.

When they saw I was serious about heading back immediately, they reluctantly put on some of their clothes. But when I explained that we were facing at least a part of the descent down Jackass Canyon in the dark, they studied the alpenglow on the cliffs and then gave me looks that said I was being a macho jerk. This irritated me. I told them to get dressed and run back to the descent into Jackass or they would hold up everybody.

The women of the friendly skies surprised me by throwing their clothes on and jogging back. But not the New Yorker. She would not even hurry. Even though we were on the road that a four-year-old could have run, she complained that she might sprain her ankle on a rock. The best I could do was convince her to walk a bit faster.

When we caught up with the group gathered at the head of the canyon, dusk had already made everyone a believer. Their faces asked me how I could have let all this happen. I asked myself the same thing. I needed a plan.

I asked Skip to hightail it down to the boats and hustle back with

---

*F*rom the South Rim at Grand Canyon Village, looking off to the northwest, there is a large, flat-topped formation known as Shiva Temple. Once it is identified for you, it is unmistakable. Thousands of years of erosion have contrived to isolate a large section of what was once a part of the Kaibab Plateau of the North Rim. It is 7,650 feet above sea level, contains a forested area of 6 square miles, and up to 1937, it had never been explored because of its presumably unscalable walls.

◆

—Edwin Corle,
Listen, Bright Angel

every flashlight he could find. Meanwhile, we crawled down, dropping half a mile through the Toroweap and the upper Coconino to the top of the waterfall. By this time, it was nearly dark. I sent Mark down next to the pool at the base of the fall to spot people from the bottom for the last tricky move. One by one, they descended, gripping the rope as if a 1,000-foot drop yawned below them. Old Herman climbed down like a mountain goat. Two really slow people gobbled all the remaining light by inching down in slow motion. The New York Princess was so worried that the only way I could get her to descend at all was to go with her. While exposing myself to a pair of broken legs by jamming my fingers into the cliff and gripping her in case she peeled off, I had alternately sweet-talked her and rough-talked her down the fall. By then it was dark. Real dark. Dark thirty.

We gathered in a little amphitheater below. Every constellation in that narrow slit of sky was crystal clear. Moonrise was not due until just before dawn. People cracked jokes, but they probably had forgotten the potentially lethal exposures in the mile below us. They had never looked back on the way up to see them. Somebody asked me if all our hikes would be like this.

Skip arrived with five flashlights for the seventeen of us. Two were almost dead. Maybe this was just as well; people could see the route in front of their noses but could not aim the beams down the drops and scare the hell out of themselves.

But a funny thing happened. Sharing the flashlights brought everyone together. Within a hundred yards, a stewardess latched onto Herman. Sometimes one held *each* of his hands. The old goat could have outclimbed any of them, but he recognized opportunity knocking. He periodically went helpless to appeal to their maternal instincts. When we got back to Flagstaff two weeks later, he thanked me for the trip, confiding that it was the greatest trip of his life, "especially," he added with a wink, "the *first* hike."

Anyway, we made it back to the fossil footprints and the beach in pitch blackness in less than an hour—amazingly, without a scratch. Not even a prickly pear spine. It was incredible luck, and a cheap lesson.

Still grateful for that smooth escape, I stared at Jackass Canyon but thought now about those fossilized footprints of reptiles. Would a few of our own footprints fossilize here in the Canyon and some-day be discovered by explorers of some strange race of intelligent life curious about the primitive creatures who preceded them? What would they guess that we were doing down here?

Michael Ghiglieri also contributed "The Green Room" to Part One and "Thunder" to Part Two.

*

The morning light reveals a miscellany of human signs. Unpleasant ones. Blackened rocks encircle partially burned debris. Beer cans, pieces of aluminum foil, pop-tops, toilet paper, and cigarette butts lie under low shrubs and are partially hidden behind rocks. The litter is an eyesore and a shock, for most of the Canyon is pristine, even with more than 16,000 people traveling through it each year. Jack Ass Canyon, however, is easily accessible from the outside world, and this camp is often used by people hiking down the side canyon.

—Patricia C. McCairen, *Canyon Solitude: A Woman's Solo River Journey Through Grand Canyon*

CHRISTA SADLER

Blacktail Ghost

There are lessons in the
sounds of the night.

THIS IS A GHOST STORY. I DON'T REALLY BELIEVE IN GHOSTS. AT least, none have ever given me any reason to believe in them. I've heard stories from other boatmen about seeing strange shapes and hearing voices in the wind off the canyon walls. Some even swear that they were chased out of some of the Canyon's Indian ruins by nameless shadows and shapeless figures with ancient voices. Yeah, right. Put the tequila down, guys. I've always been way too practical a person anyway.

It was a dark and stormy night. No kidding. It was 1992, and we were about halfway through a month-long December trip in the Canyon. This was the last third of a three-month river trip we were doing with Prescott College, as part of a field-based natural history class. Andre, Julie, and I were instructors traveling with eleven college students. We'd already been on the river since October 8, 570 miles and about 65 days ago.

We were camped at Blacktail Canyon for the night, Mile 121. Blacktail is my favorite place in the Grand Canyon. It's like a church to me. It has always been a welcoming place, if a little aloof. For years now, my river company has made a practice of doing a silent hike up the narrow, twisting side canyon. This is good, because if

225

you spend your time talking, before you know it you've walked the quarter mile to the end, and you haven't really seen anything all that unusual. But if you're quiet, the walls close in and surround you. They're plum-colored Tapeats sandstone, and they look like they bend in over your head, so that only a narrow strip of sky remains. It's absolutely still in that place, and drops of water fall with a resounding noise into the pools that you pick your way over and around. Sometimes a canyon wren sings, or thunder rumbles over the North Rim, and it sounds like it's coming right out of the walls. This is where I sing, where the string quartet plays, where any boatman with a guitar comes to make special music.

It was raining pretty hard by the time we finished dinner, and the students all retreated to their tents in the patches of soft sand scattered among the boulders of the debris fan at Blacktail's entrance. Andre and I were feeling lazy, and we knew that there was a deep overhanging ledge of sandstone at the entrance to the canyon where we could lay out our bags and sleep unmolested by rain and snow. As we settled into our niche, we could hear the sound of Blacktail Rapid reverberating off the walls behind us. The canyon's mouth at my side yawned wide and so black I couldn't see my hand in front of my face.

"Listen," Andre said, "I hear drumming." I listened. If you stretched your imagination, the deep booming waves of the rapid did sound like drumming when they echoed through the canyon. I looked over to my right. The canyon mouth got a little darker. "It's just the rapid, Andre. Let's get some sleep." He chuckled, and we settled down for the night. I probably just should have stayed awake and convinced myself that the noises I heard all had a sensible explanation. It took a long time to get to sleep....

An old man comes to me, holding a stone knife. He has long, white hair and wears something on a thong around his neck. I can't see his face. He says nothing, but somehow I know that he wants to show me something. Something horrible. I feel death, but not for me. Something has happened in this place, a long time ago. Maybe even before the Anasazi, who lived here a thousand years ago. Something has happened to someone, and it lives in these walls. I'm not supposed to be here. I should leave. Now. "They" want us out of here. The old man is telling me this, only without words. I am so scared I'm stiff. I am in that in-between sleep, where I feel like I'm awake, only I can't move, I can't talk. The only things that work are my eyes, watching the darkness of the canyon mouth, waiting to see something come out of it. I feel myself trying to move, to break the paralysis. I can't wake up. I'm awake, but I'm not. I can't wake up. I try again, and again, until I literally drag myself out of sleep. I feel like I've come back from someplace very deep and far away....

I lay there, heart pounding. The first thing I heard was the deep, resonant drumming of the rapid off the walls. I couldn't even look at the mouth of the canyon, it was too dark and bottomless, threatening. Finally, I got up enough guts to speak. God, I hoped Andre wasn't asleep. "Andre, are you awake?" I whispered anxiously.

"Yes," he said, in a tense voice that told me he had been awake for a while.

"I had a terrible nightmare," I told him.

"So did I."

I felt the hairs on the back of my neck prickle. "What was yours about?" I asked him.

"I don't know. I just know it was something horrible."

My stomach turned over. "We're not supposed to be here, Andre."

"I know."

I looked over at the darkness of the canyon mouth.

"We should leave right now," he said.

Without another word, we gathered our bags and went out into a driving rain to set up a tent near our sleeping companions. The drumming was gone.

I visit Blacktail Canyon every chance I get. It is still my favorite place in the Canyon, and it still welcomes me. In the daytime. I would never sleep there at night; I know I'm not supposed to. I've camped there since, on the debris fan. I've sat under the overhang at the entrance while our hikers were walking up the Canyon. I've never heard the drumming again.

Christa Sadler has taught at Northern Arizona University and Prescott College, and works as a geology coordinator and instructor for the Grand Canyon Field Institute. Her favorite place to teach, and learn, is the Colorado River in Grand Canyon. She is the editor of There's This River: Grand Canyon Boatman Stories, *from which this story was excerpted.*

★

I came for my favorite hands-on close-up of the Great Unconformity. In Blacktail Canyon, the Great Unconformity is at head height, 1.2 billion missing years right at eye level, a change between rock types so unmistakable and spectacular, so conceptually overwhelming, that once it engages your attention, you watch it weave throughout the Canyon, a reminder of the human ability to conjecture about what has gone before, the briefness of life on Earth compared to the eons recorded in this rock, and the need to stretch the little gray cells into new dimensions. The Great Unconformity first appears high on the walls of the Upper Granite Gorge at Mile 77.5, marked by what Stanton saw as a "black beaded fringe" of horizontal Tapeats sandstone dramatically truncating the vertical and diagonal fins of schist beneath it. At Blacktail Canyon, the ending of the Upper Granite Gorge drops the Great Unconformity to river level.

—Ann Haymond Zwinger, *Downcanyon: A Naturalist Explores the Colorado River Through the Grand Canyon*

From Anasazi to Aircraft

The lure of the vanished world is
strong and mysterious.

HE IS A SMALL MAN WITH COPPERY-BROWN SKIN WEARING A LOIN-cloth of woven cotton. It is early summer; he needs no other clothing. In one hand, he carries a carefully chosen piece of Vishnu schist. He chose it for the way it felt in his hand, heavy and oblong, easy to grip. He improved it before setting off up the Canyon by breaking bits of rock from one end, making the end a point. In his other hand, he carries a small clay pot that he filled at the last flowing water, more than a half mile down-canyon. Just last week, the stream fell strong and clear without interruption all the way from the forest on the distant rim. He brought the pot because he knew it would be dry here, and he would need water to drink.

It is time, he knows. He has waited long enough since he had the dream. It came to him early one morning, in the half-awake time, and the image remains strong in his mind. He knows he should put it on the rock.

When he gets to the right place, he climbs above the dry streambed to a flat expanse of sandstone covered with desert varnish, a natural patina of minerals. The rock gleams gunmetal blue in the desert sun, but when he chips away bits of the varnish, the reddish yellow of the sandstone shows through. Setting down his pot of water, he picks up a second piece of rock—this one to use as a mallet against the base of his pointed stone—and starts to work, tapping, pecking, ever so carefully. First a general outline, just the important points of the figures he has in mind. He wants to be sure it looks right. This is important work and should not be hurried.

He will be in good company here. Others before him have pecked figures into the sandstone cliff—figures of animals and people, geometric designs, and otherwordly shapes, like the one from his dream. All figures express inner imperatives. None are placed here capriciously. He must know—anyone living in a place like the desert Southwest, where time stretches toward an endless horizon, must know—that a thousand years from now other people will stand in this canyon, along the trail that runs from the rim to the river, and contemplate his work. All the more reason to do it well. Plan it out. Take tiny chips. Make the lines clean and deep.

As the day wears on, his son wanders up the canyon, drawn by the constant tapping and a five-year-old's curiosity. He sits for a while watching, marveling at the pictures on the wall. Some are from stories he has heard around winter fires, and seeing them etched in stone gives them reality. But soon, the canyon draws his attention elsewhere. There is so much to do here. He makes a game of shooting with his toy bow and arrows at his father's pot. The pot is empty by now. Having drunk from it, his father set it safely on a rock ledge caused by a deep horizontal crack in the cliff. It makes an appealing target but one impossible to hit with the pretend weaponry of a child. All three of the boy's arrows rattle harmlessly off the rock, but one of them stays up on the ledge. Putting down the bow, he climbs up the easy steps, collecting his arrows, proud that at least one came so close. There it is, just inches from the pot. And…ah ha! A chuckwalla! One of those big brown lizards, back in the tight crack, wedged in the way chuckwallas do when escaping predators. Maybe he can jab it out with arrows.

The chuckwalla proves resistant. The crack is too deep. If only his father would help—but his father is intent, tapping away, and after a while, the boy chases after tree lizards. If you are really quick, you can catch them. If you are only half-quick, you get nothing but a wriggling tail that the tricky lizard leaves behind.

When the man finishes the petroglyph, it is nearly dusk. His son is still here, played out and lying asleep on the warm sand. The figures look good, just as he had imagined. He sits for a few minutes, wrapped in the peaceful stillness of the canyon, watching the glow of postsunset light fade on a high, red pinnacle. The shapes of bats flick across the narrow strip of sky, and the canyon walls grow black. Time to go. Satisfied, he scoops up the yielding body of his sleeping son and starts for home. Not until the next morning, when his boy misses his bow and the arrow he jammed into the chuckwalla's refuge, does he remember the pot.

Had the arrows been his own adult arrows, carefully fletched and spirit-empowered, he would go back for them immediately. But a child's toys are easily replaced. As for the pot, it was an old one. He will pick it up some other day. If he remembers.

Centuries later, I think about that pot, and the arrows. I heard about them because I know who found them. A hiker was following a side canyon toward the river when she came to a smooth ledge at the base of a cliff. There were petroglyphs etched in the canyon wall, until something caught her attention—it looked like the chipped rim of a pot. She scrambled up to see and sure enough, there it was, along with three small arrows.

The rest is speculation. She could only guess how they got there. I thought of the little boy because I've poked at a few lizards myself, and because she said the arrows were small, without stone points. I like the story. I've thought about it for years, letting the details change according to what feels right. I also like knowing that unless someone else moved them, the pot and the arrows are still there, just as she found them, untouched and shining with the mysterious allure of lost relics.

As for the petroglyphs and the motivations behind them, no one can say for sure. When I see how carefully the best of them were made, how much effort went into their making, it seems obvious that they were taken seriously. Was it art? Communication? Perhaps both.

I recognize the unscientific nature of my imagination. I know I run the risk of misrepresenting the feelings and actions of ancient people. But at the same time, I regard such musings as the most significant value of archaeological sites in a place like the Grand Canyon. It requires nothing more than being human to imagine the personal details of ancient lives. There are thousands of petro-glyphs in the Grand Canyon, and while their direct meaning is a puzzle, the human voice speaking to us over the centuries is unmistakable.

There are not many places in America where you can find ancient history so immediately present. So tangible. The ghosts of America, as represented in our oldest settlements and artifacts, generally go back only a few hundred years. Here, they are as old as Cheops. Knowing that ancient people inhabited the Grand Canyon is important to our experience of the place in the way birds, plants, and rocks are important.

Through the simplest of artifacts, we can make a connection across the gulf of centuries and cultural differences. It takes only a hand print in the dried clay of a 10th-century wall; a warm place in the sun where you know some-

There are other pots, treasures beyond price, locked away on park study shelves, on display in the Tusayan Museum along the East Rim Drive, scattered throughout the Canyon, and at thousands of sites yet to be explored by the archaeologists—all making up the 4,000-year-old mosaic of Native American life in Canyon country.

"We've recorded more than 2,600 sites, about five percent of what we think is here," said park archaeologist Jan Balsom when I visited her in her office. "There may be more than 50,000 in the park."

—Seymour L. Fishbein,
Grand Canyon Country:
Its Majesty and Its Lore

one sat; a fragment of pottery delicately formed, appealing to us across the centuries with the quality of its craftsmanship. Through these things there comes to us a flash of recognition. These people were real, cut from the same cloth as we. And with that recognition, the flash goes the other way, back in time. From our knowledge of ourselves and how we would react to such conditions, we can imagine things for which we have no physical evidence. We can hear the sounds of voices, children laughing, mothers calling, adults talking quietly. We don't know the language those ancient people spoke, but the music of human voices is everywhere the same.

Having felt the ghosts of ancient people in some hidden spot deep in the Canyon, you can feel them from anywhere else you go. Having made the connection once, you never view the Grand Canyon quite the same again.

To know more, however, to go beyond speculation (and into details like cotton loincloths), we must listen to the professionals—the archaeologists who study these things in a disciplined manner, who corrrelate artifacts from one area with those of another, establish dates, note the passage of time, and document the growth of cultures. Only the archaeologists are able to answer specific questions like: How did these people live? Where did they come from? What did they eat? Did they trade with other cultural groups? When were they here? Without the efforts of scientists, we would have only the mystery. Thanks to them, we know more. The picture, in brief, is as follows:

There have been many people living in the Grand Canyon more or less continuously for at least 4,000 years. Although the earliest people left very little behind to mark their passing, what they did leave are some of the most evocative and lovely of all artifacts: split-twig figurines, effigies of four-legged animals resembling deer and bighorn sheep, sometimes pierced by small twigs as if in imitation of a spear or an arrow. They were set in the dim recesses of caves and covered with rocks in what seems to have been a ceremonial placement—perhaps to bring good hunting.

No one knows for sure who these people were. The figurines discovered so far have been dated by carbon-14 analysis at between 3,000 and 4,000 years ago. There is evidence connecting them with a desert culture first described in California. Most likely, they were hunter-gatherers who moved with the seasons, perhaps visiting the Canyon at a specific time each year. Their shelters would have been simple structures, not liable to endure for centuries. Below the

Canyon rims, where rock overhangs provide ample protection from the elements, they might not have had to build anything.

Not long ago, archaeologists lacked evidence for Grand Canyon habitation between about 1000 B.C. and A.D. 500. This seemed to indicate that the Canyon was deserted for all those centuries. But new evidence is surfacing all the time, and it now appears the people have indeed lived here more or less continuously. What the earliest ones left behind was just not as readily seen and dated as what came later.

Around 2,500 years ago, a new culture made its appearance on the southwestern scene—the culture now referred to as Anasazi. Derived from a Navajo term meaning "ancient ones," Anasazi can also be interpreted in the more negative sense of "enemy ancestors." That Anasazi would become the best-known name for these ancient people is ironic because they were never ancestors of the Navajo, who come from a different, northerly cultural background. The Navajo weren't even in the region at the time. The Anasazi were the ancestors of the modern Hopi (among other Pueblo tribes), who have a different, more honorific name for them: *Hisat Sinom*.

The Grand Canyon was at the edge of their world; they lived mostly to the northwest in Four Corners country, where they built the famous cliff dwellings on Mesa Verde in Colorado and many others scattered throughout the region. When the term "Indian ruin" is mentioned, it usually refers to an Anasazi structure. For many centuries, however, and in most places, they built on a much smaller scale, beginning with simple brush structures and moving up through pit houses to large stone pueblos. The cliff dwellings came toward the end of their occupation in the late 13th century.

The Anasazi were possessed of a revolutionary idea: agriculture. Someone learned how to cultivate food plants; or, as seems more likely, people arrived who already knew horticultural techniques. However it developed, the idea spread quickly and brought a new way of living for people who had previously wandered with the seasons. Growing crops meant staying in one place, improving the ground, building check dams to hold water, guarding the fields against raiders, whether human or animal. It also led to more permanent structures and new tools and appurtenances. All of these things resulted in the artifacts that inform us, through archaeologists' study, about ancient ways of life.

Over time, the Anasazi culture matured. Archaeologists have identified several distinct stages of development, as defined by changes in the tools and dwellings of these people. The earliest are called Basket Makers, named for their splendid, yucca-fiber baskets, the best of which were woven tightly enough to hold water. They applied similar skills to their woven sandals and carrying bags. Later, they learned to make pottery. They hunted with bows and arrows, replacing the spears and atlas (spear-throwing tools) of their predecessors. They built increasingly substantial dwellings that were more elegant than the modern name for them, pit houses. Set partway into the ground, they were circular or rectangular in shape. Roof beams were held up by four wooden posts, while the roof itself was made of smaller sticks covered with clay. The entrance was an opening in the top. They were easy to build and comfortable in all seasons.

An important change occurred around A.D. 750 or 800, when the people began to live in villages—first as clusters of pit houses, then as larger structures with joined living and storage rooms. This marked the beginning of the Pueblo period, the height of the Anasazi culture. Things were particularly good in the years from around A.D. 900 to 1130, a time of abundant summer rainfall. The farming was good, and the population swelled in formerly marginal country at lower elevations—including the Grand Canyon, which saw its maximum habitation around A.D. 1100.

A different cultural group, the Cohonina, moved into the western end of the Canyon around the year A.D. 600. They adopted techniques from their Anasazi neighbors and lived in a similar manner.

There were no large pueblos in the Grand Canyon, but there are hundreds—maybe thousands—of archaeological sites from the Anasazi period. They include farm sites with irrigation terraces; grain storage structures, often set beneath protective overhangs; stone pits where the hearts of agave plants were roasted; numerous petroglyph and pictograph panels; and some small cliff dwellings.

Two settlements are noteworthy: Tusayan, on the South Rim, and Waklhalla Glades on the North Rim. The latter was a summer farming outpost of a settlement located on the Unkar Creek delta, beside the river, 5,000 feet below.

Early people did little to change what we see of the Canyon today. Looking down from the rims, you might never guess that anyone ever lived down there. Walking along the rims, it takes an educated eye to pick out the old home- and farm sites. But they are there, in surprising numbers, and in their time, and in certain places, the Anasazi must have been highly visible. They had gardens, built houses, cut trees, and burned wood. Back then, you would have seen campfires winking in the night. Walking down any major side canyon, you would have encountered people, smelled the smoke of cooking fires, and heard children's laughter echoing from the cliffs.

How many lived in the Canyon at any one time? No one can say. Around A.D. 1100, there were hundreds of occupied sites. After that, the population dropped off steeply, until by 1150 the Grand Canyon was essentially abandoned. The people headed east and south, to the Hopi mesas

---

*T*he Sipapu is a sacred site, a massive travertine spring that looks like the top half of a giant pumpkin fifty feet across and half buried in the Tapeats sandstone next to the Little Colorado River four or five miles upstream from its confluence with the Colorado. About six feet down in the center of the Sipapu, clear water bubbles forth to fill a hidden pool. Despite my doctorate in biological ecology, this spring half convinces me that it *could* be a portal between our world and some other. Jammed in cracks in the travertine above the bubbling spring are prayer feathers. Hopi mythology holds that it is through this portal that the dead return to the world below. More important, Hopi mythology holds that their ancestors *emerged* here, a one-day, fifteen-mile walk from Unkar Delta.

♦

—Michael P. Ghiglieri, *Canyon*

and beyond to the Rio Grande. There is growing agreement that it was the climate that drove them out—a long drought that made life in an already marginal land impossible. The dry conditions affected Anasazi throughout the Southwest, although it's interesting to note that their most spectacular developments—the cliff dwellings like those at Navajo National Monument and Mesa Verde National Park—were built around the turn of the 13th century and abandoned some time after A.D. 1250.

There is much still unknown of that time in the Grand Canyon. Every fact learned about the Canyon's prehistory seems to raise another set of intriguing questions. Although much activity centered on springs and other sources of permanent water (where we would expect to find signs of people), there are numerous structures in more remote, waterless areas—for example, on mesa tops standing separate from the Canyon rims. Why were they here? Some structures appear to have had a defensive purpose, but no evidence has ever come to light. If they *were* built as forts, what a strange and turbulent time it must have been. Ever stranger are the food storage structures located in places that are seemingly inaccessible. One archaeologist says a helicopter is the only way she knows that anyone could build such a structure. Why so remote? So apparently hidden? Was it customary to build your private food stash in some secret place to guard against lean times?

The Anasazi lived by moving when necessary. Such was survival in an uncertain land. They moved, and they survived, and they still do in Pueblo communities from the Hopi mesas to the Rio Grande Valley. They never came back to live in the Grand Canyon, but at the same time they never totally left it. The Hopi, as they always have, regularly visit sacred sites within the Canyon; it remains very much a part of their world. Since around A.D. 1300, the Hualapai people (a redundancy; *pai* means people) have lived on the western South Rim and its canyons.

On the North Rim, Paiutes hunted deer and other animals. The name for the Kaibab Plateau comes from two Paiute words, *kaiuw* (meaning mountain) and *a-vwi* (lying down). "Mountain lying down" describes very well this high, alpine area with no clear summit and no defining pinnacles, as if a large mountain were lying on its side. In summer, Navajos would come here to trade for deerskins. From the beginning, Indians used the obvious travel routes: Bright Angel Trail began as a route to the springs now called Indian Garden—once a Havasupai farming site. The North Kaibab Trail began as an old Paiute trail down Bright Angel Creek. It was used and sporadically maintained by mapping crews, miners, and tourism operators in the early part of the century and remained in an undeveloped state until 1928, when the Park Service completed the cross-canyon Kaibab Trail.

Back in the Canyon, a thousand years ago: the Anasazi petroglyph maker is older now, in his late 40s, a grandfather. He doesn't move as easily as he did. His knees are stiff, but as an elder of the clan, he has certain prerogatives. Old men are allowed time for contemplation. Today, he sits on a flat boulder at the edge of the Inner Gorge, watching the endless river roll by, listening to the thunder of the rapids. Earth power. Water is spirit. The river is life. Never stopping, always floating away, always coming back.

He is a man of simple possessions and limited experience with the wider world. But he has at least one great thing for which I envy him. He can look at this landscape, and the future, with confidence. He can imagine the grandson of his grandson sitting on this very rock thinking these same thoughts as the old river slides past. This is the way it is, and has been, and will be. Yucca will bloom in the spring. The river will rise in muddy torrents, and in the side canyon the stream will fall cold and clear past the petroglyphs where the pot he has now long forgotten still waits on the rock shelf. Maybe that grandson, generations in the future, will tap his own figures into the desert varnish beside those of his forebears.

This is the part I envy. It would be enormously reassuring to look down through your children's lives into the future, and have confidence in the world they will inherit.

Of course, he was wrong. The world changed for his people. They left the Canyon. But he never knew that, and what a fine feeling it must have been. He believed it. We can only hope.

Jeremy Schmidt is an author of six books, including the award-winning Himalayan Passage *and several of the* Free Wheeling Road Guides to the National Parks. *This story was excerpted from* Grand Canyon National Park: A National History Guide. *He lives in Jackson, Wyoming.*

✳

It is impossible to gain a real feeling for Grand Canyon without seeing what the Anasazi left behind. Indeed, now that I have seen so many of their hidden villages and granaries, their crumbling stonework half-buried in the blowing sand and slumping soil, their sherds of elegant pottery decorated with geometric designs that trigger aesthetic neurons, I can't stay away.

I hiked along the delta, a huge, nearly level, ancient fan of soil and rock abutting the receding cliffs, then stopped at the dwellings perched on the edge of the north embankment overlooking the river above Unkar Rapid. Here, I experienced another weird time-warp sensation, as if I could forge a rapport with this vanished past if only I tried hard enough. I suppose this experience also drives archaeologists to probe in the dust for long hours— or years. It now spurred me to imagine the scene were we to travel back in time and meet these tough, little Indians dressed in brocaded cotton. We would seem like monsters: large, pale, clumsy, garishly clothed, with dark lenses hiding our eyes, and carrying strange black objects around our necks that could not possibly serve a useful function. In their world, in fact, we probably would serve no useful function.

I stepped over a pair of double-thick walls of limestone and sandstone mortared with clay and sand that had resisted a millennium of monsoonal poundings. The ruins faced a green river flowing against a bold cliff of ma-roon Dox on its far side, then plunging, roaring, into Unkar Rapid.

—Michael P. Ghiglieri, *Canyon*

DAVID R. BROWER

Let the River Run Through It

*Some say he's out of his mind. Read, visit,
investigate—and draw your own conclusions.*

"GLEN CANYON DIED, AND I WAS PARTLY RESPONSIBLE FOR ITS
needless death," I wrote in *The Place No One Knew*, a Sierra Club
book published in 1963. "Neither you nor I, nor anyone else, knew
it well enough to insist that at all costs it should endure. Then we
began to find out it was too late. On January 2, 1963, the last day
on which the execution of one of the planet's greatest scenic antiq-
uities could yet have been spared, the man who theoretically had
the power to save the place did not. I was within a few feet of his
desk in Washington that day and witnessed how the forces long at
work had their way. So, a steel gate dropped, choking off the flow
of the canyon's carotid artery, and from that moment, the canyon's
life force ebbed quickly. A huge reservoir, absolutely not needed in
this century, almost certainly not needed in the next, and conceiv-
ably never to be needed at all, began to fill."

But as surely as we made a mistake years ago, we can reverse it
now. We can drain Lake Powell and let the Colorado River run
through the dam that created it, bringing Glen Canyon and the
wonder of its side canyons back to life. We can let the river do what
it needs to do downstream in the Grand Canyon itself.

We don't need to tear the dam down, however much some

people would like to see it go. Together, the dam's two diversion tunnels can send 200,000 cubic feet of water per second downstream, twice as much as the Colorado's highest flows. Once again, Grand Canyon would make its own sounds, and, if you listened carefully, you would hear it sighing with relief. The dam itself would be left as a tourist attraction, like the Pyramids, with passers-by wondering how humanity ever built it, and why.

Glen Canyon Dam was a power project pure and simple, built to provide a bank account for the Colorado River Storage Project, which financed high-cost agriculture, wasteful dams, and violated the spirit of the water-development agreement between the Colorado River states and Mexico. Hydropower dams were the darling of developers in this century's middle decades. They are now essentially irrelevant, but dam lovers don't know it yet. Except for a minor diversion at Page, Arizona, and the 30,000 acre-feet delivered annually to the nearby coal-fired power plant, all the water not lost to evaporation or leaks is diverted to users downstream at Lake Mead and below. Lake Mead's Hoover Dam can control the Colorado River without Lake Powell and can produce more power if Powell's water is stored behind it—saving massive amounts of money, water, and wild habitat. Economics and ecology are ready to team up on this one.

Beginning with the Industrial Revolution, people have been forgetting to ask what progress costs the earth and the future. Representing the Sierra Club as "not blindly opposed to progress, but opposed to blind progress," I have long been asking what kinds of growth we must have, and what kinds we can no longer afford. I got started on this while testifying—longer than anyone else— about the proposals governing the Colorado River Storage Project, including dams in the Glen Canyon and Dinosaur National Monument. I was helped by Walter L. Huber, a former Sierra Club president and Eisenhower's key advisor on dams, who spotted the Bureau of Reclamation *under*engineering, and by U.S. Geological Survey hydrologist Luna Leopold, who spotted its *over*engineering; by General U. S. Grant III, who pointed out miscalculations on reservoir evaporation, and by other engineers, in and out of government, who didn't wish to offend, but didn't mind if I did.

There were other key players, too, including the Sierra Club's Harold Bradley and at least four of his seven sons; Howard Zahniser, the Wilderness Society's executive secretary and tireless lobbyist; and the Izaak Walton League's Joseph W. Penfold, who gave us the great line, "Bureau of Reclamation engineers are like beaver; they can't stand the sight of running water."

While serving on the Club's board in 1949, I was persuaded to vote for two Grand Canyon dams, and for building Glen Canyon reservoir as a silt trap. In the first months of the battle for Dinosaur National Monument, I even urged the construction of a higher Glen Canyon dam as a way to save Dinosaur and reduce overall evaporation from the Colorado River Storage Project. Utah river runners straightened me out. But in 1956, the Club directors instructed me, then executive director, to end the Club's opposition to the construction of the dam at Glen Canyon if the two dams proposed upstream in Dinosaur

---

*T*he tree lizard moves to the edge of a flat rock, smacking up tiny ants with its darting tongue. It saves energy by allowing the ants to come close by rather than chasing after them—any ant coming within two inches is a goner. Two ants appear on the scene from opposite directions. The lizard eyes each in turn as if deciding which to snatch first, then, thsp-thsp, it nails them both.

In the fascination of watching the lizard, I have forgotten about the ten-ton heat, which now registers again. Cicadas sputter like a static-filled radio that I can't turn off. I have no idea what time it is. My heat-registering chromosomes may have melted like butter on a hot rock.

♦

—Ann Haymond Zwinger,
Downcanyon: A Naturalist Explores the Colorado River Through the Grand Canyon

were dropped. Instead of flying home immediately and calling for a special meeting, I just sat in Washington and watched the mayhem proceed.

In a 1992 documentary in which I almost tearfully took the blame for Glen Canyon, producer John DeGraff kindly attributed my problem to my not having seen Glen before offering to give it away. I knew better: Wallace Stegner had told me, "Strictly between us, Dinosaur doesn't hold a candle to Glen." I have worn sackcloth and ashes ever since, convinced that I could have saved the place if I had simply got off my duff.

The fact is, though, Glen Canyon is still there. With that thought in mind, I've turned from regret to restoration. In 1995, I debated former Bureau of Reclamation Commissioner Floyd Dominy, builder of more dams than anybody, Glen Canyon among them. When I proposed restoring Glen Canyon, Dominy was not ready to concede, but I think the audience was. I pushed the proposal harder in 1996 before 1,600 people gathered at the University of Utah. They gave enthusiastic support. The toughest question I got was about how long it would take the tamarisk, a notoriously invasive exotic, to recover. I fudged the answer: "Twenty-five minutes."

Then on November 16, 1996, an entity that had blocked my opposition to the creation of Lake Powell in 1956, the Sierra Club board, unanimously backed my motion to drain it. I suddenly felt about 30 years younger.

One of the strongest selling points comes from the Bureau of Reclamation itself. In 1996, the Bureau found that almost a million acre-feet, or 8 percent of the river's flow, disappeared between the stations recording the reservoir's inflow and outflow. Almost 600,000 acre-feet were presumed lost to evaporation. Nobody knows for sure about the rest. The Bureau said some of the loss was a gain—being stored in the banks of the reservoir—but it has no idea how much of that gain it will ever get back. Some bank storage is recoverable, but all too likely the region's downward-slanting geological strata are leading some of Powell's waters into the dark unknown. It takes only one drain to empty a bathtub, and we don't know where, when, or how the Powell tub leaks. A million acre-feet could meet the annual domestic needs of 4 million people and at today's prices are worth $435 million in the Salt Lake City area—more than a billion on my hill in Berkeley, California.

But these numbers are moving upward. As Powell rises, fills with sediment, and spreads out across the landscape (it peaked at 88 percent of capacity last year), the losses will be even larger. They could mount to 1.5 million acre-feet per year before *Sierra's* middle-aged readers are my age (in their '80s), which won't take as long as we'd like. And what is an acre-foot likely to be worth when my grandson David Brower comes of age? When I was his age, farmers objected to having to pay $5 an acre-foot. What has happened in the last decade or two is interesting, but what will happen in the next century or two is critical. (Powell is supposed to last at least three centuries, but malpractice in the Colorado's watershed—clearcutting, grazing, and other erosive forces—will shorten its life.)

Whatever the final details of Lake Powell's water losses turn out to be, the draining of the lake simply has to happen.

I asked Bryan [an ornithologist] about the overall impact of Glen Canyon dam. "It almost sounds like heresy for me to say this," he replied. "The dam has done horrible things to the environment. But it's an undeniable fact that the dam has had some positive effects." With an upsurge in insect life and a spread of vegetation through what used to be the scour zone, the numbers of birds breeding along the river increased five- or tenfold.

Bryan Brown and Steven W. Carothers assert that the river "is no longer natural, but instead is naturalized, a blend of the old and the new, mixture of native and the exotic organisms."

A new vision is needed, the authors say, for there is currently "no guidance for coping with naturalized ecosystems."

◆

—Seymour L. Fishbein,
*Grand Canyon Country:
Its Majesty and Its Lore*

The river and the regions dependent upon it, including Baja California and the Gulf of California, can no longer afford the unconscionable loss of water. We need to get rid immediately of the illusion that the only way to protect water rights is by wasting water in Lake Powell. We can simply let the flow reach Lees Ferry, Arizona (the dividing point between the Upper and Lower basins), naturally, beautifully, and powered by gravity at no cost.

Draining Lake Powell means more water for the Colorado River states and Mexico, especially Colorado and Utah. The hundreds of millions of dollars now being lost, growing to billions in the future, should be enough to give even Bill Gates pause.

The sooner we begin, the sooner lost paradises will begin to recover—Cathedral in the Desert, Music Temple, Hidden Passage, Dove Canyon, Little Arch, Dungeon, and a hundred others. Glen Canyon itself can probably lose its ugly, white sidewalls in two or three decades. The tapestries can reemerge, along with the desert varnish, the exiled species of plants and animals, the pictographs and other mementos of people long gone. The Canyon's music will be known again, and "the sudden poetry of springs," Wallace Stegner's beautiful phrase, will be revealed again below the sculptured walls of Navajo sandstone. The phrase "as long as the rivers shall run and the grasses grow" will regain its meaning.

The candle conservationists lit to remember the things lost in Glen Canyon can be put back on the shelf, and, let us pledge, be left there. In time, Glen Canyon will reassert itself, through the action of wind and water. And we will learn what Alexander Pope knew: "And finer forms are in the quarry/Than ever Angelo evoked." Once again, for all our time, the river can run through it.

David R. Brower, executive director of the Sierra Club from 1952 to 1969, has been a Club member for more than sixty years. "If this plan works, I'll go quietly," he says.

*

It's a relatively new science, ecology; it's been only 128 years since the German Darwinian, Ernst Haeckel, even came up with the term. Given the time scale we're working with here at the Grand Canyon, that's about a nanosecond.

And, of course, once we get back to pondering environmental issues in terms of geological time, the importance of human intervention in nature's ecosystem management takes on a rather different perspective. It is undoubtedly true that in the Kaibab Plateau region man is largely, if not entirely, responsible for the demise of a number of species—the wolf, the bear, the jaguar, the condor, the burrowing owl, the Colorado squawfish, the roundtail chub, and a good many others. And it is equally true that he is guilty of massively altering the composition of the vegetation along the riparian corridor of the Colorado River, of fouling the air over most of the Canyon country, and of invading the peace and quiet of the entire region. In terms of millennia, how much will it matter?

Which is no apology or justification for insensibility. Being a Good Neighbor Sam in nature's community is still the right thing to do...but because it's right, not because it's going to make much difference in the very long run. Just stand out there at Lipan Point and wait a few million years. Another landscape Day of Judgment will surely arrive.

—Page Stegner, *Grand Canyon: The Great Abyss*

JEREMY SCHMIDT

Temples to Water

Some memories are forever.

SEVERAL MILES FROM THE COLORADO RIVER, IN A SIDE CANYON OF a side canyon, there is a grotto. You can walk to it from the river, or down from the rim. Either way, it feels like a very deep place, far beneath towering walls, a long way from roads and a long way even from trails. Deep and protected and very well hidden, it lies at the end of a narrow gorge—a cold, green pool of water the size of a large bedroom. It feels as private as a bedroom, tucked away in a cul-de-sac with no way out except the way you came in. No one who comes here is ever in a hurry to leave.

On one side of the pool is a ledge where several people can sit on smooth rock beneath an overhang. On the other side, a sheer slope of stone, layered in travertine, rises to an opening in the wall, above which lies the unknown; no way for a person to get up there and have a look. Shooting down the slope comes a narrow ribbon of water, only a few inches wide, half an inch deep, and 30 feet high. The water splashes into the pool with a gurgling sound that mixes and echoes with the hissing of its passage down the slide rock. For a ceiling, there hangs a small patch of sky, but rarely if ever does the sun shine directly into this hidden chamber.

Ask anyone who has run the Colorado River, or any hiker who

has spent enough time in the Canyon to know something of its variety, to name his or her favorite places, the side canyons will be near the top of the list. Especially the small ones, the shaded grottos where little streams flow beneath high arching walls. These are the real jewels of the Grand Canyon, made more precious by the surrounding aridity and overwhelming size of the landscape. Their intimacy makes them pleasant. Water gives them magic.

The first time I saw the grotto described above was on a hiking trip. There were four of us. We parked our cars on the broken limestone of the rim, shouldered our packs, and set off down a long rubble slope. There was no trail, and without a trail, getting into the Grand Canyon takes some route finding. It's not like a big hill that you can just walk down. To get through the cliffs, you have to follow its lines of weakness. We had only a general description of where to go, but even that was enough, because we knew we could find a way down.

The first night, we set our camp on a flat rock ledge 3,000 feet below the rim, buried in the silence of the desert. There was no water burbling in the hollows. We heard no birds. No wind. No insects. We spoke in whispers to avoid the profanity of noise.

How different it was the next day. Dropping down a series of ledges like giant steps, we entered a small canyon whose walls rose steadily above our heads the farther we went. A stream appeared, flowing intermittently at first, then strong and unbroken. As it tumbled through house-sized boulders and slid through tiny pools, it sang a canyon song that rose and filled the narrow space. It was a canyon full of echoes—not just the sound of water and frogs and birds and insects and our still-hushed voices, but also the echoes of light, and air currents.

And something more, a cultural reverberation. We found it near a spring lined with maidenhair fern and gently bobbing scarlet monkey flowers. It was a panel of petroglyphs—animals and geometric patterns and human figures pecked into the rock by people drawn like us to the mysterious presence of water in the desert.

The stream vanished again. We walked on a bed of dry gravel and boulders, knowing that if we were thirsty enough we could dig a few feet down and find water. It was obvious from the plants that grew so well here that water still flowed through the streambed beneath our feet. There were still cottonwoods and willows, which do not survive without ample moisture. There were birds also. Mourning doves, white-throated swifts, several kinds of swallows, black phoebes hawking insects from the air, broad-tailed humming-birds doing their spring mating display (superb aerial acrobatics), and one of my favorite canyon creatures, the police-whistle bird. The books call him an ash-throated flycatcher, but I've always recognized him by his call, which sounds like an old-fashioned police whistle: *Chee-beeer!*

We found deer tracks in the sand, and that made me think of mountain lions. I've never seen one in the Canyon, but their tracks haunt my thoughts. I began paying attention, looking for the big four-inch pugmarks on the soft sand and clay of the stream bank.

Soon, there was water again, and from there all the way to the Colorado River, we walked beside a permanent stream. In places, vegetation grew in dense tangles, forcing us to thrash our way through branches and hanging vines. Beneath overhung canyon walls, seeps painted the stone with patterns of algae and alkali and other minerals. There were hanging gardens of maidenhair fern, monkey flower, and columbine.

Since it was springtime, everything was in bloom, bursting and building. The flowers included those of tamarisk, that alien beauty. Sometimes I cursed the tamarisk because it was hard to move through. Its rough bark scratched my arms and legs. The tips of broken branches were sharp enough to cause puncture wounds. But I admired the tamarisk for its persistence.

Tamarisk is native to the Nile River valley, where it stabilizes riverbanks and serves other functions regarded by humans as useful. Back in the '30s, someone thought it would be a good idea to plant it along the Colorado River. It became a project of the Civilian Conservation Corps. Like many exotic species, it was too successful. It escaped into the wild, out of control of the engineers, up into side canyons throughout the Southwest, where it now defies attempts to round it up and deport it. The engineers are trying to destroy it because someone decided after the fact that tamarisk uses too much of the water that should be going into growing lettuce and other irrigated crops. They won't succeed. Tamarisk is here to stay. It's gone wild. Every spring, it bursts with purple blossoms and fills the Canyon with delicate perfume.

The walls grew even higher. On bends, great cliffs were undercut by the stream, forming huge amphitheaters like band shells for choruses of male treefrogs. The frogs sounded like sheep. Demented sheep. But to the females lured by the bellows, it must have been beautiful music.

At stream level, everything was lush. I thought of Hawaii and New Zealand. Yet only 50 feet above the canyon bottom, on baked, rocky ledges, conditions were as dry as old bones. Catclaw acacia shared space with cacti and grasses that had already grown brown, their foxtail seeds clinging to our socks when we ventured among them.

At wide places, the streambed cut through benches of sand and gravel where huge boulders had come to rest after falling from the walls above. The stream flowed 10 to 15 feet below these branches, leaving them high and dry. Nonetheless, vegetation here was as thick as a midwestern orchard, although instead of apple trees there were acacia trees. Around them grew blankets of wildflowers and grasses, and this was unusual because so often in the Southwest, anything that can be grazed has suffered from generations of cattle. One of the great values of a national park is the way it preserves a semblance of wild conditions. In Grand Canyon, we have a chance to experience natural conditions without the overwhelming influence of human industry. Once you've seen meadows like these, where the grass grows to its full height and is eaten only by native herbivores, it is possible to understand what we have done to most of our land.

Always the light! Reflecting and reverberating, rarely direct, warmed by its impact with the canyon walls. In that light, skin glows, water shimmers. Shadows are never harsh because there is so much loose light running around.

One of my friends walks across a shallow pool. Riffles from her passage gleam in gold light showering down from a bright cliff above her. She stands in a pool of gold, and I am reminded of the scatters of glitter that followed Tinkerbell in the Disney version of *Peter Pan*. If there was ever a Never-Never Land, this is it. A secret garden in the desert where water flows clear and clean. Crouching on a boulder one evening, staring into a pool of water so clear it was nearly invisible, I was startled by a river of minnows. Hundreds of them. A silver hallucinatory flow. They passed without causing so much as a shiver on the calm surface.

The days melted into one another. There wasn't much value in counting either time or distance. Somewhere along the way, I think perhaps on the fifth day, we came to a narrow side canyon. It led us to the grotto with the green pool and the ribbon waterfall. The canyon's *sanctum sanctorum*. A tiny chapel dedicated to the liturgy of water.

Jeremy Schmidt also contributed "From Anasazi to Aircraft" to Part Four.

✳

WHAT YOU NEED TO KNOW

WHEN TO GO/WEATHER

The South Rim—Open year-round, the South Rim sees the most crowds due to its close proximity to major population areas. The best time to avoid the throngs and see the Canyon in its true colors is in the spring or fall. If you plan to hike the inner canyon, do so at this time as well, but be sure to plan ahead, as permits go fast. If you must go in the summer (June, July, August), be prepared for traffic jams, lines, and hot weather. The seasonal temperatures vary tremendously, so bring enough clothing to layer effectively. In the summer, daytime temperatures can climb to 100 degrees Fahrenheit, and nighttime temperatures can dip to the 50s. Spring and fall temperatures usually range from 32 to 70 degrees, and in the winter hover around 20 degrees, with snow. Road conditions are a concern in the winter, but the roads are actively maintained and remain open as much as possible.

The North Rim—Nearly 1,200 feet higher than the South Rim, the North Rim is closed in the winter due to snowfall. The roads open in mid-May and stay open through October, weather permitting. Here, too, the best times to see the Canyon are in the spring and fall. However, since the North Rim receives only one-tenth the number of summer visitors as the South Rim, summer trips are still pleasant. Always layer, however, for the temperatures vary.

The Western Rim—Open year-round, the Western Rim is the least developed and offers the most "natural" vistas; no better view of the Colorado exists than from Guano Point. Owned by the Hualapai Indian Tribe, there are no guardrails along the Western Rim, so watch your children with an eagle's eye. Temperatures here are roughly equivalent to those at the South Rim, with a tendency for greater rainfall and higher winds.

THE NEXT STEP

GETTING THERE

Auto/recreational vehicle—These modes allow for the most flexibility, but vehicles also contribute to the increased traffic and human impact on the Grand Canyon. However, if you go this route, head first to either Williams or Flagstaff, Arizona and follow signs to the desired rim. Should you visit the Western Rim, be advised that the final 21 miles traverse a "primitive" road. Drive carefully, and no faster than 15–20 miles per hour.

Bus—Take a Greyhound bus to Flagstaff. Change to Nava-Hopi Tours, 800-892-8687 or 520-774-5003, to reach the South Rim, or the Trans-Canyon Shuttle, 520-638-2820, to reach the North Rim. There are also buses which will take you to the Western Rim.

Plane—Fly into either Phoenix or Las Vegas and catch a connecting flight to the South Rim's Grand Canyon National Park Airport. A shuttle from the airport will take you to the North Rim. You can also fly into a small airstrip operated by the Hualapai at the Western Rim; almost all flights leave from Las Vegas.

Train—Amtrak goes to Flagstaff. From there, you can rent a car, take the Nava-Hopi Tour bus to the South Rim, or ride a shuttle to the North Rim.

Antique train—A journey into times past, you can take a delightful trip from the town of Williams to the South Rim on the Grand Canyon Railway. The round trip takes approximately four hours in 1923 vintage cars pulled by old locomotives and costs $60, including the park's entrance fee. For information, call 800-843-8724.

Getting Around Once There

The Trans-Canyon Shuttle will take you 235 miles to the North Rim from the Grand Canyon Village in the South Rim. It leaves daily at 1 p.m. p.m. May 15–October 31 and costs $60 one-way, $100 round trip, per person. You must make reservations at least two weeks in advance. Call 520-638-2820.

The Fred Harvey Transportation Company offers taxi service from the Grand Canyon National Park Airport to lodgings or trailheads in the area. They also offer various tours of the Canyon. Call 520-638-2822 or 520-638-2631 ext. 6563.

Rent a car in either Flagstaff or at the airport.

The National Park Service provides a free shuttle system serving three loops within the park. For further details, see *The Guide*, the free park newspaper.

The Western canyon has a year-round bus tour. Contact the Hualapai Lodge in Peach Springs for cost, 800-255-9550.

Helicopter services, available every forty-five minutes at a cost of $100 per person, will take you to the bottom of the Canyon. Well worth the cost if you have limited time.

In September 2000, the National Park Service hopes to institute a light rail service/bus system. This will enable visitors to travel more easily within the park without a car and protect the Grand Canyon's natural beauty and resources from increased auto traffic.

*L*ODGING

For suggestions about accommodations in the park, contact Amfac Parks & Resorts, 14001 E. Iliff, Ste. 600, Aurora, CO 80013; 303-297-2757. Outside the Park, on the South Rim, contact The Grand Canyon Chamber of Commerce, Hwy. 64, Tusayan, AZ 86023; 520-638-2901. For the North Rim, get in touch with Kane County Travel Council, 78 S. 100 E. Kanab, UT 84731; 800-733-5263. The Hualapai Lodge (about 58 miles from the Western Rim) provides accommodations for the Western Rim, which is not owned by the park service. Contact the Hualapai Tourist Office in Peach Springs, 888-255-9550.

The Havasupai Tribal Area of the Grand Canyon, containing Havasu Canyon, is not operated by the park service. Contact the Havasupai Lodge, 520-448-2201.

THE NEXT STEP

There are many opportunities to camp. Three backcountry campgrounds in the park stay open year-round: Indian Garden (15 sites), Cottonwood (12 sites), and Bright Angel (33 sites). Each requires a backcountry permit which also serves as a reservation. Backcountry permits cost $20, plus $4 per person, per night. These can be purchased through the Backcountry Office, Box 129, Grand Canyon, AZ 86023; 520-638-7888. Additional sites exist in the nearby Kaibab National Forest, which also require permits. Plan ahead.

Auto/RV camping on the South Rim varies in regards to the existence of hook-ups and the need for reservations. It is best to call ahead of time and double check. The campgrounds:

- Desert View Campground—50 RV/tent sites. 520-638-7888; no hook-ups; open April–November; $12 per night.
- Mather Campground—319 RV/tent sites. 520-638-7888; no hook-ups; open year-round; $15 per night; reservations needed (the site closest to the visitor center, this is the busiest campground during the summer months). For reservations, call 800-365-2267 or Amfac.
- Trailer Village—50 RV sites. 520-638-2631; full hook-ups; open year-round; $19 per night, reservations needed.

Auto/RV camping on the North Rim:

- North Rim Campground—83 RV/tent sites. 520-638-7888; no hook-ups; open mid-May through mid-October, depending upon snow conditions; $12 per night, on a first-come, first-served basis.
- DeMotte Campground—22 RV/tent sites. 520-643-7395; no hook-ups; open mid-May through mid-October; $10 per night, on a first-come, first-served basis.
- Jacob Lake Campground—53 RV/tent sites. 520-643-7395; no hook-ups; open mid-May through mid-October; $10 per night, on a first-come, first-served basis.
- Kaibab Lodge Camper Village—80 RV and 50 tent sites. 520-643-7804; full hook-ups; open mid-May through mid-October; $12–$22 per night; reservations needed.

Auto/RV camping on the Western Rim:

• Contact the Hualapai Tourist Office in Peach Springs, 888-255-9550, for camping locations and permits.

ARK FEES, PERMITS, PASSES

Fees—The park charges $20 if traveling by car, or $10 if by bike or on foot; fees are only collected during peak seasons, mid-May through mid-October. The gates are open 24 hours a day; if no one is on duty, just drive in.

Permits—If you are planning only a day hike into the Canyon or if you are going to Phantom Ranch, a permit is not necessary. However, if you backpack overnight, you must obtain a backcountry permit from the Backcountry Office, Box 129, Grand Canyon, AZ 86023; 520-638-7888. To speak to a "live" person, call 520-638-7875, or fax them, 520-638-2125. The cost is $20, plus a camping fee of $4 per person, per night. Plan ahead, as permits go fast. A Frequent Hiker Membership is also available for $50, which waives the $20 permit fee for up to one year.

Passes—A variety of park passes are available:

• The Grand Canyon Park Pass is for frequent visitors. If you plan to visit the Grand Canyon repeatedly throughout the year, this one's for you. The $40 entrance fee gives you free access for a calendar year.

• The Golden Eagle Pass entitles the bearer and his/her passengers free entrance to any U.S. national park for a calendar year. Costing $50, this pass can be purchased at any National Park Headquarters.

• The Golden Age Passport is for U.S. citizens 62 years of age and older. The fee is $10, and the pass can be purchased at any U.S. national park entrance. Good for life, this pass offers free entrance into all U.S. national parks, as well as a 50 percent discount on park services and facilities, excluding private concession stands.

• The Golden Access Passport is for people with permanent disabilities and is free. Good for life, this pass can be obtained at any U.S. national park that has an entrance fee. To qualify, you must provide written documentation of your disability in the form of a doctor's letter, and proof of your disability. This pass entitles the bearer to a 50 percent discount on all park services and facilities, excluding private concessions. Disabled visitors can check *The Guide*, the free Park newspaper, for services, facilities, and programs that meet their needs.

ℋEALTH AND HAZARDS

A visit to the Grand Canyon involves various hazards. Be prepared and be careful. Don't be stupid. The dangers include:

- Car accidents—With so many vehicles, especially during the summer months, trouble between car and car, car and person, and car and animal becomes inevitable. Always be alert and drive at a reasonable speed. Or, better yet, don't drive, and seek other means of transportation.
- Falling —The Canyon is *very* deep. One slip or poor decision to go off the trail, and you may be in trouble. Be sure of your footing and stay away from the edge. Wear good hiking boots with adequate tread.
- Drownings—For those descending to the Colorado River, the water in places is fast and very cold. Always check temperature and current before taking a dip.
- Animal encounters—Stay at a reasonable distance from any wild animal you meet. *Do not feed the animals.* (To minimize possibilities of an encounter with a big cat, avoid hiking at dawn and dusk, their prime hunting hours.) If there is a threat of attack, *slowly* back away. *Never run.* If bitten by a snake, stay calm, don't move, and have a companion seek medical assistance as soon as possible.
- Hiking Solo—There is safety in numbers. When possible, always hike with at least one companion. Give friends and family a copy of your itinerary.
- Dehydration—When hiking, you should drink a bare minimum of two quarts of water per day, and a gallon is recommended. (In especially hot conditions, some suggest a quart of water an hour.) Many water sources in the wild are contaminated with a bacteria called *Giardia* which can cause severe diarrhea and other health problems. To avoid getting sick, even if the water looks clean, always purify your water by boiling, filtering, or using chemical tablets.

- Heat stroke—On a hot summer day the temperature can exceed 100 degrees Fahrenheit. Drink a lot of water, as severe dehydration can lead to heat stroke, which can be fatal. Should you experience headaches, dizziness and/or fatigue, rest in shade, wrap your forehead with a cool, wet bandanna, and *drink* until the symptoms subside. If the symptoms don't subside, seek help. Come prepared for the sun by wearing a hat with a brim, sunglasses, and use plenty of sunscreen, even on cloudy days, and especially in snow.
- Hypothermia—At the other extreme, the cold can get you, too. Hypothermia is a condition in which the core body temperature plummets, and mental confusion, uncontrollable shaking and, if un-treated, death ensue. The first signs of hypothermia include feeling chilly and tired, a warning to put on more dry clothes and drink warm liquids. If confusion develops, immediately find shelter, wrap up in a sleeping bag, and drink tepid liquids (not too hot). If extreme confusion and shaking occur, it is imperative to a) create as much warmth as possible (strip naked with your hiking companion and share a sleeping bag to generate body heat), and b) send for help. To avoid hypothermia, wear dry clothes, drink warm liquids, and eat high-caloric food. Bring multiple layers and rain gear. In the winter, particularly, make sure you are overprepared with clothing. (Avoid cotton; wool, fleece pile, silk, and wicking polyester fabrics stay drier and retain heat better.) Remember, hypothermia can occur even in mild temperatures, and especially in wet conditions.
- Plants—Look out for cacti. Taking a pratfall into one of the many kinds of cacti can be a nasty experience.
- Know your limitations—Challenge yourself, but don't be stupid. Have a good idea of the rigors involved with your trip. Talk to a ranger or other knowledgeable person prior to setting out.

Emergency Assistance:

There are phones located in the visitor centers and all around the Park. Call 911 for 24-hour medical help. The Grand Canyon Clinic also has 24-hour emergency services, 520-638-2551 or 520-638-2469. Cell phones are handy to pack, although if you are planning a descent into

THE NEXT STEP

the Canyon, check for reception. Or, for the old-fashioned way to signal for help, bring a mirror. Helicopter evacuations exist for extreme emergencies, although due to the air currents and narrow width of parts of the Canyon, this is a very dangerous procedure. And then there are always the ubiquitous rangers. Do not be shy about asking them for help—that is part of their job.

TIME

The Grand Canyon lies in the Mountain Time Zone.

Greenwich Mean Time (GMT) is seven hours ahead of the Mountain Time Zone. Thus, when it is noon in the Grand Canyon, it is:

11 a.m. in San Francisco
2 p.m. in New York
7 p.m. in London
8 p.m. in Paris
3 a.m. the following day in Hong Kong
4 a.m. the following day in Tokyo
5 a.m. the following day in Sydney

HOURS

The entrance gates to the park are open 24 hours a day, 7 days a week. Most of the park's visitor centers and facilities are open daily from 9 a.m. to 5 p.m. and stay open into the late fall, depending upon demand. Open daily, year-round, Babbitt's General Store, 520-638-2262, on the South Rim in the Grand Canyon Village provides most anything one could need. During the summer, it is open from 8 a.m. to 8 p.m., and in the winter, from 9 a.m. to 6 p.m. On the North Rim, the North Rim General Store, 520-638-2611, ext. 270, near the Grand Canyon Lodge, provides supplies for travelers, but it is closed during the winter months.

$\mathcal{T}$HE NEXT STEP

$\mathcal{E}$LECTRICITY

Power runs on 110–120 volts AC, 60 cycles. If you come from a country that uses 220–250 volts AC, 50 cycles, bring your own adapter with two flat vertical plugs because converters that change from 220 to 110 are difficult to find here.

$\mathcal{M}$EDIA

The best source of information comes from *The Guide*, a free paper given at the gate upon entrance to the park. The visitor centers sell various books on such topics as native plant life, animal behavior, and Canyon history.

$\mathcal{L}$OCAL CUSTOMS: DOS AND DON'TS

- Don't feed the animals.
- Keep a respectful distance from animals.
- Tread lightly.
- Stay on the trails.
- Use caution near the edge.
- Test for river and stream currents.
- Be smart about fire.
- Pack your garbage out.
- Hang your food when in the backcountry.
- Be reverent in this sacred place.

$\mathcal{E}$VENTS

For current event listings and schedules, refer to *The Guide*, the free newspaper handed out at the entrance gates and at the visitor centers. It includes maps, an activity list, phone numbers, etc. You can also contact the Flagstaff Chamber of Commerce, 520-774-9541, for nearby activities including the Flagstaff Summerfest and Festival of the Arts, which happen in August.

☉HE NEXT STEP

IMPORTANT CONTACTS

☉OURIST INFORMATION ────────────────────────

General tourist information:

- Flagstaff Chamber of Commerce—Flagstaff, AZ; 520-774-9451
- Grand Canyon Chamber of Commerce—Tusayan, AZ; 520-638-2901
- Williams Chamber of Commerce—Williams, AZ; 520-635-4061
- Hualapai Lodge—Peach Springs, AZ; 888-255-9550 (Western Rim information only)
- Havasupai Lodge—Supai, AZ; 520-448-2201

For general information and brochures about the park:

- National Park Service, Office of Public Inquiries, Box 37127, Rm. 1013, Washington, D.C. 20013-7127; 202-208-4747
- Intermountain Field Office, 12795 Alameda Pkwy., Denver, CO 80225; 303-969-2500

For more detailed information on the Canyon:

- Grand Canyon National Park, Box 129, Grand Canyon, AZ 86023; 520-638-7888

For information on lodging and recreation within the park:

- Amfac Parks and Resorts, 14001 E. Iliff, Ste. 600, Aurora, CO 80013; 303-297-2757

For information and permits on backcountry hiking:

- Backcountry Office, P.O. Box 129, Grand Canyon, AZ 86023; 520-638-7888

For information on river trips:

- Wilderness River Adventures, P.O. Box 717, Page, AZ 86040; 800-992-8022
- Grand Canyon River Guides, P.O. Box 1934, Flagstaff, AZ 86002; 520-773-1075

For information on fishing:

- Colorado River Guide Service, 520-355-2247
- Bubba's Guide Service, 888-741-2822
- Lake Powell Charter/Lees Ferry, 520-645-5505
- Lees Ferry Anglers (Guide and Fly Shop), 800-962-9755
- Gunn Terry Trophy Trout Tours, 520-355-2220
- Wahweep Lodge and Marina, 520-645-2433

For information on education and preservation resources and opportunities:

- Grand Canyon Field Institute, P.O. Box 399, Grand Canyon, AZ 86023; 520-638-2485
- Grand Canyon National Park Visitor Centers—throughout the Park
- Earthwatch, 680 Mount Auburn St., Watertown, MA 02272; 617-926-8200
- Sierra Club, 85 2nd St., San Francisco, CA 94105; 415-977-5500
- National Wildlife Federation, 8925 Leesburg Pike, Vienna, VA 22184; 800-822-9919
- Grand Canyon Monitoring and Research Center, P.O. Box 22459, Flagstaff, AZ 86001; 520-556-7363
- Grand Canyon Natural History Association, P.O. Box 399, Grand Canyon, AZ 86023; 520-638-2481

FUN THINGS TO DO

- Free, daily guided hikes, tours, lectures, and interpretive programs are provided by the National Park Service (great for families), and most are listed in *The Guide*.
- In-depth classes and tours by private companies are available from April through November, covering such topics as geology, ornithology, and native cultures. Classes last anywhere from one to eight days. Check with the Grand Canyon Field Institute, P.O. Box 399, Grand Canyon, AZ 86023; 520-638-2485.
- Mule rides into the Canyon are available for one- and three-day trips. Reservations are needed. Call 520-638-2631 or 303-297-2757.

THE NEXT STEP

- White-water river trips are popular. For information, call 800-959-9164, or contact the Grand Canyon River Guides, P.O. Box 1934, Flagstaff, AZ 86002; 520-773-1075.
- A multitude of bus and van tours are available from various companies, including Fred Harvey Transportation, offering tours ranging anywhere from 90 minutes to 4 hours. Contact the Grand Canyon National Park Lodges, P.O. Box 699, Grand Canyon, AZ 86023; 520-638-2401. The Hualapai Indian Nation, 888-255-9550, also gives tours.
- Take the East Rim Drive to some of the most breathtaking vista turn-outs and overlooks. To get there, enter the park from the south, drive three miles north and turn right on Rte. 64E. The West Rim Drive is open to private vehicles between late October and Memorial Day only. During the summer months, due to the high volume of traffic, a free shuttle provides service along the rim.
- Hikes abound, with a trail for everyone. Difficulty levels vary, from a half-mile stroll through level terrain to rigorous backpacking through drastic elevation changes. Know your ability, plan ahead, and be pre-pared. For more information, contact the Grand Canyon National Park, 520-638-7888, for a trip planner, or read *Hiking the Grand Canyon* by Scott Thybony, a 1994 publication published by the Grand Canyon Natural History Association. Call 520-638-2481.
- Biking is a great way to see the park rim, but can be deadly in the summer months due to the high volume of vehicles. Bicycles are prohibited on park trails; bikers must therefore ride on the roads. Be safe. Wear a helmet and bright clothing.
- Horseback riding is available for both long and short excursions. For information and reservations, call 520-638-2891.
- Fishing is excellent on the Colorado around Lees Ferry and further downriver into the Canyon.
- Volunteer as a short-term assistant on a research expedition through Earthwatch, 680 Mount Auburn St., Watertown, MA 02272; 617-926-8200.
- Go to the IMAX Theater in Tusayan and see *Grand Canyon: The Hidden Secrets* as an introduction to your visit. Tickets are $7.50. Open daily from 8:30 a.m. to 8:30 p.m.

- Take a helicopter tour with Papillon Grand Canyon Helicopters, 520-638-2419 or 800-528-2418. A list of other air-tour operators is available at the visitor centers. Depending upon the length of the tour, prices range from $80 to $100 and up. These tours fly over the Canyon. If you want to descend into the Canyon, contact the Hualapai-owned Western Rim Airport, 888-255-9550.
- Put the camera away and try this: using a plain-paged journal (no lines) and colored pencils, sit in one place for no less than an hour. Sink into yourself and the setting and see what you can capture in word and image.
- Pretend you're a naturalist and learn to identify and describe ten different plants and ten different animals.
- Skinny-dip in the great Colorado River (but test the currents first).
- For a real treat after a long day in the sun, visit the classic el Tovar Hotel at the South Rim for afternoon tea or for dinner.
- Escape the crowds and travel to the nearby Havasupai Reservation for an eight-mile hike beginning at Hualapai Hilltop and descending into the Canyon to the village of Supai. A permit and entrance fee of $15 per person to access the trail are required. For information, call the Havasupai Nation, 520-448-2121 or 800-622-4409.
- Take a plane ride to the Bar 10 Ranch on the Arizona strip and stay the night. This is a particularly lovely spot. Call 435-628-4010.
- Visit Mooney Falls in Havasu Canyon and take a dip in the many travertine pools.

GRAND CANYON ONLINE

There are a number of websites featuring information on the Grand Canyon. Start with the basics provided below:

- **The Grand Canyon**: comprehensive information on the Park
  http://www.thecanyon.com
- **The Grand Canyon Field Institute**: course and tour information
  http://www.grandcanyon.org/fieldinstitute/

𝒯HE NEXT STEP

- **The Grand Canyon National Park Foundation**: for financial contribution information
  http://www.grandcanyonfund.org
- **National Park Service**: extensive information on all parks
  http://www.nps.gov
- **American Park Network**: publisher of park guides
  http://www.AmericanParkNetwork.com
- **National Park Foundation**: general park information
  http://www.nationalparks.org

GIVING BACK

There are three things the Park really needs from you: your respect, your time, and your money.

- Financial contributions can be sent to The National Park Service Budget Division, P.O. Box 37127, Washington, DC 20013, or contact the Grand Canyon National Park Foundation, 520-774-1760.
- For $20 per year, you can become a member of the Grand Canyon Association (GCA), a non-profit organization operating bookstores around the park. All sale proceeds support the park and its resources. Your membership entitles you to 20 percent off at the Association bookstores and a newsletter which lists special member events and park news. For more information, call 520-638-2485.
- Join the Habitat Restoration Team for an hour, or for a week or more; help restore the Canyon by planting native plants in trampled areas, removing invading plant species, or cleaning up trails. Call 520-638-7857 for information.
- Participate in the "Volunteers in the Park," a program designed to access the many talents of the park's visitors. Whether you help with paperwork, lecture on the rare boogabooga plant found halfway up on the north side, pick up litter, pour coffee, or lead a hike, there's a job for you. Contact the program's coordinator at the park for an application. Call 520-638-7888 for assistance.

• Anytime you enter the park, be respectful of the flora and the fauna. Tread lightly. Open yourself to the wonders which abound in this extraordinary place. If you see someone else abusing the Park, don't be silent—say something or get a ranger. The Grand Canyon is yours to protect and preserve.

RECOMMENDED READING

Annerino, John. *Adventuring in Arizona: The Sierra Club Travel Guide to the Grand Canyon State*. San Francisco: Sierra Club Books, 1991.

Annerino, John. *Hiking the Grand Canyon*. San Francisco: Sierra Club Books, 1993.

Annerino, John. *Running Wild: Through the Grand Canyon on the Ancient Path*. Tucson: Harbinger House, Inc., 1992.

Babbitt, Jim, and Scott Thybony. *Bass Trail, North & South*. Grand Canyon: Grand Canyon Association, 1991.

Babbitt, Bruce. *Grand Canyon: An Anthology*. Flagstaff, Ariz.: Northland Press, 1978.

Berkowitz, Alan. *Bright Angel Trail*. Grand Canyon: Grand Canyon Association, 1980.

Berkowitz, Alan. *North Kaibab Trail*. Grand Canyon: Grand Canyon Association, 1980.

Butchart, Harvey. *Grand Canyon Treks: 12,000 Miles Through the Grand Canyon*. Bishop, Calif.: Spotted Dog Press, 1997.

Collier, Michael. *An Introduction to Grand Canyon Geology*. Grand Canyon: Grand Canyon Association, 1980.

Corle, Edwin. *Listen, Bright Angel*. New York: Duell, Sloan and Pearce, 1946.

Euler, Robert C. and Frank Tikalsky, eds. *The Grand Canyon: Intimate Views*. Tucson: The University of Arizona Press, 1992.

𝒯HE NEXT STEP

Fishbein, Seymour L. *Grand Canyon: Its Majesty and Its Lore.*
Washington, D.C.: National Geographic Society, 1991.

Fletcher, Colin. *The Man Who Walked Through Time.* New York:
Vintage Books, 1989.

Ghiglieri, Michael P. *Canyon.* Tucson: The University of Arizona
Press, 1992.

Goldwater, Barry M. *Delightful Journey: Down the Green & Colorado
Rivers.* Tempe: Arizona Historical Foundation, 1970.

Good, John. *Grandview Trail.* Grand Canyon: Grand Canyon
Association, 1985.

Houk, Rose. *South Kaibab Trail.* Grand Canyon: Grand Canyon
Association, 1981.

Hughs, Donald. *In the House of Stone and Light.* Grand Canyon:
Grand Canyon Association, 1978.

Jones, Anne Trinkle, and Robert Euler. *A Sketch of Grand Canyon
Prehistory.* Grand Canyon: Grand Canyon Association, 1979.

Krutch, Joseph Wood. *Grand Canyon: Today and All Its Yesterdays.*
Tucson: The University of Arizona Press, 1989.

Lamb, Susan, ed. *Nature Notes: The Best of Grand Canyon 1926–1935.*
Grand Canyon: Grand Canyon Natural History Association, 1994.

Lavender, David. *River Runners of the Grand Canyon.* Grand Canyon:
Grand Canyon Natural History Association, 1985.

Lopez, Barry. *Open Crossing Ground.* New York: Vintage Books, 1988.

McCairen, Patricia C. *Canyon Solitude: A Woman's Solo River Journey
Through Grand Canyon.* Seattle: Adventura, 1998.

Philips, Arthur II. *Grand Canyon Wildflowers.* Grand Canyon: Grand
Canyon Association, 1990.

Pyne, Stephen J. *Fire on the Rim: A Firefighter's Season at the Grand
Canyon.* Seattle: University of Washington Press, 1989.

Pyne, Stephen J. *How the Canyon Became Grand: A Short History.*
New York: Viking Penguin, 1998.

Reisner, Marc. *Cadillac Desert: The American West and Its Disappearing Water.* New York: Penguin Books, 1987.

Ryan, Kathleen Jo. *Writing Down the River: Into the Heart of the Grand Canyon.* Flagstaff, Ariz.: Northland Publishing, 1998.

Sadler, Christa. *There's This River…Grand Canyon Boatman Stories.* Flagstaff, Ariz.: Red Lake Books, 1994.

Schmidt, Jeremy. *Grand Canyon National Park: A Natural History Guide.* New York: Houghton Mifflin Company, 1993.

Schullery, Paul. *The Grand Canyon: Early Impressions.* Boulder: Colorado Associated University Press, 1981.

Snyder, Gary. *A Place in Space: Ethics, Aesthetics, and Watersheds: New and Selected Prose.* Washington, D.C.: Counterpoint, 1995.

Steck, George. *Grand Canyon Loop Hikes.* Helena, Mont.: Chockstone Press, 1989.

Steck, George. *Loop Hikes II.* Helena, Mont.: Chockstone Press, 1997.

Stegner, Page. *Grand Canyon: The Great Abyss.* New York: Tehabi Books, 1995.

Stevens, Larry, ed. *Colorado River in Grand Canyon: A Comprehensive Guide to Its Natural and Human History* (5th ed.). Red Lake Books, 1998.

Teal, Louise. *Breaking into the Current: Boatwomen of the Grand Canyon.* Tucson: The University of Arizona Press, 1994.

Thybony, Scott. *Havasu Canyon Trail.* Grand Canyon: Grand Canyon Association, 1989.

Thybony, Scott. *Hermit Trail.* Grand Canyon: Grand Canyon Association, 1989.

Thybony, Scott. *Official Guide to Hiking the Grand Canyon.* Grand Canyon: Grand Canyon Natural History Association, 1994.

Welch, Vince, Cort Conley, and Brad Dimock. *The Doing of the Thing: The Brief Brilliant Whitewater Career of Buzz Holmstrom.* Flagstaff, Ariz.: Fretwater Press, 1998.

THE NEXT STEP

Williams, Terry Tempest. *An Unspoken Hunger: Stories From the Field.*
    New York: Vintage Books, 1994.

Zwinger, Ann Haymond. *Downcanyon: A Naturalist Explores the
    Colorado River Through the Grand Canyon.* Tucson: The University
    of Arizona Press, 1995.

Index

air tours 157
Anasazi 234
Apache Trail 190
Arizona Strip 142

Badger Creek Rapid 220
Bass Trail 111
Bass, William 193
Bat Cave 61
bats 59
Beaver Falls 41
bird watching 127
Blacktail Canyon 225, 228
Brahma Temple 48

camping 3, 10, 125, 176, 187, 250
Cape Solitude 81
caving/spelunking 106
Colorado River 13, 15, 35, 40, 64,
    129, 150, 203
Crystal Hole 72
Crystal Rapid 70

de Cárdenas, García López 193

Echo Cliffs 221
Elves Chasm 14, 23
Esplanade 138

flora and fauna 5, 125, 251
Fossil Canyon 188

Glen Canyon 240
Glen Canyon Dam 20, 133, 166, 241
Grand Canyon Railway 115
Granite Rapid 65
Great Havasupai Sacred Peach
    Festival 178

Great Unconformity 228
Green Room 41

Hance, John 174, 193
Harvey, Fred 117
Havasu 175, 203
Havasu Canyon 40, 180, 203, 209
Havasupai Indians 176
Havasupai Reservation 209
Hermit Rapid 69
hiking 3, 6, 103, 110, 169, 180,
    221, 250

Ives, Joseph Christmas 193

Jackass Canyon 220

Kaibab Plateau 95
Kaibab Trail 95, 169
Ken Patrick Trail 148
Kolb Arch 8

Lake Mead 133
Lake Powell 243
Lava Falls 212
Lee, John Doyle 119
Lower Bass Camp 76

Marathon Friendship Dance 178
Marion Point 10
mining 121
Mystic Eye 103

Nankoweap Beach 125
Nankoweap Canyon 6
Nankoweap Creek 11
Nankoweap Trail 8

Phantom Ranch 96
pictographs 138, 230
Point Imperial 148
Point Sublime 200
Powell, John Wesley 8, 162, 193
Precipice View 113

rafting 15, 35, 40, 86, 161, 203, 211
rail travel 115
Ramparts Cave 140
Redwall Cavern 17
rock art 138, 230
rock climbing 44

Shamans' Gallery 137
Shiva Temple 222
Sipapu 236
spelunking/caving 106
Stanton, Robert Brewster 193

Stone Creek 35
Surprise Valley 109

Thunder Cave 106
Thunder River 105
Tilted Mesa 11
Tonto Plateau 3
Tonto Platform 5
Toroweap Overlook 143
Toroweap Valley 146
trail running 92
Travertine Falls 86
Tusayan Museum 232

White, George 162
Williams, Arizona 115

Zoroaster Temple 44, 48, 57

Index of Contributors

Abbey, Edward 175–185
Aleshire, Peter 59–62
Annerino, John 44–57, 62, 74

Bishop, William W. 121
Brower, David R. 240–245

Carlson, Raymond 84–85
Carothers, Steven W. 133–134
Cook, Nana 152–155
Corle, Edwin 101, 124, 174, 222
Crumbo, Kim 163

Dixon, Winifred Hawkridge 191
Dudley, Gail 6–12

Fishbein, Seymour L. 178, 209–210,
        215, 232, 244
Fletcher, Colin 187–199

Ghiglieri, Michael P. 40–43,
        102–108, 126, 150–151, 168, 182,
        185–186, 220–224, 236, 239
Goldberger, Gail 211–219
Goldwater, Barry M. 23–24
Grey, Zane 172

Hafford, William 142–150
Hawkins, Harold H. 113–114
Holmstrom, Buzz 65, 88

James, G. Wharton 34
Janecek, Tom 203–209
Jenkins, Mark 43
Jones, W. Paul 169–174

Kardong, Don 92–101
Kerry, Bob 57–58
Kreutz, Douglas 148
Krutch, Joseph Wood 17

Lavender, David 13
Lopez, Barry 14–23

Madison, Charlotte 152–155
McCairen, Patricia C. 63–77, 224
Miller, Joaquin 139

O'Reilly, Sean 115–117

Powell, John Wesley vii, 159–160
Priestley, J. B. 195
Pyne, Stephen J. 33, 109, 140–141,
        156, 200

Qwerta, Sylvia 219

Richfield, Paul 157–159

Sadler, Christa 225–227
Schmidt, Jeremy 5, 95, 229–238,
        249–253
Smith, Dean 119–123
Snyder, Gary 56
Stegner, Page 19, 25–33, 245–246

Teal, Louise 39, 83, 77, 90–91,
        161–168, 213
Thybony, Scott 3–5, 8, 30, 112,
        137–140

Udall, Stewart 110–113

Waesche, Hugh H. 122
Williams, Terry Tempest 35–38
Winter, Larry 81–84

Zimmerman, Karl 117–118
Zwinger, Ann Haymond 61,
    125–133, 242
Zwinger, Susan 86–90

Acknowledgements

We would like to thank our families and friends for their usual forbearance while we are putting a book together. Thanks also to the staff at Travelers' Tales and O'Reilly & Associates, including especially Susan Brady, Deborah Greco, Jennifer Leo, Lisa Bach, Amy Greimann Carlson, Natanya Pearlman, Tara Weaver, Kathryn Heflin, Susan Bailey, Leili Eghbal, Cindy Cohen, and Tim O'Reilly. Special thanks also to Barbara Urlaub, Sarah Stebbins, librarian for the Grand Canyon National Research Library, Julia M. V. Andrick of the Grand Canyon Railway, Sylvia Qwerta, Hualapai tribal member, Patricia Cesspooch, director of the Hualapai Tourist Office, Holly Ethier, the staff of the periodical department of the Phoenix Central Library, and the Luke Air Force Base library.

We'd also like to express our gratitude for the fine boatmanship and excellent company (tall tales included) provided by Karen Bellinger, Mike Reyes, Christian Seamans, and Mike Bullock (who pulled James out of the drink in Hermit Rapid). A final note: If you have the opportunity to go down the Colorado River, don't forget to tip your boatmen well! Your smooth, awesome trip will flow not just from the natural wonders of the Canyon, but from their hard work and knowledge.

"Beneath the Rim" by Scott Thybony reprinted from *Men's Journal*, May-June 1993. Copyright © 1993 by *Men's Journal*, all rights reserved. Reprinted by permission.

"Nankoweap" by Gail Dudley reprinted from the October 1996 issue of *Arizona Highways*. Copyright © 1996 by Gail Dudley. Reprinted by permission of the author.

"Gone Back into the Earth" by Barry Lopez excerpted from *Crossing Open Ground* by Barry Lopez. Copyright © 1978 by Barry Lopez. Reprinted by permission of Sterling Lord Literistic, Inc. and the author.

"Revelation" by Page Stegner excerpted from *Grand Canyon: The Great Abyss* by Page Stegner. Copyright © 1995 by Tehabi Books. Reprinted by permission of HarpersCollins Publishers, Inc.

"Stone Creek Woman" by Terry Tempest Williams excerpted from *An Unspoken*

Ghiglieri. Copyright © 1992 by Michael P. Ghiglieri. Reprinted by permission of the University of Arizona Press.

"Legends of the Lost" by Dean Smith reprinted from the February 1994 issue of *Arizona Highways*. Copyright © 1994 by Dean Smith. Reprinted by permission of the author.

"Shamans Gallery" by Scott Thybony reprinted from "Grand Canyon: Beneath the Rim," *Men's Journal*, May–June 1993. Copyright © 1993 by *Men's Journal*, all rights reserved. Reprinted by permission.

"The Journey's End" by William Hafford reprinted from the September 1992 issue of *Arizona Highways*. Copyright © 1993 by William Hafford. Reprinted by permission of the estate of William Hafford.

"Women in the Canyon" by Louise Teal excerpted from *Breaking into the Current: Boatwomen of the Grand Canyon* by Louise Teal. Copyright © 1994 by Louise Teal. Reprinted by permission of the University of Arizona Press.

"Trinitarian Thoughts" by W. Paul Jones reprinted from the October 1992 issue of *Theology Today*. Copyright © 1992 by *Theology Today*. Reprinted by permission of *Theology Today*.

"Transition" by Colin Fletcher excerpted from *The Man Who Walked Through Time* by Colin Fletcher. Copyright © 1967 by Colin Fletcher. Reprinted by permission of Alfred A. Knopf, Inc. and Brandt & Brandt Literary Agents, Inc.

"Flash Flood" by Tom Janecek reprinted from the Fall 1997 issue of *Boatman's Quarterly Review*. Copyright © 1997 by Tom Janecek. Reprinted by permission of the author.

"Under Lava" by Gail Goldberger published with permission from the author. Copyright © 1999 by Gail Goldberger.

"Jackass Canyon" by Michael P. Ghiglieri excerpted from *Canyon* by Michael P. Ghiglieri. Copyright © 1992 by Michael P. Ghiglieri. Reprinted by permission of the University of Arizona Press.

"Blacktail Ghost" by Christa Sadler excerpted from *There's This River...Grand Canyon Boatman Stories* by Christa Sadler. Copyright © 1994 by Christa Sadler. Reprinted by permission of the author.

"Let the River Run Through It" by David R. Brower reprinted from the March/April 1997 issue of *Sierra* magazine. Copyright © 1997 by David R. Brower. Reprinted by permission of the author.

"Temples to Water" by Jeremy Schmidt excerpted from *Grand Canyon National Park: A Natural History Guide*. Copyright © 1993 by Jeremy Schmidt. Reprinted by permission of Houghton Mifflin Company. All rights reserved.

Additional Credits (Arranged alphabetically by title)

Selection from *Adventuring in Arizona: The Sierra Club Travel Guide to the Grand Canyon State* by John Annerino copyright © 1991 by John Annerino. Reprinted by permission of Sierra Club Books.

Selection from "All Aboard for the South Rim" by Karl Zimmerman reprinted from the August 1992 issue of *Americana*. Copyright © 1992 by *Americana*.

Selection from "An Appreciation of Grand Canyon" by Zane Grey excerpted from *The Grand Canyon: Early Impressions* by Paul Schullery. Copyright © 1981 by Paul

mission of the author.

Selections from *Nature Notes: The Best of Grand Canyon 1926–1935* edited by Susan Lamb copyright © 1994 by Grand Canyon Natural History Association. Reprinted by permission of Grand Canyon Natural History Association.

Selection from "A New Wonder of the World" by Joaquin Miller excerpted from *The Grand Canyon of Arizona*. Copyright © 1909 by Joaquin Miller.

Selections from *Official Guide to Hiking the Grand Canyon* by Scott Thybony copyright © 1994 by Grand Canyon Natural History Association. Reprinted by permission of Grand Canyon Natural History Association.

Selection from "A Pilgrimage to Zoroaster" by Bob Kerry reprinted from *Arizona Highways*. Copyright © by Robert Kerry. Reprinted by permission of the author.

Selection from *A Place in Space: Ethics, Aesthetics, and Watersheds: New and Selected Prose* by Gary Snyder copyright © 1995 by Gary Snyder. Reprinted by permission of Counterpoint Press, a member of Perseus Books, L. L. C.

Selection from *River Runners of the Grand Canyon* by David Lavender copyright © 1985 by David Lavender. Reprinted by permission of the author.

Selections from *Running Wild: Through the Grand Canyon on the Ancient Path* by John Annerino copyright © 1992 by John Annerino. Reprinted by permission of the author.

Selection from "Static Electricity" by Harold H. Hawkins excerpted from *Nature Notes: The Best of Grand Canyon 1926–1935* edited by Susan Lamb. Copyright © 1994 by Grand Canyon Natural History Association. Reprinted by permission of Grand Canyon Natural History Association.

Selection from "The Living Canyon" by Steven W. Carothers as excerpted from *The Grand Canyon: Intimate Views* edited by Robert C. Euler and Frank Tikalsky. Copyright © 1992 by Frank D. Tikalsky and Robert C. Euler. Reprinted by permission of the University of Arizona Press.

Selection from *Westward Hoboes* by Winifred Hawkridge Dixon excerpted from *Grand Canyon Deeps* by Benjamin J. Kimber. Copyright © 1921 by Winifred Hawkridge Dixon.

About the Editor

Sean O'Reilly is a former seminarian, stockbroker, and prison instructor who lives in Arizona with his wife Brenda and their four small boys. He's had a life-long interest in philosophy and theology, and is at work on a book called *How to Manage Your Dick: A Guide for the Soul*, which makes the proposition that classic Greek, Roman, and Christian moral philosophies, allied with post-quantum physics, form the building blocks of a new ethics and psychology. Widely traveled, Sean most recently completed an 18,000-mile van journey around the United States, sharing the treasures of the open road with his family. He is editor-at-large and director of international sales for Travelers' Tales.

Larry Habegger, executive editor of Travelers' Tales, has been writing about travel since 1980. He has visited almost fifty countries and five of the six continents, traveling from the frozen arctic to equatorial rain forest, the high Himalayas to the Dead Sea. In the early 1980s he co-authored mystery serials for the *San Francisco Examiner* with James O'Reilly, and in 1985 the two of them began a syndicated newspaper column, "World Travel Watch," which still appears in major newspapers throughout the USA. He was born and raised in Minnesota and lives with his family on Telegraph Hill in San Francisco.

James O'Reilly, president and co-publisher of Travelers' Tales, wrote mystery serials before becoming a travel writer in the early 1980s. He's visited more than forty countries, along the way meditating with monks in Tibet, participating in West African voodoo rituals, and hanging out the laundry with nuns in Florence. He travels extensively with his wife Wenda and their three daughters. They live in Palo Alto, California when they're not in Leavenworth, Washington.

TRAVELERS' TALES GUIDES

LOOK FOR THESE TITLES IN THE SERIES

 FOOTSTEPS: THE SOUL OF TRAVEL
A NEW IMPRINT FROM TRAVELERS' TALES GUIDES

An imprint of Travelers' Tales Guides, the Footsteps series unveils new works by first-time authors, established writers, and reprints of works whose time has come...again. Each book will fire your imagination, disturb your sleep, and feed your soul.

 **KITE STRINGS OF THE SOUTHERN CROSS**
A Woman's Travel Odyssey
By Laurie Gough
ISBN 1-885211-30-9, 400 pages, $24.00, hardcover
A TRAVELERS' TALES FOOTSTEPS BOOK

SPECIAL INTEREST

THE PENNY PINCHER'S PASSPORT TO LUXURY TRAVEL
The Art of Cultivating Preferred Customer Status
By Joel L. Widzer
ISBN 1-885211-31-7, 253 pages, $12.95

DANGER!
Ttue Stories of Trouble and Survival
Edited by James O'Reilly, Larry Habegger, & Sean O'Reilly
ISBN 1-885211-32-5, 336 pages, $17.95

$\mathscr{S}$PECIAL INTEREST

FAMILY TRAVEL:
The Farther You Go, the Closer You Get
Edited by Laura Manske
ISBN 1-885211-33-3, 375 pages, $17.95

THE GIFT OF TRAVEL:
The Best of Travelers' Tales
Edited by Larry Habegger, James O'Reilly & Sean O'Reilly
ISBN 1-885211-25-2, 240 pages, $14.95

THERE'S NO TOILET PAPER ON THE ROAD LESS TRAVELED:
The Best of Travel Humor and Misadventure
Edited by Doug Lansky
ISBN 1-885211-27-9, 207 pages, $12.95

A DOG'S WORLD:
True Stories of Man's Best Friend on the Road
Edited by Christine Hunsicker
ISBN 1-885211-23-6, 257 pages, $12.95

$\mathscr{W}$OMEN'S TRAVEL

SAFETY AND SECURITY FOR WOMEN WHO TRAVEL
By Sheila Swan & Peter Laufer
ISBN 1-885211-29-5, 159 pages, $12.95

$\mathcal{W}$OMEN'S TRAVEL

WOMEN IN THE WILD:
True Stories of Adventure and Connection
Edited by Lucy McCauley
ISBN 1-885211-21-X, 307 pages, $17.95

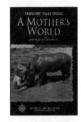

A MOTHER'S WORLD:
Journeys of the Heart
Edited by Marybeth Bond & Pamela Michael
ISBN 1-885211-26-0, 233 pages, $14.95

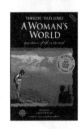

──── ★ *★* ★ ────

Winner of the Lowell
Thomas Award for Best
Travel Book – Society of
American Travel Writers

A WOMAN'S WORLD:
True Stories of Life on the Road
Edited by Marybeth Bond
Introduction by Dervla Murphy
ISBN 1-885211-06-6
475 pages, $17.95

GUTSY WOMEN:
Travel Tips and Wisdom for the Road
By Marybeth Bond
ISBN 1-885211-15-5, 123 pages, $7.95

GUTSY MAMAS:
Travel Tips and Wisdom for
Mothers on the Road
By Marybeth Bond
ISBN 1-885211-20-1, 139 pages, $7.95

$\mathcal{B}$ODY & SOUL

THE ROAD WITHIN:
True Stories of Transformation and the Soul
Edited by Sean O'Reilly, James O'Reilly & Tim O'Reilly
ISBN 1-885211-19-8, 459 pages, $17.95

★ ★ ★

Small Press Book Award Winner and Benjamin Franklin Award Finalist

LOVE & ROMANCE:
True Stories of Passion on the Road
Edited by Judith Babcock Wylie
ISBN 1-885211-18-X, 319 pages, $17.95

FOOD:
A Taste of the Road
Edited by Richard Sterling
Introduction by Margo True
ISBN 1-885211-09-0
467 pages, $17.95

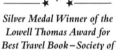

Silver Medal Winner of the Lowell Thomas Award for Best Travel Book – Society of American Travel Writers

THE FEARLESS DINER:
Travel Tips and Wisdom for Eating around the World
By Richard Sterling
ISBN 1-885211-22-8, 139 pages, $7.95

$\mathscr{C}$OUNTRY GUIDES

AMERICA
Edited by Fred Setterberg
ISBN 1-885211-28-7, 550 pages, $19.95

JAPAN
Edited by Donald W. George
& Amy Greimann Carlson
ISBN 1-885211-04-X, 437 pages, $17.95

ITALY
Edited by Anne Calcagno
Introduction by Jan Morris
ISBN 1-885211-16-3, 463 pages, $17.95

INDIA
Edited by James O'Reilly & Larry Habegger
ISBN 1-885211-01-5, 538 pages, $17.95

FRANCE
Edited by James O'Reilly, Larry Habegger
& Sean O'Reilly
ISBN 1-885211-02-3, 517 pages, $17.95

*C*OUNTRY GUIDES

MEXICO
Edited by James O'Reilly & Larry Habegger
ISBN 1-885211-00-7, 463 pages, $17.95

THAILAND
Edited by James O'Reilly
& Larry Habegger
ISBN 1-885211-05-8
483 pages, $17.95

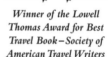

Winner of the Lowell
Thomas Award for Best
Travel Book – Society of
American Travel Writers

SPAIN
Edited by Lucy McCauley
ISBN 1-885211-07-4, 495 pages, $17.95

NEPAL
Edited by Rajendra S. Khadka
ISBN 1-885211-14-7, 423 pages, $17.95

BRAZIL
Edited by Annette Haddad & Scott Doggett
Introduction by Alex Shoumatoff
ISBN 1-885211-11-2
452 pages, $17.95

Benjamin Franklin
Award Winner

*R*EGIONAL GUIDES

HAWAII
True Stories of the Island Spirit
Edited by Rick & Marcie Carroll
ISBN 1-885211-35-X, 375 pages, $17.95

GRAND CANYON
True Stories of Life Below the Rim
Edited by Sean O'Reilly & James O'Reilly
ISBN 1-885211-34-1, 375 pages, $17.95

*C*ITY GUIDES

HONG KONG
Edited by James O'Reilly, Larry Habegger & Sean O'Reilly
ISBN 1-885211-03-1, 439 pages, $17.95

PARIS
Edited by James O'Reilly, Larry Habegger & Sean O'Reilly
ISBN 1-885211-10-4, 417 pages, $17.95

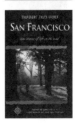

SAN FRANCISCO
Edited by James O'Reilly, Larry Habegger & Sean O'Reilly
ISBN 1-885211-08-2, 491 pages, $17.95

SUBMIT YOUR OWN TRAVEL TALE

Do you have a tale of your own that you would like to submit to Travelers' Tales? We highly recommend that you first read one or more of our books to get a feel for the kind of story we're looking for. For submission guidelines and a list of titles in the works, send a SASE to:

Travelers' Tales Submission Guidelines
330 Townsend Street, Suite 208, San Francisco, CA 94107

or send email to *guidelines@travelerstales.com*
or visit our Web site at **www.travelerstales.com**

You can send your story to the address above or via email to *submit@travelerstales.com*. On the outside of the envelope, *please indicate what country/topic your story is about*. If your story is selected for one of our titles, we will contact you about rights and payment.

We hope to hear from you. In the meantime, enjoy the stories!